Praise for Diane L. Moore's *Overcoming Religious Illiteracy: A Cultural Studies Approach to the Study of Religion in Secondary Education*

"Moore's new book is a vitally important contribution to the growing international literature on educating the public–especially the young–about religions. At a time when learning about religion is being debated in Asian, African and Middle Eastern countries and when international bodies such as UNESCO, the Council of Europe and the Office for Security and Cooperation in Europe are giving close attention to teaching and learning about religions, Moore's important book will attract much attention internationally."—Robert Jackson, DLitt Director, Warwick Religions and Education Research Unit, Institute of Education, University of Warwick and Editor of the *British Journal of Religious Education*

"Moore has brought insight, clarity, common sense, and long experience to one of the most important and contentious issues of our day-the question of religion in the public schools. Religious literacy goes to the heart of the purpose of education in a democracy that can no longer afford to remain uneducated about the world's religions. This book is a must-read for teachers, school administrators, parents, and every citizen concerned with the quality of American education."—Diana L. Eck, Professor of Comparative Religion and Indian Studies and Director of The Pluralism Project, Harvard University

"Moore's lucid, thoughtful book wrestles with a fundamental educational question-what should we teach our children? She argues persuasively the critical importance of religious literacy for survival in the 21st century and goes deeply into the contentious debates around the teaching of religion in public schools. Moore convinces that we keep the teaching of world religions out of our schools at our own peril. Read it, debate it, act on it."—Steve Seidel, Bauman and Bryant Chair in Arts and Education, Graduate School of Education, and Director of Project Zero, Harvard University

"In a world fraught with religious and cultural conflicts, Moore models how to teach about religion respectfully as part of the goal of educating for democratic citizenship. What is unique about this book is that the author explores both the philosophy as well as the pedagogical challenges of using a cultural studies approach to teach about religion. This important book will be of interest to educators and any citizen concerned about our country's religious illiteracy."—Marya R. Levenson, Professor of the Practice in Education and the Harry S. Levitan Director of the Education Program, Brandeis University

"*Overcoming Religious Illiteracy* is unique. Moore not only persuades us about *why* we ought to teach about religion in our public schools, but she also tells us *how* to do it-practically, sensitively, and effectively."—James W. Fraser, Professor, Steinhardt School of Culture, Education, and Human Development, New York University

"Religious illiteracy in our country and in the world is rampant. Ignorance of the faith and cultural practices of others is the source of great misunderstanding and suffering. Moore's book proposes an inquiry-based approach for American public schools that opens the door to religious discussion and reflection in an atmosphere of respect and cultural awareness. This book is pioneering. It offers a strong base of theory and concrete foundations for practice to bring a new dimension to teaching about diversity."—Renee Cherow-O'Leary, Assistant Professor of English Education, Teachers College, Columbia University

"In recent years religion has become a dominant feature of global politics and American public life. Today active participation as informed citizens in our multicultural society demands knowledge of the world's religious traditions. Moore's *Overcoming Religious Illiteracy* offers a template for achieving that goal. It should be required reading for all secondary school educators."—Donald K. Swearer, Director of the Center for the Study of World Religions and Distinguished Visiting Professor of Buddhist Studies, Harvard Divinity School

"Moore convincingly argues that religion should be taught in public schools by giving both solid theoretical reasons and productive examples of how to do so practically. I am sure this fascinating study will enrich the debate not only in academic circles but in public discourse as well. This is a remarkable and innovative book that should be widely read by Americans and Europeans alike."—Wolfram Weisse, Professor of Religious Education, University of Hamburg and Director of the Centre for World Religions in Dialogue

"In a world marked by the inability of societies to engage with religious difference, the need to combat religious and cultural illiteracy has become urgent. Diane Moore presents a strong and convincing case for the inclusion of the study of religion as a cultural phenomenon in the curricula of schools and, indeed, for a liberal arts college education. She persuasively demonstrates the destabilizing consequences of religious illiteracy for the proper functioning of democratic societies. A must read for anyone concerned with the crucial role of education in fostering healthy multiracial, multicultural and multireligious societies."—Ali S. Asani, Professor of the Practice of Indo-Muslim Languages and Cultures, Harvard University

"*Overcoming Religious Illiteracy* is a must read for those concerned with the future of public education in a multi-religious society. Moore offers thoughtful suggestions for educators preparing to tackle this difficult subject."—Adam Strom, Director of Research and Development, Facing History and Ourselves

"Teachers everywhere should welcome *Overcoming Religious Illiteracy*. Finally here is a text that gives instructors the perspective and tools they need to teach about religion in a way that avoids the shrill stereotypes, over simplistic assumptions, and unexamined sectarianism that too often beleaguers this topic. Moore links theory with practice, offering educators both methodologies and resources to teach responsibly and creatively about religion."—Susan McCaslin, Instructor in Philosophy and Religious Studies and Associate Dean of Faculty, Phillips Academy

"Moore's well-written and very readable book, *Overcoming Religious Illiteracy*, is important for two reasons. It is a cogent guide for any district, school or teacher looking to integrate the study or discussion of religion into the curriculum and it outlines clear steps for making any class a learning-centered, inquiry based experience where students participate fully in the teaching and learning process."—Charles Skidmore, Principal, Arlington High School

"Concerned by the detrimental consequences of religious illiteracy and the divisive nature of the culture wars, Moore appeals to teachers in particular for change. She argues that teachers should be 'treated as professionals, supported as scholars, recognized as moral agents, and given voice as public intellectuals.' An award winning educator, Moore offers teaching models for constructing learning communities to stimulate student-centered inquiry about religions while remaining respectful of religious beliefs. How refreshing! This is a book of fundamental importance to those interested in educational reform."—Heidi Roupp, World History teacher and founding member of the World History Association

"Moore takes her readers seriously, as she does her students, and challenges us to debate the purpose of education, especially vis-à-vis democracy and the possibilities inherent in talking to each other across differences. Her contributions to this conversation are based on years of classroom teaching as well as scholarship, but she ultimately defies stale scholarly logic: she deftly bridges the chasm between theory and practice, and she dares express an optimism so profound that it is a form of resistance in itself."—Shipley Robertson Salewski, Teacher, 8th Grade English, KIPP Summit Academy

"Moore's in-depth case studies provide teachers with what is often the missing element in substantial theoretical work-how to transfer the intellectual concepts they find compelling into the classroom. Moore does so in a way that will have impact for both teachers and students."—Clare R. Sisisky, Director and Teacher, Center for the Humanities, Henrico County Public Schools

Overcoming Religious Illiteracy

A Cultural Studies Approach to the Study of Religion in Secondary Education

Diane L. Moore

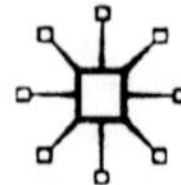

OVERCOMING RELIGIOUS ILLITERACY

First published in 2007 by
PALGRAVE MACMILLAN™
175 Fifth Avenue, New York, N.Y. 10010 and
Houndmills, Basingstoke, Hampshire, England RG21 6XS
Companies and representatives throughout the world.

PALGRAVE MACMILLAN is the global academic imprint of the Palgrave Macmillan division of St. Martin's Press, LLC and of Palgrave Macmillan Ltd. Macmillan® is a registered trademark in the United States, United Kingdom and other countries. Palgrave is a registered trademark in the European Union and other countries.

ISBN-13: 978–1–4039–6348–2 (hardcover)
ISBN-10: 1–4039–6348–7 (hardcover)
ISBN-13: 978–1–4039–6349–9 (paperback)
ISBN-10: 1–4039–6349–5 (paperback)

Library of Congress Cataloging-in-Publication Data is available from the Library of Congress.

A catalogue record for this book is available from the British Library.

Design by Newgen Imaging Systems (P) Ltd., Chennai, India.

First edition: October 2007

10 9 8 7 6 5 4 3 2 1

Transferred to digital printing in 2008.

For our nation's educators
and my daughter Lily and her generation

CONTENTS

ACKNOWLEDGMENTS

This is an impossible task, for there are many, many hands that have shaped this project in direct and indirect ways over the years. This is so with all creative endeavors and I am fully cognizant of this truth now more than ever. Though I cannot possibly begin to recognize all those who have helped bring this work to fruition, the following deserve special recognition for their significant contributions.

For my foundational association of the ways that religion is imbedded in all dimensions of our lives, I am indebted, first, to my parents Milton and Dolores Moore who have lived lives both simple and profound as individuals of tremendous faith and integrity; second to my earliest and most influential mentor Reverend Russell Fuller who modeled (and continues to model) a life of prophetic faith tempered by humility and gentle kindness; and third, my intellectual mentor Beverly Harrison who taught me how to hold the dangers inherent in religion in tension with its possibilities. My gratitude to these four extraordinary individuals is boundless.

In 1993, I accepted what was to be a one-year sabbatical leave replacement position in the Philosophy and Religious Studies department at Phillips Andover Academy. I was finishing my doctoral dissertation in ethics and missed working with adolescents, so I thought this would be a nice change of pace before launching into a full time career working with undergraduate and graduate level students. As the product of a working class family and the public school system, the world of elite boarding schools was completely foreign to me and, frankly, I did not know what to expect. I was completely surprised by the rich diversity of the student body and soon grew to know my faculty colleagues as dedicated, creative, and exemplary professionals. Much in this text is inspired by the hundreds of students and dozens of educators from Phillips Academy who have taught me much over the years about the transforming power of education. Special thanks to the late Pete Joel who was instrumental in hiring me in 1993, and for my colleagues in the Philosophy and Religious Studies Department: Vincent Avery, Thomas Hodgson, and Susan McCaslin. I am personally indebted to these remarkable educators who have enriched my life deeply in both personal and professional ways.

In 1997, Nancy Richardson, who was then the Director of the Program in Religion and Secondary Education (PRSE) at Harvard called to ask if I would teach the *Colloquium in Religion and Secondary Education* as a visiting lecturer. Nancy was a pivotal force in reinvigorating the intellectual core of the PRSE and was eager to involve scholar practitioners in the training of preservice teachers. The program has consistently attracted remarkable applicants who are unique in their desire to pursue teaching as a vocation in concert with their training in religious and theological studies. The combination of working with preservice educators while continuing to teach secondary school students at Phillips has given me a unique insight into both educational arenas and I am deeply grateful to Nancy for the initial invitation and for her constant support and friendship over the years.

The manuscript itself began to take explicit shape in early 2001 when I assumed the directorship of the PRSE and became more familiar with the available resources as well as what was missing in the field. My dear friend, mentor, and colleague James Fraser was especially supportive of this project and recommended that I submit a proposal for review to his editor Amanda Johnson Moon at Palgrave Macmillan. Amanda was enthusiastic from the start and I am very grateful to her and to Jim for encouraging me at these pivotal, early stages.

Jim remained supportive throughout the writing process and, as readers will see, his own work has informed mine in important ways. Though we do not always agree, our discussions over the years have helped to sharpen my thinking more than any other scholar in this small but growing field. He is a wise, generous, and dedicated educator who has been a personal inspiration to me in my own vocational path.

Students in the PRSE have helped to shape many of the ideas here through our work together. The following individuals read and engaged parts of the manuscript in PRSE related coursework and through our discussions helped me recognize areas for revision and clarification: Christy Cummings, Alyson Dame, Alexis Dare-Attanasio, Cati de los Rios, Kate Dugan, Emily Fleig, Helena Fleig, Lara Freeman, Eliot Friesen, Abigail Henderson, Andrew Housieaux, Matthew Nelson,

Sam Potolicchio, Marielle Ramsey, Shipley Robertson, Fernando Silva, Tracy Wells, and Emily Wright-Timko.

Other colleagues and friends read all or parts of the manuscript and provided extremely insightful comments. They include Ali Asani, Vincent Avery, Jocelyn Beh, Elizabeth Bounds, Renee Cherow-O'Leary, Bruce Grelle, Jamie Hamilton, Paul Hanson, Duncan Hilton, Susan Moore Johnson, Victor Kazanjian, Stephanie McAllister, Susan McCaslin, Paul McKnight, Stephanie Paulsell, Deborah Quitt, Heidi Roupp, Karen Russell, David Schwartz, Clare Sisisky, Charles Skidmore, T.J. Skulstad-Brown, and Rebecca Sykes. I owe a special debt of gratitude to my dear friend Elizabeth Carl who read through Part One with special care, attentiveness, and insight and provided me with astute comments and helpful suggestions. Wendy McDowell also deserves special recognition for her editing assistance during the final stages of the project. She combined her consummate expertise as a professional journalist with her generous support of the project to offer keen insight and critical comments that have strengthened this text tremendously. The astute suggestions and corrections by the Newgen team have improved the book in significant ways.

I am especially indebted to the 11 Phillips Andover Academy students who enrolled in the Islamic Cultural Studies class that serves as a case study for Chapters Five and Six. They are typical of the students at Phillips Academy that I have come to know and respect over the years and who serve as a continual reminder to me of how privileged I am to be a teacher.

Without the material and emotional support of my family, this project would never have seen the light of day. Milton and Dolores Moore seemed to instinctively know when to ask about my progress and when to remain silent but ready to hear any news that I wished to share. Dave and Em Eissenberg offered their lovely cabin by the brook for family summers and individual writing retreats where much of this manuscript came to life. My life partner Judith Eissenberg has not only helped to make the "space" for me to write but has also provided extremely helpful feedback on critical chapters of the text itself. As an intellectually gifted professional musician with deeply ethical sensibilities, she brings a unique lens to all of her endeavors. Our partnership through the years has helped me think in some new and creative ways about the many passions we share, and the strongest aspects of this text were deeply influenced by her in direct and indirect ways. Finally, our daughter Lily is a constant source of joy and a daily reminder to me that our present is brighter than it sometimes seems and our future potentially more promising. This book is dedicated to Lily, her peers, and the teachers who partner with parents like us to nurture our children into adults with courage inspired by compassion, vision inspired by hope, and ambition inspired by empathy.

PREFACE

In the face of the current escalating culture wars in the United States regarding religion in the public square, many might legitimately wonder why anyone would choose to step into the crossfire between the "Christian Right" and the "liberal secularist Left" in the especially contentious issues related to religion and public education. Controversies such as the evolution/creationism/intelligent design debates, school prayer, sex education, and questions about how U.S. history should be taught are increasingly common in school communities all across the nation while the quality of discourse about these topics has simultaneously diminished to the extent that caricature and vitriol are commonplace.

For example, in November 2004 in Cupertino California, a fifth grade teacher named Stephen Williams claimed that he had been stopped from distributing historical documents to his students because the documents mentioned God. He brought a federal civil rights suit against the Cupertino Union School District and his principal claiming that he had been discriminated against because he is a devout Christian.[1] The principal, herself a Christian, alleged that Williams was presenting the material out of context and that he was promoting a conservative Christian agenda in ways that were in violation of the Establishment clause of the First Amendment prohibiting government sponsorship of religion.[2] The Alliance Defense Fund (ADF) represented Williams in the case and issued a press release with the inaccurate heading "Declaration of Independence Banned at California School"[3] that was picked up by Reuters. Within days there were scores of commentaries posted on several conservative Web sites condemning the alleged discrimination and focusing explicitly on the "fact" that the Declaration was banned. Many commentaries on these sites urged supporters of Williams to voice their protests directly and provided contact information for the principal and other administrators.[4] The principal received a barrage of emails in protest, including the following that represent the most disturbing extreme: "I can only say, you people up there are wayyyyy f----- up. Thank you." "Run Patricia, Run!! . . . F--- you very much communist c--t!!!!! Hope to see you soon."[5] Fox News ran several stories on the case and the program Hannity and Colmes moved their entire show to Cupertino and staged a rally to "Take America Back." Fox News repeatedly reported that the Declaration was banned from the school in spite of the fact that Williams never made that claim in the lawsuit itself.[6] Parents of the school also made an open plea to the ADF to apologize for misrepresenting the case, but the ADF never responded.[7] In April 2005, U.S. District Judge James Ware dismissed three of the four charges filed in the original suit. The remaining charge was one claiming that Williams had been discriminated against as a Christian.[8] In August 2005, the parties reached a settlement and the case was dismissed. In contrast to the media blitz that brought this case to the attention of the conservative community, relatively scant attention was given to the settlement and many Web sites still retained the original charge that the Declaration was banned months after the incident had been resolved. The ADF press release announcing the settlement is entitled "Settlement: Historic American Documents Can Be Taught in Cupertino Schools"[9] implying that the lawsuit led to a change in policy which, in fact, it did not.[10]

Incidents such as this one in Cupertino fuel both "Religious Right" proponents who claim there is a "secular conspiracy" to keep religion out of the schools and "liberal secularists" who equate religion with right-wing fanaticism. This debate is increasingly polarized to the extent that all other voices are rendered unintelligible because they fall outside of the context of these narrowly designated spheres of discourse. This fact alone is reason enough for any concerned citizen to get involved with this debate if only to challenge the legitimacy of the terms of discourse themselves. In truth, the study of religion should be more integrated into public school curricula across the disciplines and throughout the full span of compulsory K-8 or K-12 education. It is also true, however, that teachers should never promote a particular religious perspective over others or privilege religious over nonreligious world-views. It is my firm conviction that the current debate itself is allowed to flourish precisely because it is predicated on a widespread religious illiteracy that is being exploited by those who reside on its extremes.

This book is written for the vast majority of well-intentioned and thoughtful educators, parents, and citizens who are frustrated with the current state of public discourse about issues of such significant importance. Though not everyone will agree with the priorities and positions that I put forth here, it is my earnest hope that this book will serve as a method for a more respectful and transparent public conversation whereby foundational assumptions are exposed and positions are promoted in a spirit of dialogue rather than antagonism. The only people benefiting from these culture wars are those who are intentionally exploiting our vulnerability toward zealous and sometimes even nefarious ends. The most profound victims are our children who are learning that false representation of the facts, demonization of the "other," and simplistic (often self-righteous) absolutism are acceptable terms of public discourse about matters of tremendous importance and complexity. We owe them and ourselves more than that, and I have every confidence that we can do better. My hope is that this book will be received as a small contribution toward that goal, and it is therefore dedicated to educators who inspire us to realize our highest aspirations and to my daughter Lily and her generation who are ready for the challenge.

Notes

1. *Stephen J. Williams v. Patricia Vidmar, et al*, USDC, Northern District, San Jose, Case No. C044946, November 22, 2004.
2. Peter J. Boyer, "Jesus in the Classroom," The New Yorker, March 21, 2005.
3. Alliance Defense Fund, "Declaration of Independence Banned from Classroom," news release,November 23, 2004. http://www.alliancedefensefund.org/news/pressrelease.aspx?cid5 3218, accessed March 3, 2005.
4. See, for example, "Declaration of Independence Banned at California School!" The Drudge Report, November 24, 2004, http://www.drudgereportarchives.com/data/2004/11/24/ 20041124_220000.htm, accessed March 20, 2005; "Is Declaration of Independence Unconstitutional?" WorldNetDaily, November 23, 2004, http://www. worldnetdaily.com/news/article.asp?ARTICLE_ID=41623,accessed March 20, 2005; "Anti-God Squad Hits U.S. Classrooms!" USA Next, November 23, 2005, http://www.usanext.org/full_story.cfm?article_id=94&category_id=3, accessed March 20, 2005; "Battle over God in U.S. history class/Cupertino teacher sues to tell role of Christianity," The Scriptorium, December 9, 2005, http://rightwingerz.com/?m=20041209, accessed March 20, 2005; "A history lesson for the Cupertino Union School District" The American Thinker, December 15, 2005, http://www.americanthinker.com/articles.php?article_id=4099, accessed March 20, 2005.
5. Boyer, "Jesus in the Classroom," 62.
6. See "Fox peddles false report that California school 'banned Declaration of Independence because it mentions God,'" Media Matters for America, December 8, 2004, http://mediamatters.org/items/200412090002, accessed March 20, 2005. See, also, *Williams v. Vidmar, et. al*, November 22, 2004.
7. A copy of the parents' letter with a contextual introduction can be found at "California Parents Request Retraction and Apology from Alliance Defense Fund," http://www.stevenscreek parents.org/pr012505.htm, accessed March 20, 2005.
8. *Williams v. Vidmar, et. al*, April 28, 2005.
9. Ibid.

10. It was always legal and appropriate to teach about religion in American history classes and that policy did not change. The *San Jose Mercury News* ran an editorial entitled "The Cupertino Settlement Proves Case Was Weak," where the editors made the following assertion: "The agreement ending the suit simply reaffirms existing district practice: Educational material with religious content, including historical documents, can be used as long as it is objective, age-appropriate and in compliance with the curriculum prescribed by the district, and not being used to influence a student's religious beliefs (or lack thereof)." *San Jose Mercury News*, 22A, August 17, 2005.

PART ONE

Foundations

Introduction

Though the United States is one of the most religiously diverse nations in the world,[1] the vast majority of citizens are woefully ignorant about religion itself and the basic tenets of the world's major religious traditions. The consequences of this religious illiteracy are significant and include fueling the culture wars, curtailing historical and cultural understanding, and promoting religious and racial bigotry. The attacks on September 11, 2001 and their aftermath provide one lens through which to recognize some of these debilitating consequences. It is well known that in the wake of the terrorist attacks Muslims, Sikhs, Hindus, and people who were perceived by others to be of Middle Eastern and South Asian descents were targeted with hate crimes due to their presumed affiliation with terrorism. Less public attention is given to the fact that this form of misrepresentation and bigotry existed prior to 9/11 and continues to persist.[2]

Following the attacks many Americans experienced earnest feelings of shock and confusion that were represented through the oft-repeated phrase "Why do they hate us?" Attempts to help answer that question by anything more complex than "They hate our freedoms . . ."[3] were often silenced by accusations that proponents were "blaming America first" and were therefore unpatriotic and "anti-American." Efforts to discuss, for example, the historical complexities of U.S. involvement in the Israeli-Palestinian conflicts, our economic and political partnership with Saudi Arabia, or our role in supporting the establishment of the Taliban in Afghanistan during the Soviet-Afghan conflicts were often characterized as attempts to justify the terrorist acts themselves rather than help explain them.[4] Though I am not suggesting that our widespread religious illiteracy is the sole cause of these phenomena, I do contend that our lack of understanding about the ways that religion itself is an integral dimension of social/historical/political experience coupled with our ignorance about the specific tenets of the world's religious traditions significantly hinder our capacity to function as engaged, informed, and responsible citizens of our democracy. In these ways, religious illiteracy has helped to foster a climate that is both politically dangerous and intellectually debilitating.

There is a growing consensus that knowledge about religion and the world's religious traditions should be an integral part of a K-12 curriculum in public education. Contrary to popular understanding, teaching about religion in public schools is not unconstitutional. In fact, the failure to include religion in the curriculum can itself be interpreted as a violation of First Amendment guidelines. In the pivotal 1963 *Abington Township v. Schempp* Supreme Court decision banning state-sponsored prayer and Bible readings in public schools, Associate Justice Tom Clark wrote the following for the court:

> It might well be said that one's education is not complete without a study of comparative religion or the history of religion and its relationship to the advancement of civilization. It certainly may be said that the Bible is worthy of study for its literary and historic qualities. Nothing we have said here indicates that such study of the Bible or of religion, when presented objectively as part of a secular program of education, may not be effected consistently with the First Amendment.[5]

This decision highlights the difference between *teaching religion* or promoting a particular religious worldview and *teaching about religion* from a nonsectarian perspective. Though this distinction is extremely important and useful, putting this distinction into practice is a complex endeavor and that complexity will be addressed throughout this book. It is important to note at the outset, however, that the Constitution does not prohibit the study of religion in the schools.

Indeed, the study of religion has been increasingly incorporated in state standards and frameworks, especially in history, social studies, and English.[6] There are, however, correspondingly few teacher training opportunities or resources available for teachers to learn for themselves about the study of religion as it pertains to their discipline. Consequently, much of what passes as instruction in religion (well meaning though it may be) is informed by ignorance, stereotype, and unexamined sectarianism. Given the complexity of this topic, teachers and administrators often try to avoid the danger of a misstep by simply avoiding the topic altogether. They understand that this is a climate ripe for misunderstanding and exploitation and the current culture wars are but one dramatic consequence. The aim of this book is to give educators, parents, and other citizens some tools to begin to overcome this debilitating religious illiteracy. The specific goals are as follows:

1. To present a strong argument in support of including the academic study of religion in public schools from a comparative and multicultural lens that emphasizes diversity;
2. To construct methodologies and resources for secondary school teachers and teacher educators to gain the knowledge base and skills necessary to creatively teach about religion in constitutionally sound, intellectually responsible, and educationally innovative ways; and
3. To link theory with practice by illustrating some of the common mistakes and best practices of teachers who incorporate the academic study of religion in secondary school classrooms.

Context and Background

There are three complementary rationales for promoting religious literacy in the schools. The first is that without a basic understanding of the beliefs, symbols, literature, and practices related to the world's religious traditions, much of history and culture is rendered incomprehensible. Religion has always been and continues to be woven into the fabric of cultures and civilizations in ways that are inextricable. The failure to recognize this fact impoverishes our understanding of human experience and sends the false message that religion is primarily an individual as opposed to a social phenomenon. In fact, the very notion that religious devotion can be characterized as a "private" affair is itself a Protestant Christian construct and speaks to its cultural hegemony.

Second, religious worldviews provide alternative frameworks from which to critique normative cultural assumptions. In this way (contrary to popular belief) the study of religion can serve to enhance rather than thwart critical thinking and cultural imagination regarding human agency and capacity.

Third, knowledge of the basic tenets and structures of the world's religions is essential to a functioning democracy in our increasingly pluralistic age. This has always been true, but it is especially pronounced over the past few decades. As my colleague Diana Eck has so clearly articulated, since the 1965 *Immigration and Naturalization Act*, America's religious landscape has become increasingly diverse. Along with the indigenous populations of Native Americans and the early immigrant populations of Protestants, Catholics, and Jews, the United States is now home to a substantial number of Sikhs, Hindus, Buddhists, Baha'i, Muslims, Pagans, and Jains as well as people who claim no religious belief or affiliation. Having a basic knowledge of the world's religious traditions will deepen our understanding of multiculturalism and enhance our ability to embrace rather than fear our differences.

Other scholars in the field have provided important contributions that have helped frame the broad discussion outlined above.[7] Though several current volumes help illuminate significant dimensions of the issue, none of them delve deeply into the complexities of what it means to root these frameworks in actual practice from the perspective of religious pluralism. It is one thing to recognize the importance of religious literacy and quite another to teach about religion responsibly. This is the challenge that will be engaged in *Overcoming Religious Illiteracy*.

One final contextual note is in order. Though there is a growing consensus regarding the need to teach about religion in public schools, there are strong dissenting voices across the ideological spectrum. Many orthodox practitioners from a variety of traditions object on the grounds that they believe the academic approach to the study of religion (as opposed to the devotional approach) contradicts their theological convictions. Furthermore, many do not want their children to be taught about their own faith tradition (or others) in school because they feel that is the responsibility of the parents in concert with their faith communities. On the other hand, many progressive religious and secular voices fear that sectarian biases will inevitably prevail when religion is taught in public school, in spite of the best intentions of teachers, administrators, and school boards. It is important to note at the outset, however, that religion is *already* being taught in the schools in spite of these concerns. Unintentional sectarianism, antireligious biases and the intentional promotion of particular religious worldviews are already manifest in schools across the nation, though often unwittingly and/or without understanding the problematic nature of these practices. The aim of this book is to help educators recognize how religion is deeply imbedded in culture and to be more transparent about how it is addressed and engaged.

In Part One I lay out the basic frameworks regarding religion and education in American society. In the first chapter I ground this inquiry in my own theoretical framework by engaging the question of what the purpose of education *should* be. Here I draw upon the work of political philosopher Amy Gutmann and critical education theorist Paulo Freire to articulate the foundations of my own claims while simultaneously urging readers to articulate their own as well. In the second chapter I put forward several different arguments regarding why promoting religious literacy is an important and worthwhile endeavor in ways that challenge the extremes on both sides of the current debate about the role of religion in the schools. I include examples of how both repression and censorship are often promoted in the name of religious liberty in ways that are actually in violation of fundamental First Amendment protections. In the third chapter, I develop a cultural studies model for teaching about religion that emerges out of multicultural frameworks but also forges new ground in relationship to them. In the fourth chapter I discuss the implications that my assertions hold for both inservice and preservice teacher education programs.

In Part Two I explore the practical implementation of these ideas by offering experiences and reflections from my own classroom practices with secondary school students. I begin with a detailed focus on the importance of establishing a sound foundation during the first few days of a new course. Classroom cultures are often defined during these early meetings by either design or default, thus attention to how to construct an environment that is consistent with a cultural studies methodology is critical. I focus on a particular iteration of a course entitled Islamic Cultural Studies as a case study and continue to focus on this same course in Chapter Six where I identify and address common issues that arise when teaching about religion in the context of widespread religious illiteracy. In this chapter I also outline how I constructed the Islamic Cultural Studies syllabus and review student evaluations of the course. It is important to include reflections from students themselves about their own learning as well as their experience of the course methodology and this section provides significant and helpful information to balance my own reflections. In Chapter Seven I expand the discussion with suggestions regarding how to teach about religion in courses that are not focused on religion per se. I have chosen American history, economics, biology, and literature as examples representing the humanities, sciences, and social sciences. I close with a brief epilogue that focuses on a report issued by the First Amendment Center regarding a required world religions course for ninth grade students piloted in Modesto, California.

I hope that parents, students, educators, and other concerned citizens will find helpful resources in this book to address the challenging issues regarding religion and education that are manifested in classrooms across the country and that represent wider national tensions. We simply must cultivate more knowledge about and respect for the religious differences that represent an important dimension of our national identity. And we must do so in ways that will enhance rather than undermine the democratic ideals that unite us in multicultural, multireligious America.

CHAPTER ONE

The Purpose of Education

All of the students who go through the program I direct at Harvard Divinity School, the Program in Religion and Secondary Education, are required to articulate and periodically review their own answer to the following question: What is the purpose of education? My hope is that they will continue to do so throughout their teaching careers as one way to remind them why they were drawn to education in the first place and to inspire them to help create environments where their beliefs are aligned with their practices. There are, of course, a variety of often competing answers to this question and this has always been the case. Another reason I urge students in the Program and educators in general to articulate these fundamental assumptions is to encourage more transparency regarding the values that underlie policies and priorities in all educational arenas. In keeping with this call for transparency, it is only fitting that I begin by answering the question myself so that readers will understand the underlying values and beliefs that inform this project.

I believe that the purpose of mandatory K-8 or K-12 education in the United States should be for students to acquire the skills and experiences that will enable them 1) to function as active citizens who promote the ideals of democracy; 2) to act as thoughtful and informed moral agents; and 3) to lead fulfilling lives. These three goals are not discrete. Indeed, I will argue throughout this text that they are interrelated and even interdependent. First, however, a clear explication of each is required.

The Ideals of Democracy

The ideals embodied in the Declaration of Independence, the Constitution, and the Bill of Rights are noble ones worthy of our highest aspirations. The assertions that all humans are created equal and deserve to be afforded fundamental respect, dignity, and the conditions that will enable the flourishing of life, liberty, and the pursuit of happiness are grounded in a profoundly optimistic view of human capacity and purposefulness. The following definition of "democracy" that flows directly from these assertions is one I also affirm: "A state of society characterized by tolerance toward minorities, freedom of expression, and respect for the essential dignity and worth of the human individual with equal opportunity for each to develop freely to his [or her] fullest human capacity in a cooperative community."[1] In a general way, these values are ones that very few Americans would contest as worthy of our collective embrace. As such, it seems altogether appropriate that the promotion of these values should reside at the heart of the educational enterprise.

As history has proven, however, *how* these values are specifically defined, represented, and made manifest has always been and continues to remain hotly contested. Four arenas of interpretation that have proven to be contentious are 1) differing representations of what "tolerance toward minorities" should entail; 2) whether "freedom of expression" should ever be limited and, if so, under what circumstances; 3) debates regarding how "fullest human capacity" is ascertained given distinctions related to race, ethnicity, sex, sexual orientation, class, religion, physical ability, and other dimensions of human difference; and, in a related point, 4) competing notions of how "equal opportunity" should be defined and measured. It is instructive, for example, to understand how the founding fathers could wholeheartedly affirm the values put forth in the Declaration of Independence while at the same time justify the ownership of human beings as slaves. In a more contemporary example, how "democratic values" are defined is hotly contested in the current culture wars. This is why thoughtful, honest, and transparent discourse is required so that fundamental assertions regarding what constitutes democratic values can be exposed and debated on their merits.

Political philosopher Amy Gutmann has made an important contribution to this discussion in her text, *Democratic Education*.[2] Her central assertion is that democratic education in a deliberative democracy requires that the principles and methods promoted must be "compatible with our commitment to share the rights and the obligations of citizenship with people who do not share our complete conception of the good life."[3] A primary aim of education, then, must be to promote the skills and virtues of deliberation that will enable citizens in a pluralistic democracy to engage in what she defines as "conscious social reproduction in its most inclusive form."[4] By conscious social reproduction, Gutmann is referring to the necessity for citizens to continually review, interrogate, and debate the underlying values that are promoted in the name of democracy as a central expression of democracy itself.

> A guiding principle of deliberative democracy is reciprocity among free and equal individuals: citizens and their accountable representatives owe one another justifications for the laws that collectively bind them. A democracy is deliberative to the extent that citizens and their accountable representatives offer one another morally defensible reasons for mutually binding laws in an ongoing process of mutual justification.[5]

Thus, given that there will inevitably be competing beliefs among citizens regarding the values that should be promoted in the name of democracy, the principle of reciprocity must be enforced to ensure transparent engagement of and justification for the values that inform mutually binding laws In order for the principle of reciprocity to be made manifest, citizens must possess the skills and virtues associated with deliberation. They must be able to articulate their own assumptions and beliefs and to evaluate the articulations of others. The ability to deliberate must be cultivated and the act of deliberation promotes skills and virtues common to a well-functioning democracy.

> Deliberation is not a single skill or virtue. It calls upon skills of literacy, numeracy, and critical thinking, as well as contextual knowledge, understanding, and appreciation of other people's perspectives. The virtues that deliberation encompasses include veracity, nonviolence, practical judgment, civic integrity and magnanimity. By cultivating these and other deliberative skills and virtues, a democratic society helps secure both the basic opportunity of individuals and its collective capacity to pursue justice.[6]

Deliberation thus defined promotes both moral character and civic responsibility. "The willingness and ability to deliberate sets morally serious people apart from both sophists, who use clever argument to elevate their own interests into self-righteous causes, and traditionalists, who invoke established authority to subordinate their own reason to unjust cause."[7] Deliberation is essential to democracy and as such it must be widely cultivated for democracy itself to be sustained. It is incumbent upon schools to take on this responsibility, and in fact, cultivating the skills and values required to insure the future of democracy has been and continues to be a primary justification for *mandatory* K-8 or K-12 education.

Though the principle of reciprocity and the skills and virtues inherent in deliberation are necessary dimensions of education that will promote the ideals of democracy, they are themselves insufficient. For a society to be engaged in conscious social reproduction in its most inclusive form, citizens and future citizens must be *informed* about the differing conceptions of the good life that a multicultural democracy will inevitably inspire. There are three popular theories of education that address this issue that are rooted in differing conceptions of democracy. Gutmann considers and challenges all three and instead formulates what she calls "democratic education" that incorporates aspects of each while minimizing their antidemocratic expressions. The following is a brief summary of her argument, which is crucial in my own understanding of what constitutes a democratic education.

The first theory she represents and critiques is the "family state" which gives ultimate authority for education to the state based on the assumption that those in positions of authority know what is best for citizens and can therefore impose this understanding on the populace at large. In contrast, the "state of families" gives ultimate authority for education to parents based on the assumptions that they have a natural right of authority over their children. A third theory, the "state of individuals," champions individual autonomy and challenges any framework that would either hinder the range of choices regarding conceptions of "the good life" for students to pursue or any that would bias them toward one or more conceptions over others. Opportunity for *choice* and *neutrality* among choices are the values promoted by those who support this third theoretical framework.[8]

Gutmann rightly argues that all three fundamentally undermine democratic values even though all are all rooted in different representations of democratic theory. Educational manifestations based on both the family state and the state of families fail to expose children to competing claims of what constitutes the good life which, in turn, limits their ability to cultivate the skills of discernment and deliberation that will help them make responsible and informed choices as adult citizens in a multicultural democracy. On the other hand, when freedom of choice is itself considered paramount (represented in the state of individuals) moral relativism is promoted in ways that undermine the foundations of democracy itself. For example, if racial bigotry and mutual respect are represented as equally valid moral choices, then the foundational assumptions of democracy that promote equality and human dignity are undermined.

Gutmann, instead, supports what she calls democratic education that includes the fundamental assumption that educational authority must be shared among parents, citizens, and professional educators because this idea supports the core value of democracy as conscious social reproduction in its most inclusive form.

> Unlike a family state, a democratic state recognizes the value of parental education in perpetuating particular conceptions of the good life. Unlike a state of families, a democratic state recognizes the value of professional authority in enabling children to appreciate and to evaluate ways of life other than those favored by their families. Unlike a state of individuals, a democratic state recognizes the value of political education in predisposing children to accept those ways of life that are consistent with sharing the rights and responsibilities of citizenship in a democratic society. A democratic state is therefore committed to allocating educational authority in such a way as to provide its members with an education adequate to participating in democratic politics, to choosing among (a limited range of) good lives, and to sharing in the several sub-communities, such as families, that impart identity to the lives of its citizens.[9]

According to Gutmann, in order for conscious social reproduction to be achieved in its most inclusive form, two principled limits on parental and state control over education must be imposed by professional educators. These limits are *nonrepression* and *nondiscrimination*.

The principle of nonrepression is that which "prevents the state, or any group within it, from using education to restrict rational deliberation of competing conceptions of the good life and the good society."[10] Citizens must be free to engage a variety of competing claims in order to make informed and intelligent choices in a multicultural democracy. Democratic education, therefore, must expose children to a wide variety of options (consistent with the values of democracy) and to instill in them the tools of rational deliberation in consideration of those options. "Adults must therefore be prevented from using their present deliberative freedom to undermine the future deliberative freedom of children . . . Because *conscious* social reproduction is the primary ideal of democratic education, communities must be prevented from using education to stifle rational deliberation of competing conceptions of the good life and the good society."[11] Though I will develop this notion more fully in the next chapter, it is important to note here that the principle of nonrepression can be used to both support the inclusion of study about religion in the schools as well as to challenge educational practices that privilege what I have defined as "exclusive" sectarian over "inclusive" sectarian and/or nonsectarian dimensions of education.[12]

The second limit on democratic authority that Gutmann cites is that of nondiscrimination. Fundamentally, this principle supports the notion that "all educable children must be educated." Nondiscrimination challenges the legitimacy of overt and covert forms of discrimination whereby racial minorities and/or other historically marginalized or disfavored groups are denied adequate forms of education. "The effect of discrimination is often to repress, at least temporarily, the capacity and even the desire of these groups to participate in the processes that structure choice . . . Applied to those forms of education necessary to prepare children for future citizenship (participation in conscious social reproduction), the nondiscrimination principle becomes a principle of nonexclusion. No educable child may be excluded from an education adequate to participating in the political processes that structure choice among good lives."[13] This also applies to subtle forms of exclusion such as race or gender biases whereby some children are considered less capable and/or less "worthy" than others.

Significant to my purposes, the principle of nondiscrimination applies to both the structure and *content* of education. Structurally, all children should be afforded access to quality education, including the conditions that allow them to flourish. Regarding content, the contributions of historically marginalized groups need to be included in the curriculum to accurately represent the multicultural dimensions of human civilizations, both past and present.[14] This principle also applies directly to issues related to the inclusion of religion and religious worldviews into the curriculum.

These two principles, nonrepression and nondiscrimination are foundational to the primary ends of democratic education: conscious social reproduction in its most inclusive form. According to Gutmann, democratic education builds upon the best of the three prominent political theories outlined above while minimizing the antidemocratic tendencies implicit in them all.

> Like the family state, a democratic state of education tries to teach virtue—not the virtue of the family state (power based upon knowledge), but what might best be called *democratic* virtue: the

> ability to deliberate, and hence to participate in conscious social reproduction. Like the state of families, a democratic state upholds a degree of parental authority over education, resisting the strong communitarian view that children are creatures of the state. But in recognizing that children are future citizens, the democratic state resists the view, implicit in the state of families, that children are creatures of their parents. Like the state of individuals, a democratic state defends a degree of professional authority over education—not on grounds of liberal neutrality, but to the extent necessary to provide children with the capacity to evaluate those ways of life most favored by parental and political authorities.[15]

Democratic education as defined above is a method intended to promote the conditions that will enable democracy to flourish in present and future contexts. Nonrepression and nondiscrimination are limits that are imposed in the name of democracy itself and must be enforced if conscious social reproduction in its most inclusive form is to be honestly enabled. The alternatives of limiting exposure to competing conceptions of the good life and/or limiting participation of all citizens as participants in democratic discourse and discernment erode the foundations of democracy and threaten its future. I am firmly convinced that Gutmann's understanding of democratic education provides the basic minimum requirements to cultivate democratic values within our future citizens.

Before moving on, I want to say a brief word about the role of independent schools and homeschooling in relation to democratic education. I will elaborate upon them further in Chapter Three, but it is important to note here that in a multicultural democracy, *all* forms of education should be required to at least minimally promote the fundamental values of democracy as outlined above. This includes (but is not restricted to) educational contexts that are explicitly religious. When parents are allowed to keep their children from exposure to those who are different and/or shield them from respectful consideration of reasonable views they oppose, then democratic values are compromised in the service of the state of families. At the same time, the family state cannot deny the rights of parents to choose an educational venue that represents their values, including religious ones. All forms of accredited schooling (public or independent) should be required to meet the minimum standards of democratic education as outlined above to insure that future citizens will both value democracy and have the tools to actively engage in its conscious social reproduction. Precisely how these minimal standards are defined and how they should be determined are questions that need to be deliberated, but no child should be denied the experience and skills that will enable her or him to participate as an informed and active citizen of our multicultural democracy.

Finally, it is important to note that the interests of the state and that of parents need not be interpreted as antagonistic. As Gutmann states, "Parents acting individually and citizens acting collectively both have valuable and largely complementary roles to play in the moral education of children: the former in teaching children what it means to be committed to particular people and one way of life among many; the latter in teaching responsibilities and rights within a larger and more diverse community. Moral education in a democracy is best viewed as a shared trust of the family and the polity, mutually beneficial to everyone who appreciates the values of both family life and democratic citizenship."[16] This understanding of complementarity is also critical to a well-functioning multicultural democracy where diversity and individuality are both centrally valued.

Cultivating Moral Agency

The maintenance and promotion of the democratic values outlined above depend on an active and informed citizenry. Schools should inspire and empower students to take themselves seriously as moral agents capable of making a positive difference in the world. In my view, this requires the development of 1) critical thinking skills; 2) self-confidence; and 3) humility.

Critical Thinking Skills

It is well documented that many atrocities have historically been and continue to be justified in the name of democracy and/or morality. Claiming to act in the service of high ideals is no guarantee that those ideals are being represented; indeed, such claims are often used to mask nefarious action and intent. Essential to a well-functioning democracy is the capacity for its citizens to think critically and independently so as to discern and interrogate the underlying assumptions that inform all value claims. This transparency will not lead to clear consensus, but it will provide the foundations for a more informed deliberation about which values are appropriate ones to promote in the context of our multicultural democracy. Actions or assumptions promoted in the name of patriotism, religion, science, and/or human nature should all be able to withstand public scrutiny based on whether they promote democratic values as defined above. Students need to be taught critical thinking skills so that they can ask these fundamental questions and evaluate the responses they receive.

Like broad definitions of democracy, there are few who would challenge the notion that critical thinking is an essential skill that should be highlighted throughout K-12 education and beyond. Much more controversial are discussions about *how* critical thinking should be fostered. In my view, critical thinking must be modeled in the classroom and this requires a shift from what educational theorist Paulo Freire called "banking models" of education to those that focus instead on "problem-posing" methods. He outlined these distinctions in his classic text *Pedagogy of the Oppressed* and his understanding is worth discussing at length.

Banking models of education are teacher rather than learner-centered and make the following assumptions:

1. the teacher teaches and the students are taught;
2. the teacher knows everything and the students know nothing;
3. the teacher thinks and the students are thought about;
4. the teacher talks and the students listen;
5. the teacher disciplines and the students are disciplined;
6. the teacher chooses and enforces her/his choice, and the students comply;
7. the teacher acts and the students have the illusion of acting through the action of the teacher;
8. the teacher chooses the program contents, and the students (who were not consulted) adapt to it;
9. the teacher confuses the authority of knowledge with her/his own professional authority, which she/he sets in opposition to the freedom of the students;
10. the teacher is the Subject of the learning process, while the pupils are mere objects.[17]

Freire argues that this method of teaching promotes passivity and knowledge accumulation rather than critical thinking. "The more students work at storing the deposits entrusted to them, the less they develop the critical consciousness which would result from their intervention in the world as transformers of that world. The more completely they accept the passive role imposed on them, the more they tend simply to adapt to the world as it is and to the fragmented view of reality deposited in them."[18]

Problem-posing education, in contrast, is learner-centered and invites (indeed, requires) learners to be active participants in the educational enterprise. The emphasis is on asking questions and posing problems to ponder rather than the accumulation of knowledge defined as objective facts or the uncritical acceptance of authority. Thus, in contrast to the banking model outlined above, assumptions that inform a problem-posing method of education include the following:

1. both teacher and students teach;
2. both teacher and students have knowledge and important perspectives to share;
3. both teacher and students think and are thought about;
4. teacher and students engage in dialogue together;
5. teacher and students share responsibility for creating a classroom atmosphere of respect;
6. teacher and students choose and are transparent about their choices and the foundations that inform them;
7. both teacher and students act;
8. the teacher is transparent about program content and the students have choices within a problem-posing framework;
9. the teacher is clear about the distinction between her/his experience and knowledge of a particular field and her/his freedom;
10. teacher and students are Subjects.[19]

Freire is often misunderstood as promoting the simplistic notion that there are no fundamental differences between teacher and student regarding roles and responsibilities in the classroom. This is not the case as is clearly represented in points 8 and 9 as defined above. What he is asserting, however, is that teacher and students should be consciously working toward the common goal of promoting humanization amidst the dehumanizing structures of oppression that Freire rightly insists are harmful to everyone.[20] Banking models of education are problematic because they promote the uncritical reproduction of both knowledge itself and a form of blind acceptance of authority. Problem-posing methods, on the other hand, require that students and teachers engage together in a process of ever deepening consciousness (*conscientization*) by interrogating the underlying ideologies that give legitimacy to knowledge claims.

To illustrate these distinctions, consider the subject of slavery in the United States. Banking Model A: The teacher might have students read about slavery in a standard textbook and/or see a film that recreates some aspect of the life of slavery. The teacher might then lead a discussion about the content of the reading and/or film with an emphasis on the facts presented, including the horrors of slavery itself. Students might then be asked to write an essay or take a test about what they learned.

Banking Model B: The teacher might have students read a different account of slavery that is explicitly critical of the economic factors that drove the industry and the underlying values regarding race, class, and gender that gave legitimacy to the institution. The teacher might then lead a discussion about the content of the reading with an emphasis on the facts presented. Students might then be asked to write an essay or take a test about what they learned.

Regardless of the content of the lesson, both models are banking models because 1) all knowledge is transferred uncritically through a designated authority whether it be the teacher, the author of the text or the narrator of the film; 2) the lessons are content versus process driven; 3) they fail to encourage students to interrogate the underlying assumptions of the perspectives represented; 4) they fail to engage students as subjects who are expected to respond to the material from their own perspectives and assumptions; and 5) they fail to address how the study of slavery is relevant to our lives today.

As an alternative to the banking model, problem-posing methods require the active engagement of students who are treated with respect as subjects who are capable of wrestling with challenging issues. For example, the teacher might ask the students to break into groups to brainstorm answers to the question "How was slavery in the U.S. justified?" Answers could be compiled and students could choose specific dimensions to explore more fully in pairs or groups and report their findings to the class. The teacher would work with the students and the librarians to help the students find credible resources that represent the complexity of the dimensions explored to avoid simplistic characterizations of "good" versus "bad" people. Instead, students would explore and confront the structural dimensions of power that gave social legitimacy to an institution that most Americans now consider abhorrent. The class could then generate further questions that include applying these tools of critical reflection to contemporary issues we face today. The overarching questions that guide the entire enterprise would be "Are we as a society living up to the values affirmed in our founding documents?" "If so, how?" "What are the factors that support us in manifesting these ideals?" "What are the factors that hinder our ability to achieve those aspirations?" Problem-posing methods promote critical thinking by inviting students to ask and attempt to answer questions of real significance. The difference between knowing facts about slavery and wrestling with the complex questions regarding *how* the institution arose and was sustained is a profound one. The former promotes passivity regardless of the ideological content of the facts presented while the latter promotes active agency by encouraging the interrogation of the underlying assumptions that inform all knowledge claims.

Some might argue that banking methods are needed to first give students the basic material that they can then ponder and interrogate. It is true that students need information and a basic point of departure to give context to anything they study. It is, appropriately, the role of the teacher to provide that context. *How* this is achieved marks the difference between banking and problem-posing methods. In the example cited above, the context could be established by having the students read *both* sources cited in my illustration of banking models A and B and to have *them* comment on the similarities and differences in presentation. This in itself provides both context and an example of how knowledge claims are, by necessity, always subjective. The work of the critical thinker is to recognize this and to attempt to discern what the underlying values are of the perspective being represented.

This same assumption applies to teachers and the ways that curricula is constructed and implemented. From the problem-posing perspective, teachers should always be explicitly transparent with their students about what they are hoping to achieve through each lesson in particular and in education in general. As a result of the teacher's articulation, students should be able to 1) understand what the teacher's guiding principles and assumptions are regarding the content and methods that are adopted and/or reproduced[21] and 2) answer the basic question "Why does this matter?" in a way that they will find convincing and compelling. Problem-posing methods require that education be meaningful and relevant to students themselves. The fact that this notion may seem radical and/or ill-fated is a measure of how students are often treated as objects versus subjects in the educational enterprise.

One of Freire's greatest contributions is his understanding of how structures of oppression are reproduced unwittingly when critical thinking is not fostered. The simple demonization of slave owners (or Nazis or members of the Taliban, etc.) fails to recognize how social structures arose in the service of certain ideological assumptions that gave contemporary social legitimacy to actions and values that we, in hindsight, find reprehensible. By demonizing those in the past, we fail to recognize their similarities to us in our own contemporary context. What are the social structures that are currently operative in our own time that lend social legitimacy to practices and values that future generations (or perhaps we ourselves in hindsight) will consider immoral? His assertions that 1) the vocation of humanity is humanization; 2) structures of oppression dehumanize; 3) dehumanization is harmful to *both* those who are oppressed as well as those who are agents of oppression; 4) structures of oppression are often unwittingly reproduced; and 5) structures of oppression can be transformed by human agency, all closely mirror the optimistic view of human nature and capacity that are represented in the democratic ideals outlined above. Students should be encouraged to foster this optimism and the critical thinking skills necessary to recognize and interrogate contemporary social values and assumptions to ensure that the values promoted are consistent with those they consciously wish to promote.

Confidence and Humility

In order to act as thoughtful moral agents, citizens must also develop confidence that their voices and perspectives matter. Problem-posing forms of education can promote deep confidence in students because teachers and peers take them seriously as subjects who have important perspectives to share and contributions to make. When discernment and deliberation replace recitation of facts and/or perspectives as the focus of the educational enterprise, each voice is valued as a contributing member of the debate. Encouraging students to take themselves seriously and inspiring in them the confidence to do so are two of the most important roles of an educator in a multicultural democracy.

Classrooms that promote critical thinking should also mirror the process of social discourse itself whereby differing views are engaged in an atmosphere of mutual respect and dialogue. Students will learn how to listen attentively, agree or disagree respectfully, and work toward enhancing understanding toward ideals that are commonly forged. Cultivating confidence by honestly valuing the contributions of everyone, even (and perhaps especially) those with whom we disagree is another cornerstone of a well-functioning democracy.

Another important contribution that Freire made was his recognition that our work as moral agents requires humility.[22] Though good intention is important, this alone will not dismantle the structures of oppression that continue to thwart our ability to fully manifest democratic ideals. The ideological assumptions that lend social legitimacy to all value claims are deeply rooted and broadly influential. For example, my own longstanding commitment to antiracism is not in itself sufficient to keep me from holding racist beliefs or acting on racist assumptions. As a white woman in a society where whiteness is still privileged, I have been exposed to overt and covert forms of racism and racist ideologies all of my life. One of the consequences of white privilege, however, is that I do not always recognize racism when I see it and I often perpetuate racist assumptions unwittingly. On the other hand, as a feminist and lesbian, I encounter blatant forms of discrimination daily at the hands of people who are not always aware of their assumptions and who would often be appalled to realize the effects of their unconscious actions.

Freire recognized that the ideological assumptions that give social legitimacy to various forms of oppression are deeply rooted and require conscientization to recognize and interrogate those assumptions. He suggests *praxis* as the method of ongoing conscientization, and praxis is defined as a continual process of reflection, action, and further reflection that will inspire a new action.[23] This method of action, reflection, and action is done in communities and requires humility as well as conviction and confidence on the part of all participants: confidence to take oneself seriously as an active moral agent involved in a process of discernment, and humility to realize that there is always more to learn about the complex ways that we ourselves often embody and practice ideologies of discrimination unwittingly. If good intention alone were sufficient to dismantle the structures of dehumanization we would have achieved our goal long ago. Though good intention matters (one can consciously choose to promote racist or sexist beliefs, for example) it is only the beginning of the work. Engaging in praxis with both confidence and humility is required to imagine and construct new ways of being in relationship to one another.

If we take seriously the assumptions that 1) good intentions alone will not dismantle the structural dimensions that continue to thwart our ability to fully manifest democratic ideals; 2) dehumanization is often reproduced unwittingly; and 3) promoting humanization requires conscious reflection regarding our own actions and assumptions and interrogating them in light of our beliefs; then we must always be open to learning about the ways that we ourselves fall short of living out our own ideals with integrity. Ethicist Sharon Welch has coined a phrase that captures beautifully how moral agents can hold both confidence and humility in tension: in our moral convictions we must be "whole hearted and half sure."[24] Dogmatic and unyielding assertions presume an absolutism that is neither intellectually nor morally credible, yet weak and/or relativist claims are void of conviction and integrity. Fostering humility is not a sign of weakness but of strength. We should cultivate in students a sense of passionate conviction about the ideals of our multicultural democracy while helping them remember that the manifestation of those ideals must be forged through praxis in democratic community that is defined in dialogue and deliberation with others.

If an important goal of education is to foster active citizens who are both eager to participate in and capable of shaping our multicultural democracy, then schools must cultivate in students a sense of their own moral agency. Moral agency in the service of democratic ideals requires critical thinking, self-confidence, and humility, and these traits and skills should be encouraged and modeled throughout the K-12 curriculum.

To Lead Fulfilling Lives

Finally, K-12 education should also be promoted in the service of providing citizens with the skills and tools to be able to lead fulfilling lives. Promoting democratic ideals and encouraging citizens to recognize their role as moral agents in fostering those ideals are certainly important dimensions of a meaningful and purposeful life. Education should also, however, inspire individual imagination, creativity, the thrill of discovery and an empowering sense of self-determination. This enterprise is fraught with complexity within the context of a society whose social conditions do not yet authentically foster equal opportunities for all. Indeed, Jonathan Kozol captures the heartbreaking irony of how schools themselves symbolically represent the promise of equal opportunity when in reality they are a stark demonstration of the nation's profound economic and material disparity.[25] Remember that one of Gutmann's main assertions is that in a democracy "all educable students should be [adequately] educated." Though we are a long way from manifesting this fundamental right, students should still feel empowered in schools and encouraged to discover and cultivate skills and talents that will enable them to be lifelong learners. Literacy of all kinds (numeric, artistic, scientific, religious, linguistic, cultural) should be consistently promoted and evaluated in ways that are meaningful and relevant. There is simply no reason for education to feel burdensome to students if it is learner-centered and purposeful. Children of all ages are naturally curious and eager to be taken seriously. Engaging in learner-centered approaches to education does not mean sacrificing rigor. As teachers (and parents) well know, students who are personally invested in the learning process and feel supported and encouraged are often motivated to excel. It could, in fact, be argued that intellectual rigor is sacrificed when education is solely or even primarily content (in the form of "banking") versus process (in the form of "problem-posing") driven.

In conclusion, I believe that the purpose of education in our multicultural/multireligious democracy is to foster the skills, values, interest, and confidence in students to be able to participate as active moral agents in the conscious social reproduction of society in its most inclusive form. The skills and virtues that are promoted toward this end are also those consistent with the cultivation of a personally meaningful and fulfilling life. The central moral values that form the foundation of this conception of education are "tolerance toward minorities, freedom of expression," and the belief that "all humans are created equal" with "essential dignity and worth" and should therefore be granted "equal opportunity . . . to develop freely to [their] fullest human capacity in a cooperative community."[26] The cultivation of a society where these values can be realized is a worthy and potentially unifying goal amidst our vast and complex diversities. Though there will inevitably be disagreement about how to promote these values and what forms they will take, by fostering the skills of democratic discourse and deliberation we can promote a method of constructive engagement of our differences which may itself be the defining feature of a healthy and vibrant democracy.

It is important to note here that the structural dimensions of public education in the form of unequal funding and resources, high stakes testing, wide disparities regarding student preparation, large class sizes, and so on place enormous burden on educators who often feel unable to significantly impact the larger forces that shape the context of their individual practices. In this climate, my articulations regarding the primary purposes of education as promoting the ideals of democracy, moral agency, and the conditions that will foster a love of learning may seem unrealistic to teachers who might otherwise share these values. My comments are not intended to minimize or ignore the larger structural challenges that teachers face today. Indeed, I believe that these larger realities should be directly acknowledged and addressed in our own educational communities (including, where appropriate, in our classrooms) as a critical aspect of deliberative democracy. These burdens are real ones and often place teachers in untenable situations. The reason I urge educators to articulate what they believe should be the purpose of education is so that they will be able to be more explicit about how the structural dimensions that shape the context of their teaching either enhance or hinder their ability to align their beliefs with their practices. This consciousness can provide the foundation for teachers to become more active in public policy debates from their perspective as professionals with expertise to share. Classroom educators are too often absent from these policy debates and their voices need to be heard, respected, and engaged.

All citizens and especially educators and educational theorists should be encouraged to articulate and defend what they believe should be the purpose of education. Though I do not expect that all readers will agree with the values that I promote here, I hope that these ideas will be openly engaged and debated in the spirit of honest, respectful, deliberative discourse. There is a lot at stake in this question and it deserves our serious, collective consideration. What we are ultimately educating our children *for* should be of significant concern to us all.

CHAPTER TWO

Why Religion Should Be Included in Public School Education

"Islam promotes violence and discrimination against women."
"Hinduism is a cult."
"America is a Christian nation."
"Homosexuality is a sin."
"In their heart of hearts, all Muslims are terrorists."
"Buddhists aren't violent."
"Mormons aren't Christian."
"Religion and reason are incompatible."
"Christianity is a peaceful religion."
"Jews killed Christ."

One of the greatest ironies of our intellectual life in the Unites States is that though we are the world's most religiously diverse nation we are also its most religiously illiterate. Because the two primary sources of information about religion are the media and people's own faith traditions (or none), relatively few people possess even a basic understanding of the tenets of the world's religious traditions, let alone an understanding of the complex ways that religion influences and is influenced by social, cultural, and historical forces. Public debates about religion are often painfully misguided and/or superficial because relatively few people possess the knowledge to critically assess sectarian claims or to intelligently challenge those who dismiss religion altogether as the product of blind naiveté or fanaticism. The quotes cited at the beginning of this chapter are typical of students, friends, and professional colleagues (outside of religious studies). Very few (if any) of the authors of these statements would make similarly unqualified pronouncements about any other topic, yet when engaging issues related to religion they speak with unfettered confidence as though their assertions were self-evident.

In this chapter, I will address these concerns by articulating how the promotion of religious literacy will enhance democratic discourse by cultivating discernment, understanding, and respect as they relate to religion in American public life. In the first part of the chapter I will discuss how inclusion of the study of religion in schools will help promote intellectual rigor, critical thinking, and deep multiculturalism. As noted in Chapter One, these are values that are central to the perpetuation of a healthy democracy as well as to the promotion of a meaningful life. In the second part of the chapter, I will demonstrate through a series of examples associated with the culture wars how religious illiteracy can and often does thwart democratic discourse in schools by creating conditions whereby the violation of the principles of nonrepression and nondiscrimination are widespread. Here I argue that public schools need to help future citizens develop the tools to deliberate about controversial matters from an informed perspective and in contexts aimed at deepening understanding rather than fueling antagonism. The culture wars are themselves predicated on ignorance and fueled by misrepresentation. Both tactics are at cross-purposes with deliberative democracy and therefore need to be exposed and challenged.

By presenting positive examples of how the study of religion will enhance the educational enterprise as well as negative illustrations of how religious illiteracy thwarts understanding and diminishes the ability to engage in rational deliberation, I hope to convince readers of the urgent need to promote religious literacy in the schools.

Promoting Religious Literacy

There are several reasons why the study of religion should be included in public school curricula across the K-12 spectrum. The most fundamental and comprehensive is that religion has always been and continues to function as a powerful dimension of human experience. Religious beliefs, expressions, and worldviews have inspired and affected the full spectrum of human agency in artistic, philosophical, ethical, political, scientific, and economic arenas. Attempts to "extract" religion from experience or to ignore its influences are not only futile but also misguided. Such an approach leads to subjects of inquiry being presented in a fragmented light and understanding is therefore significantly diminished if not altogether thwarted. In this way, religion is similar to race, ethnicity, gender, and class. For example, just as it is impossible to understand and interpret the founding documents of U.S. history accurately without acknowledging that all women, men of color, and poor white men were originally excluded from citizenship rights, it is equally impossible to adequately comprehend these documents without an understanding of the religious context out of which they were forged. Increasing our collective understanding of that context would both deepen our appreciation of the complexity of those early years of the Republic while simultaneously giving students the tools to critically engage current debates regarding the ideological foundations of the nation and the proper role of religion in American public life.

Another example comes from the realm of literature. In a general way, when the religious contexts and/or sensibilities of texts and authors are explored, understanding is enhanced. Familiar texts can become alive in new ways, and students learn the tools to engage similar sets of questions from their own interpretive lenses. More specifically, understanding can also be enhanced when students are exposed to the foundational literature of the world's religious traditions from a nonsectarian perspective. For example, in a recent study commissioned by the Bible Literacy Project under a grant from the John Templeton Foundation, ninety percent of the high school English teachers surveyed believed that basic biblical literacy was important for students as a foundation to understanding Western literature.[1] One teacher made the comment that "It is difficult to pick up a piece of [Western] literature that doesn't have some reference to the Bible."[2] Yet, amajority of the teachers in the study estimated that fewer than one quarter of their current students were biblically literate.[3] Though "Bible as Literature" courses are not uncommon in secondary classrooms, more could be offered and their overall quality could be enhanced.[4] It would also be beneficial to offer similar courses on other foundational religious texts that have themselves influenced world literature, such as the *Qur'an*, the *Mahabharata*, and the *Tao Te Ching*. All of these texts, including the Bible, have literary merit in their own right as well as for their significant cultural influences. Religious literacy should include exposure to "sacred" texts from a variety of traditions that are studied from a nonsectarian perspective.

In truth, religious influences have always been and continue to be intimately woven into the fabric of human cultures and have therefore impacted human experiences in ways that include but go well beyond individual expressions of belief. When the religious dimensions of experience are recognized, then rich avenues of exploration are revealed and the intellectual enterprise across the curriculum can be significantly enhanced.

A second reason why the study of religion should be incorporated into curricula is that it invites students to identify and question underlying foundations of assumption in ways that inspire engaged reflection and critical thinking. This dimension of understanding includes both the "why" of human agency as well as the "why" of existence itself.[5] The answers to these questions are, of course, as varied as humanity itself and include both religious and nonreligious motivations and claims. The Holocaust provides a helpful lens to illustrate this critical aspect of the educational enterprise.

Though it is possible to study the Holocaust as a compilation of facts and figures, it would be a shallow and arguably an extremely troubling endeavor if "why" questions were not also engaged. The study of the Holocaust is the study of human capacity in its extremes where ordinary people sometimes acted in extraordinary ways as agents of both heinous cruelty and nearly unfathomable courage and compassion. How does one make sense of this spectrum in relationship to larger questions of meaning? Answers to this question are widely varied, including assertions that it is impossible to affirm "meaning" in the face of this horror[6] to speculative claims of meaning found through suffering[7] to justifications of extermination and repression represented in overt and covert beliefs that victims deserved their fate.[8] What motivated the Nazis to act in the ways that they did and what rationales did they employ to justify their actions? What assumptions about human nature were these rationales based upon and how were they represented and justified? How did "ordinary" citizens respond? How did those who survived sustain themselves against tremendous odds? What motivated rescuers and resistors? Religion plays an important role in pondering these questions; a role that includes but goes well beyond the fact that the majority of the victims of the Holocaust were Jews and the majority of perpetrators were Christian.

An example of this kind of complex thinking is Irving Greenberg's classic essay "Cloud of Smoke, Pillar of Fire" in which he offers a searing indictment of pre-Holocaust Judaism, Christianity, and Enlightenment secularism as failed systems that actually helped give rise to the "legitimization" of the Nazi state. He challenges the simplistic dichotomy between "secular" and "religious" and calls instead for a "postmodern faith" that can speak meaningfully to the specter of the crematorium. "Neither classical theism nor atheism is adequate to incorporate the incommensurability of the Holocaust; neither produced a consistently proper response; neither is credible alone—in the presence of the burning children."[9] Whether one finds Greenberg's specific assertions compelling or not,[10] he offers an example of someone who articulates and engages important *questions* that need to be considered if we are to take the study of human experience seriously. The failure to include the religious dimensions of these experiences and questions impoverishes understanding and diminishes opportunities for critical thinking and reflection.

A third reason why the study of religion should be incorporated more fully into curricula is that ignorance about religion itself and the world's religious traditions promotes misunderstanding that diminishes respect for diversity. As noted in the "Introduction", following 9/11 hate crimes against Muslims, Sikhs, and those perceived to be of Middle Eastern or South Asian descents were widely publicized and still persist. Similarly, the patriotism of non-Christians and especially nonbelievers is sometimes questioned while, conversely, many who profess no religious faith equate religion with right-wing fanaticism and/or ignorance, irrationality, and arrogant self-righteousness. Stereotypes abound and are easily perpetuated in the face of widespread ignorance and misrepresentation. Consider the following examples of what can happen when there is ignorance of the world's religious traditions and their appropriate expressions.

1. On February 4, 2005, a 15-year-old Sikh honors student at Woodlands High School in Hartsdale, New York was charged with carrying a weapon and suspended from school for eight days. Amandeep Singh had worn the kirpan (a ceremonial dagger that all male initiated Sikhs wear) since taking *amrit* (vows) at eight years of age and never had any difficulties until this incident. A fellow classmate saw it and decided to report it to the principal. Amandeep's 22-year-old brother Kamaldeep stated, "He never had any disciplinary problems. Teachers loved him. They knew about the kirpan. It is ironic, because it is a place of education, but if the school had the knowledge about a kirpan, this would never have happened. They saw it as a weapon, and we view it as an article of faith comparable to a yarmulke or a cross." On April 1, 2005, the suspension record was revoked and authorities allowed him to wear a smaller version of the sacred symbol.[11]
2. In 2001, as part of the reauthorization of the *Elementary and Secondary Education Act* (No Child Left Behind) the U.S. Department of

Education issued a statement entitled *Guidance on Constitutionally Protected Prayer in Elementary and Secondary Schools.*[12] These guidelines articulate what is and is not allowed regarding First Amendment protections for students and teachers. They clearly state that students are free to form religious clubs, bring their books of faith to school and read them, incorporate their religious views into classroom assignments where relevant, and to pray before or between classes. Schools that do not comply with these guidelines are threatened with the loss of federal funding. In spite of these clear articulations, teachers are still often confused about what constitutes acceptable practices. For example, a secondary school teacher in a suburban school in Texas assigned an essay on "The person you admire most." She rejected a student's submission on Jesus because the teacher mistakenly believed it to be unconstitutional. The instructor reversed her decision after consultation with her principal and colleagues, but she later reported that the student was "really upset about it all in a deep way. She poured her heart into that essay and believed that I rejected her faith. She never quite opened up again throughout the rest of the term. I really blew it."[13]

3. Samieh Shalash is a reporter for the *Lexington Herald Leader* and published an article recounting her experiences growing up as a Muslim in Lexington, Kentucky.

> Most 5-year-old girls run from the bully on the playground who wants to yank their pigtails. As a kindergartener, I ran from the bully who wanted to tug off my hijab, the Islamic head cover. "Is Saddam Hussein your daddy?" I was asked in fourth grade. Seventh grade brought frequent taunts of "towelhead" from a gang of boys.

She and her family are still frequently mistaken for being "foreign born" as the following incidents reveal:

> Strangers often ask where we're from, expecting "Saudi Arabia" or "Iraq." The answer—born and raised in Lexington—usually surprises them. A saleswoman once complimented my language skills: "Wow, you speak really good English." In another incident, a sweet older gentleman was shocked when I answered, "I'm Muslim" after he asked why

> I cover my hair. "You can't be Muslim, young lady. You've got freckles," he said earnestly.[14]

These incidents speak for themselves. Exposing students to a more informed and sophisticated understanding of religion will not, in itself, end discrimination or unintended harm perpetuated through ignorance. It will, however, help diminish discriminatory practices while also providing information to help educators proactively shape their educational environments so that *all* students feel a sense of belonging. Though ensuring the safety of students by enforcing minimum standards of tolerance may be legally required; this minimum is grossly inadequate as the foundation for a learning community responsible for promoting the ideals of deliberative democracy in a multicultural society. Even in schools where the population is seemingly (or perhaps truly) religiously homogenous, cultivating an informed respect for religious differences will equip students with the skills and temperaments to function more meaningfully and effectively within their home communities and the workplace realities they are likely to encounter in the future.

Promoting religious literacy in the schools will enhance intellectual rigor, sharpen critical thinking skills, and further advance deep multiculturalism by giving students the tools to understand religion and the plurality of religious experiences across the curriculum and within the school community itself. In the next chapter I will outline some fundamental guidelines about how to advance religious literacy in constitutionally sound, intellectually responsible, and educationally innovative ways. First, however, a more general discussion is needed regarding how religious illiteracy can and often does thwart democratic discourse in the schools by violating the principles of nonrepression and nondiscrimination.

Religious Illiteracy: Manifestations and Consequences

Remember that the form of freedom that nonrepression secures "is not a freedom to pursue the singularly correct way of personal or political life, but the freedom to deliberate rationally among differing ways of life."[15] The principle of nonrepression as it relates to religion and education is frequently violated in ways that both "conservative" and "progressive" voices in the culture wars have tried to convey.[16] For example, repression is sanctioned when teaching about religion in the schools is prohibited or seriously restricted by either intention or consequence. This assertion is shared by many conservatives and a few moderates who have challenged what they perceive to be the "antireligious" sentiments that "permeate" contemporary life and culture, including secular education.[17] Though I do not agree with the magnitude of this charge, I do believe that secular forms of education are often wrongly promoted and/or interpreted as antireligious. I will illustrate this form of indirect repression through an example from my own secondary school classroom. A second example of repression that I will explore relates to overt forms of censorship in the name of religion. Here I will focus on the conservative religious campaign against what proponents have defined as the "homosexual agenda" that "activists" are "promoting" in the public schools. I will close this chapter with the consideration of a third type of repression that is conversely related to the second and practiced when sectarian religious perspectives are privileged over other religious and nonreligious frameworks in educational settings. Many progressives in the culture wars have voiced this concern by citing examples of what they perceive to be the inappropriate adoption of explicitly sectarian materials into public school curricula. The third set of illustrations focuses on the efforts to promote teaching about intelligent design and attempts to include sectarian Bible courses as history or literature electives.

The Dismissal of Religious Worldviews as Unsophisticated and Irrational

In the spring of 1999 I introduced a new senior level elective into our curriculum at Phillips Academy entitled *Advanced Topics in Religion: Islamic Cultural Studies.*[18] The intention of the course is to explore the diversity of Muslim expressions of faith and the ways that religion is both shaped by and helps to shape social, historical, and cultural phenomena. The course went well the first year I taught it. In the spring of 2000 I was looking forward to a second opportunity after tweaking it a bit based on my own reflections and student evaluations. I became even more excited about teaching it again when I realized that three of the ten students enrolled that term were all people I had worked with in previous philosophy or religious studies courses. In addition, I knew that several others had been exposed to Islam in their 9th grade world history classes. These facts coupled with the small class size made for a promising beginning.

Given that most of the students had previous exposure to either the method (religious studies) and/or the content (Islam), I decided not to assign one of several "point of departure" exercises that I utilize at the start of almost every class I teach. The intention of these exercises is to help students identify previous knowledge, articulate questions of inquiry they would like to explore, and to name what conscious (and sometimes unconscious) assumptions they bring to the topic under investigation. Though these exercises are always useful, given their background experiences I decided we could use the day or two of class time usually devoted to them in a more productive manner. I soon discovered that this was a big mistake.

The first introductory classes were animated and engaged, but by the third or fourth session the seminar discussions gradually became uncharacteristically strained and unfocused. Students had a difficult time representing the readings accurately and conversations regularly strayed off topic and degenerated into lackluster generalizations. My specific requests to return to the topics at hand were always honored in a good-natured way, but the conversation would again eventually digress. I asked students directly whether the readings were too difficult and/or if they found them uninteresting. They responded that the readings were "compelling" and the workload "fine." I was baffled.

During the beginning of the third week of the course we read a case study of a *pesantren*[19] in rural Indonesia where birth control and reproductive health were part of the curriculum. Though students initially began by focusing on the reading, they soon launched into an animated discussion about how Islam discriminates against women. Many of their assertions directly contradicted information they read in the article as well as other information already covered in the class. (For example, we had studied how well respected scholars, clerics, and practitioners within the tradition can and do disagree about the interpretations of pivotal verses in the Qur'an, including those about women.) A central goal of the course is to convey the fact that there is a wide diversity of opinions and practices within the tradition itself that need to be represented and acknowledged.

Aside from the fact that they were ignoring evidence that challenged their claims, their sweeping generalizations were intellectually troublesome regardless of the topic. I intervened to articulate these concerns and to invite their reflections about the source or sources that informed their views. They were honestly confused by my question, but responded with what to them seemed to be obvious and widespread examples of discrimination against women in Islam such as wearing hijab, inheritance rights, and other "restrictions" that were "dictated" in the Qur'an. They inferred that the article about the *pesantren* and other "more progressive" examples of women in the tradition were simply exceptions to an otherwise nearly universal set of rules and practices.

The conversation then moved into a more general discussion about religion. Here it was revealed that four of the ten members of the class believed that religion itself represents worldviews that they characterized as "unsophisticated, irrational, and oppressive." They classified themselves (in direct contrast) as "secular humanists" (read sophisticated, rational, and nonoppressive) and implied that "all intelligent" people share this self-definition. The other six members of the class ranged between general sympathy with this belief to overt disagreement. It became immediately apparent to all of us, however, that the source of our strained and unfocused discussions up to this point in the course was the fact that what students were learning about Islam in particular and religion in general directly contradicted or at least challenged many of their own deep-rooted (and largely unarticulated) assumptions.

When members of the class heard themselves characterize religion so simplistically and in such broad generalities, they became uncomfortable. Though they knew intellectually that these assumptions were flawed, they still felt them to be at least partially true and they had few tools to help them address this dilemma directly. Together, we decided that the best course of action was to take a few class periods to examine (and by definition interrogate) their underlying assumptions before moving forward in the course. This proved to be an invaluable exercise and our work throughout the rest of the term was much more productive and focused as a result. One student summarized the experience in the final evaluation:

> It was humbling to see how biased I was against Islam and, actually, all religions . . . My prejudices against Islam were so strong that I literally couldn't "take in" any perspectives outside of my own. I'd been exposed to other ideas (here and in other places) but there wasn't any room for them to live. I still classify myself as a secular humanist, but I learned that I have biases that need to be challenged. There's a lot more to Islam than I thought before taking this course, and a lot more to religion . . . The diversity of expression is something that I guess I "knew" but never thought about or incorporated. After all, I was raised as a Christian and though I don't really believe anymore I know that the Christianity I learned growing up and that my parents still practice is very different than the Christianity of the people who bomb abortion clinics.[20]

I learned a lot from this experience. One of the students who expressed the belief that religion was "irrational and unsophisticated" had just completed another one of my classes the previous term entitled *Approaching the Holocaust*. Though the two courses were quite different in content, a similar method was employed in each that emphasized the social/historical contexts that shape a diversity of religious expressions, including how religion can be utilized to inspire and justify a full range of human agency from the heinous to the heroic. My error with her and the entire class was that I assumed too much from their previous exposure in religious studies in general or Islam in particular. As the quote from the evaluation cited above states so clearly, just because someone learns about the complexities of religion and religious experience in one context does not necessarily mean that s/he will automatically transfer that understanding to another. This is not a comment about intellectual capacity but rather one that reflects how assumptions about religion in our culture are deeply rooted and difficult to self-consciously engage.

I clearly should have followed through with my original plan of beginning the course with a "point of departure" exercise. Though we did participate in a version of this exploration approximately three weeks into the term, it would have been much more fruitful and productive to have done so at the outset. Given the depth of feeling about Islam in particular and religion in general that some of these students held, I doubt that the initial exercises would have fully uncovered the deeply rooted assumptions that were later articulated. The exercises would, however, have given us some collective *language* to more readily address the ways that these assumptions were hindering our exploration of the material. Conscientization is a process that must be taken seriously as such, no matter what ideological assumptions one is trying to uncover and interrogate. Religion is an especially complicated topic in our culture precisely because there are so few opportunities for people to identify and explore their assumptions about religion itself or particular faith traditions in settings that encourage the conscious interrogation of those assumptions toward the goal of deeper understanding. Schools should provide this opportunity while also teaching students about the world's religions from an approach that emphasizes the diversity within traditions. I will more fully elaborate on this method and my rationale for promoting its use in the following chapter.

Censorship in the Name of Religion

Another manifestation of religious illiteracy is the degree to which campaigns that promote certain forms of censorship in the name of religion are successful in defining the terms of the debates themselves. There are several examples of this form of censorship in the schools but I have chosen to focus on the religious opposition to positive depictions of homosexuality in the curriculum and/or in extracurricular clubs and activities. I have chosen to focus on these controversies because they are widespread, contentious, fueled by religious illiteracy, and dangerous.

Conservatives in the culture wars have long opposed civil rights legislation and educational initiatives that present homosexuality in a favorable light.[21] The 2004 decision of the Massachusetts Supreme Judicial Court granting marriage rights to same sex couples has served as a catalyst to further invigorate this well-organized opposition. A 2005 article in the *New York Times* entitled "Gay Rights Battlefields Spread to Public Schools" highlights how conservative religious groups such as the Alliance Defense Fund (ADF) and the Liberty Council are mounting challenges to educational initiatives that promote what they call the "homosexual agenda." Chief targets are health education programs that include discussions of homosexuality, extracurricular clubs where gay, lesbian, bisexual, and straight students join together, and humanities and social science curricula that engage homosexual themes and/or present homosexuality in a positive light. I will focus here on two organizations that have engaged in targeted campaigns against these types of activities in the schools: The ADF and the Southern Baptist Convention (SBC).

The Alliance Defense Fund

According to their website, the ADF was founded in 1993 "for a unique and, we believe, God-given purpose. We exist to empower our allies, through an alliance, to accomplish far more than they could alone. This means we assist them in common areas, but do not assist them in areas outside the scope of our mission. And that is one of the reasons the Alliance is so effective. Since 1994, we have been blessed to work with more than 125 organizations, helping to coordinate an allied effort, to avoid duplication, and to provide resources and strategic direction on cases related to our mission."[22] Their mission is focused in three areas: religious freedom, right to life, and family values.[23] They have been involved in key actions and decisions since their inception, including the 1995 Supreme Court decision in *Rosenberger v. Rector and Visitors of the University of Virginia* involving discrimination against a conservative Christian group on the UVA campus and the pivotal *Hurley v. Irish-American Gay, Lesbian, and Bisexual Group of Boston* that granted the right of organizers of the St. Patrick's Day Parade in Boston to exclude the participation of the Irish-American Gay, Lesbian and Bisexual Group.

This case was cited in the 2000 Supreme Court decision that granted the Boy Scouts the right to exclude homosexuals from leadership positions.[24] In 2004, the ADF played a central role through funding, organization, and training that led to the ballot initiatives in 13 states that voted to restrict the rights of gays and lesbians to marry.[25] Readers may recall from the "Preface" that the ADF is the organization that represented Stephen Williams, the fifth grade teacher in Cupertino, California who sued his principal and district alleging religious discrimination.

The ADF has been at the forefront of several recent initiatives in the schools that are aimed at challenging the legitimacy of programs, policies, and/or curricula that present homosexuality in a positive light. The president and general counsel of the ADF, Alan Sears, and his colleague Craig Osten (vice president of creative services) published a book in 2003 entitled *The Homosexual Agenda: The Principal Threat to Religious Freedom*.[26] This book is featured on the ADF website as well as in other conservative publications.[27] The following excerpts are taken from Chapter Three, "Stupid Parents, Enlightened Kids," and reveals much about their ideological foundations.

> Every fall, millions of parents drop their children off at taxpayer-funded public schools, assuming that their children's education will provide what they need to be successful in life: strong academics, civility, and responsibility. Unfortunately, many of these same parents have little or no idea of what is happening to their children once they pass through the classroom door. Instead of learning the three R's or how to be good citizens like many of us were taught, they are learning how to reject the values that many of their parents have tried hard to instill in them. Sadly, many of these parents refuse to believe that this is happening, even when you produce evidence of how the radical homosexual activists are targeting children in public schools to accept, affirm, and be recruited into homosexual behavior.[28]

The entire text is riddled with claims of an intentional, usually undercover campaign by radicals that are aimed at manipulating children away from the moral values of their parents and recruiting them into the homosexual lifestyle. This language builds upon and bolsters the worst stereotypes of homosexuals as stealth predators and the schools as havens of immorality. Later in the same chapter, the authors lament recent survey results that indicate widespread acceptance of homosexuality among high school seniors. They claim that these attitudes are the result of successful "indoctrination."

> The indoctrination that takes place in our public schools has definitely had an effect in shaping teens' attitudes toward homosexual behavior. In 2001, Zogby International released a poll that found that 85 percent of high school seniors thought homosexual men and lesbians should be accepted by society; 68 percent said homosexual couples should be allowed to adopt children; 88 percent supported so-called hate-crimes legislation, and two-thirds thought same-sex "marriage" should be allowed. Even 80 percent of evangelical Christians supported hate-crimes legislation, which in its many proposed forms will be used to silence religious speech about homosexual behavior.[29]

They indicate that acceptance of homosexuality is itself an assault on the religious freedoms of Christians and call on parents to form an "army" to "rise up in righteous anger" to "take back our schools from the radical homosexual activists for the sake of our children."

> One of parents' key religious freedoms is the ability to raise their children to accept Jesus Christ into their lives and to train them to hold biblically based beliefs. In our public schools today, this religious freedom is under daily assault. Sad to say, large numbers of children may have already been lost to the pro-homosexual efforts that have been quietly implemented in our public schools over the past decade. But harm to future generations can still be prevented. Confused children can still be redeemed. However, it is going to take an army of parents, not just one individual here and there, who will rise up in righteous anger over what is happening to our children. The day when we can trust our public school system to affirm America's traditional values is over. It is time to take back our schools from the radical homosexual activists for the sake of our children.[30]

The ADF has led several campaigns in the service of countering the "Homosexual Agenda" in the schools that is depicted above. For example, in a highly publicized case in Boyd County Kentucky, a group of students at Boyd High School wanted to form a Gay-Straight Alliance (GSA) as an extracurricular club. Administrators first refused and then when pressured by the American Civil Liberties Union (ACLU) regarding equal access clauses, the school banned all extracurricular clubs altogether rather than grant approval for the GSA. The ACLU was eventually able to negotiate a settlement requiring 1) that the district treat all student clubs equally and 2) that it mandate antiharassment trainings for all students and staff. The school district agreed to implement the training after the judge found that there was a widespread problem with antigay harassment in the school, where students in an English class once stated that they needed to "take all the f—king faggots out in the back woods and kill them."[31]

In February of 2005, the district was sued by the ADF who sought to shut down the required training and who challenged the policy requiring that all clubs be treated equally. The ACLU has agreed to represent the school.[32]

In another example, in 1996, the Gay, Lesbian and Straight Education Network (GLSEN) organized a National Day of Silence in secondary schools in an effort to highlight the plight of gay, lesbian, bisexual, and transgendered (GLBT) youth who are often "silenced" due to overt and covert forms of discrimination in the schools.[33] In 2003 the ADF began organizing counterprotests and their efforts have gained support. In 2005 they organized a counter protest entitled the National Day of Truth. "We needed to present a counter or Christian perspective,'" said J. Michael Johnson, spokesman for the ADF. Mr. Johnson said that 340 schools participated.[34] One was a public high school in a Boston suburb where parents and students gathered at the entrance to the school on the day of the protest with buttons and banners featuring the silhouette of a man and a woman holding hands with the caption "The Way it is Meant to Be."[35]

The Southern Baptist Convention

The SBC was organized in 1845 in Augusta, Georgia when it split with the Baptist General Convention over organizational, economic, and political issues, including the issue of slavery. For Baptists in the South, slavery was a part of their legal, cultural, and economic life and many believed that God intended for the races to be separate while many in the North became increasingly convinced that the institution of slavery was immoral.[36]

The SBC claims over 16 million members who worship in more than 42,000 churches in the United States. They sponsor about 5,000 home missionaries serving the United States, Canada, Guam, and the Caribbean, as well as sponsoring more than 5,000 foreign missionaries in 153 nations of the world.[37]

The SBC has long opposed homosexuality and they have passed numerous resolutions over the past 30 years condemning civil rights legislation, educational initiatives, and policies that support domestic partnership benefits. For example, according to the Human Rights Watch, in a 1996 "Resolution on a Christian Response to Homosexuality," the SBC declared that "even a desire to engage in a homosexual relationship is always sinful, impure, degrading, shameful, unnatural, indecent and perverted." In 1997 it launched a boycott of the Walt Disney Co. "for its airing of the *Ellen* show, for offering domestic partner benefits for its employees and for allowing the annual 'Gay Day' celebrations." (The SBC voted to end the boycott at the 2005 annual meeting claiming that they "made their point.") In 2000 the SBC passed a Baptist Faith and Message statement that equated homosexuality with pornography and adultery, and in 2003 they introduced a program urging gays and lesbians to "accept Jesus Christ as their Savior" to "free them" from what key leader Richard Land called "this sinful, destructive lifestyle."[38]

In April of 2005 two members of the SBC sent a resolution entitled "Resolution on Homosexuality in Public Schools" for consideration by the delegates at the Annual Meeting of the SBC scheduled for that June. The resolution accuses "homosexual activists" of "aggressively working to transform the moral foundation of our culture by promoting homosexuality as an acceptable lifestyle" through "programs that use such deceptive labels as "Safe Sex," "Diversity Training," "Multicultural Education," "Anti-Bullying," and "Safe Schools." It also declares, "any school district that recognizes homosexual clubs or treats homosexuality as an acceptable lifestyle is a clear and present danger to all of its children and is violating the community's trust." The resolution called for members of the SBC to "rebuke homosexual activists for slandering minorities by claiming that homosexual behavior has any authentic connection with the civil rights movement" and "to investigate diligently whether the school district . . . has either one or more homosexual clubs or curricula or programs in any of their schools that present homosexuality as an acceptable 'lifestyle.'" If they find any such evidence, the resolution encourages parents to "remove their children from the school district's schools immediately."[39]

The proposed resolution received a great deal of press and was endorsed by leaders of over 40 state-wide family groups including state affiliates of the following prominent conservative organizations: Focus on the Family, the American Family Association, The Eagle Forum, and Concerned Women of America.[40]

Though the resolution itself did not pass, an amended version that did (entitled "Resolution on Educating Children"), uses much of the same language but stops short of calling for parents to remove their children from public schools. The final version encourages Southern Baptists to "investigate diligently the curricula, textbooks and programs in our community schools and to demand discontinuation of offensive material and programs."[41]

The examples cited above are only a small representation of the activities that are taking place in schools, at school board meetings, in legislatures, and in the courts across the country. Conservative Christian groups that include (but are no means limited to) the ADF and the SBC have mounted a religiously defined and inspired campaign against schools and school districts that advocate for the health, well-being, and civil liberties of gay and lesbian people. From the perspective of promoting the ideals of democracy in public education, these activities are deeply troubling on several fronts, but I will highlight the following: they violate the principles of nonrepression and nondiscrimination, and they rely on misrepresentation of the facts and demonization of their opponents to advance their cause.

I will deal with the latter charge first and in swift order. Given that these issues are already deeply divisive and heart wrenching for people of good will across the ideological spectrum, I find the characterization of those in support of gays and lesbians as militant activists promoting a stealth campaign to lure children into homosexuality to be morally reprehensible. Inflaming the debate by characterizing the opposition in such caricatured and villainous ways is profoundly antidemocratic, disrespectful, and dishonest. Those on the left who practice similar tactics against those with whom they disagree should also be reprimanded. We simply must hold ourselves and each other to a higher standard that includes the honest representation of opposing views, respect, and, at the very least, minimal standards of tolerance.

In regard to nonrepression and nondiscrimination, censorship of the magnitude promoted by the SBC, the ADF, and the other examples cited above are extremely difficult if not impossible to morally justify in a democratic society. First, the arguments in support of these restrictions are all theologically based upon particular sectarian perspectives. The theological assumptions that give justification to the claims that homosexuality is sinful and that any positive depiction of homosexuality is therefore immoral are not universally held even among Christians, let alone those of other faiths or none.[42] A number of religious groups and individuals have articulated religiously inspired moral arguments that are in direct contradiction to the positions represented above.[43] Indeed, it is another example of religious illiteracy that homosexuality is often uncritically equated with "sin" which renders silent the myriad religious perspectives that challenge that claim.

However, even if there were a religious consensus regarding the immorality of homosexuality, it would be a violation of the Establishment Clause of the First Amendment for schools to enforce policies based upon a religiously justified moral conviction *that has no moral secular equivalent.* Several political theorists have argued that it is appropriate (indeed beneficial) for religiously inspired positions to be included in public discourse about a full range of issues, including highly contentious ones. In order for these positions to be democratically sound, however, they must also have a secular equivalent and/or be morally persuasive to others who do not share the same (or any) theological foundations for the positions advanced.[44] This stipulation honors the importance of religious convictions to be included in public discourse in a multicultural democracy by enforcing the principle of nonrepression while simultaneously protecting against its violation. I agree with Michael Perry's claim that there are no sound secular equivalents to religiously inspired moral arguments against homosexuality;[45] therefore, censorship of exposure to positive depictions of gays and lesbians in particular or homosexuality in general in the schools has no basis in a multicultural democracy.

A second reason why the positions advanced by the ADF and SBC above violate democratic ideals is that these positions presume the *exclusive* right of parents to control the education of children (the state of parents). This assumption is in direct contradiction to the position advanced in Chapter One that parents, citizens, and professional educators must share this responsibility if the future of democracy is to be promoted. Though parents do have a central voice in the education of their children, the principle of nonrepression is violated when children are not exposed to rationally legitimate perspectives of the good life and good society that differ from those of their families. In the language of the positions advanced by the ADF and SBC, *exposure* to differing values is equated with intentionally undermining the moral authority of parents. This is not a valid equation from the perspective of democratic ideals. If citizens are expected to have the tools to engage in conscious social reproduction in its most inclusive form, they must be exposed to legitimate views that differ from those advanced by their parents. Political theorist Rob Reich has articulated a similar claim in his assertion that education should guarantee that students will be able to develop the tools to exercise "minimal autonomy" as a fundamental right of citizenship. Though parents do have an important right to shape the values of their children, I agree with Reich when he argues that they do not have the right to restrict their children from exercising their own minimal autonomy as citizens.[46]

Third, the policies promoted by the ADF and the SBC violate the principle of nondiscrimination as defined by the basic right of "every educable child to be educated."[47] Gay and lesbian students (or those who are perceived to be gay or lesbian) are often the victims of overt and covert forms of harassment in schools that threaten both their physical and psychological health. Policies that either promote discrimination of this nature and/or that fail to address the conditions whereby such harassment is sanctioned directly violate the basic civil liberties of GLBT youth while also violating the principle of nondiscrimination as noted above. In addition, denying students positive exposure to gays and lesbians in the curriculum is a further violation of nondiscrimination because such an omission fails to recognize them as functioning and contributing members of our multicultural democracy. Such an omission serves to promote ignorance, stereotype, and misinformation that give sanction to further forms of discrimination that perpetuates a vicious cycle.

Furthermore, contrary to the assertions advanced in the SBC "Resolution on Homosexuality in the Schools" cited above, this cycle *is* comparable in obvious and less obvious ways to other forms of discrimination in American history, including discrimination based on race, ethnicity, religion, and gender. They are most obviously comparable in relation to the civil rights issues that are at stake; so much so that further defense of this connection seems unnecessary. A less obvious way that these issues are linked is that in each of these debates, religion has been invoked to justify positions along the full spectrum of ideological beliefs, including those on the extremes. For example, it is well documented that Christians were morally divided on the issues of both slavery and women's suffrage.[48] A more substantial focus on the religious influences of these historical debates would give us better tools to engage our own current discourses from more informed and nuanced perspectives. At the very least, the tacit assumption that any religious tradition holds a uniform view on moral issues would itself, hopefully, be more readily challenged than it currently is today.

To summarize, there are strong, rationally sound secular and religious moral arguments that support granting gay men and lesbians the same fundamental rights, dignity, and respect due all humans as articulated in our founding documents. The principle of nonrepression supports the inclusion of ideologies and worldviews that are rationally sound and conducive to democracy. Because the arguments that promote discrimination are based on particular religious claims that do not have any secular equivalent, there is no democratically sound justification for allowing gays and lesbians to be discriminated against in the public school context. In this regard, just as it would not be morally permissible to consider the pros and cons of racism in a contemporary public school classroom, I argue that it is equally inappropriate to sanction anti-gay/lesbian sentiments as one legitimate perspective among many. In this way, I disagree with Kent Greenwalt who takes a more cautious stance by promoting the civil rights of gays and lesbians but not asserting their moral equality with heterosexuals.[49]

Having taken this stand I also want to articulate the importance of respecting students who hold different views based on their religious convictions. When issues related to homosexuality arise, it is important to acknowledge that some people believe that homosexuality is immoral and that those convictions are rooted in particular religious beliefs that people are free to hold and that parents are free to foster. It is also important, however, to distinguish between the right of individuals to hold these beliefs and school policies that legitimately enforce nondiscrimination based on respect for pluralism in our multicultural democracy.

For example, to revisit the analogy offered above, some religions still promote the belief that discrimination against African Americans is theologically justified, if not mandated.[50] In a multicultural democracy, individuals and groups are free to hold unpopular beliefs but it is not incumbent upon the state to give moral sanction to those beliefs by giving them social legitimacy. In the context of the schools, students are free to hold and express their religious beliefs so long as they are not harmful or discriminatory to others. Gutmann makes a similar claim in her advocacy for accommodations to be granted for some children to be exempted from activities that are opposed to their religious convictions. There are compelling reasons for granting certain accommodations, but there are limits to how the parameters of what is considered "acceptable" are defined.

> Public schools would more effectively teach democratic values . . . if they were willing to exempt some children from practices to which their parents object as long as those practices do not require public schools to be discriminatory or repressive. On this argument, public schools should accommodate children who

> refuse to salute the flag but not those who refuse to sit next to blacks (assuming both refusals are based on principle rather than mere preference.)

She goes on to offer another relevant example: This standard does "not permit schools to 'recognize a right' of white adolescents not to associate with blacks; recognizing such a right indirectly discriminates against black students."[51] Similarly, I argue here that heterosexual students do not have a "right" not to associate with gays, lesbians, or bisexual students for such a standard constitutes an indirect form of discrimination.

Before moving on, I want to state that though it is not appropriate for schools to sanction discriminatory behavior against gay, lesbian, and bisexual students, it is also never appropriate to belittle or denigrate the religious beliefs of anyone, including and especially the beliefs of particular individuals. I will also return to this issue in the next chapter where I will offer specific examples of how to balance these challenging conflicts in a respectful way when they arise in our nation's classrooms.

Privileging Sectarian Perspectives

Another consequence of religious illiteracy is when sectarian perspectives are privileged in school curricula. At first glance, it may appear that the inclusion of the theory of intelligent design in biological science classes and/or the adoption of a sectarian "Bible as history" course would represent efforts to uphold the democratic principle of nonrepression. Both efforts would, after all, promote consideration of worldviews that most students in public school classrooms would not otherwise engage. This is, in fact, one of the main arguments that proponents of these and similar initiatives put forward in support of their efforts.

Intelligent Design

For example, in October of 2004, the Dover Pennsylvania Area School Board voted to require biology teachers in their district to present intelligent design as an alternative to the scientific theory of evolution.[52] They also mandated that teachers read the following statement to their ninth grade biology classes:

> Because Darwin's Theory is a theory, it is still being tested as new evidence is discovered. The Theory is not a fact. Gaps in the

> Theory exist for which there is no evidence. A theory is defined as a well-tested explanation that unifies a broad range of observations.
>
> Intelligent design is an explanation of the origin of life that differs from Darwin's view. The reference book, *Of Pandas and People* is available for students to see if they would like to explore this view in an effort to gain an understanding of what intelligent design actually involves. As is true with any theory, students are encouraged to keep an open mind.[53]

This view was endorsed by President Bush in August 2005, as reported in the *New York Times*. He was speaking with Texas journalists and was asked about his stance on teaching intelligent design. "Recalling his days as Texas governor, Mr. Bush said in the interview, according to a transcript, 'I felt like both sides ought to be properly taught.' Asked again by a reporter whether he believed that both sides in the debate between evolution and intelligent design should be taught in the schools, Mr. Bush replied that he did, 'so people can understand what the debate is about.' "[54]

The court came to a different conclusion. On December 20, 2005, District Court Judge Jones issued a ruling in *Kitzmiller v. Dover Area School District*, USDC, 342 (2005) that the Intelligent Design curriculum was unconstitutional. "The proper application of both the endorsement and Lemon tests to the facts of this case makes it abundantly clear that the Board's ID Policy violates the Establishment Clause. In making this determination, we have addressed the seminal question of whether ID is science. We have concluded that it is not, and moreover that ID cannot uncouple itself from its creationist, and thus religious, antecedents."[55]

Bible Curricula

In a similar type of issue, in April of 2005, the Odessa, Texas School Board voted unanimously to add an elective course on the Bible to their 2006 curriculum. Though at the time the specific curriculum for the course had yet to be selected, there was a heavy lobby for the adoption of one written by the National Council on Bible Curriculum in Public Schools (NCBCPS).[56] The NCBCPS contends that its curriculum is "concerned with education rather than indoctrination" and that the approach is "appropriate in a comprehensive program of secular education."

When visiting the NCBCPS web site, one is first greeted with a rousing trumpet fanfare and a rapidly expanding phrase that reads "IT'S

COMING BACK" before the page changes to a letter from the founding president of the organization, Elizabeth Ridenour.[57] The letter reads as follows:

> Dear Friend,
>
> A program is underway to serve the public through educational efforts concerning a First Amendment right and religious freedom issue. This is to bring a state certified Bible course (elective) into the public high schools nationwide.
>
> The curriculum for the program shows a concern to convey the content of the Bible as compared to literature and history. The program is concerned with education rather than indoctrination of students. The central approach of the class is simply to study the Bible as a foundation document of society, and that approach is altogether appropriate in a comprehensive program of secular education.
>
> The world is watching to see if we will be motivated to impact our culture, to deal with the moral crises in our society, and reclaim our families and children.
>
> Please help us to restore our religious and civil liberties in this nation.[58]

In another section of the site entitled "Founding Fathers," the following claim is made: "The Bible was the foundation and blueprint for our Constitution, Declaration of Independence, our educational system, and our entire history until the last 20 to 30 years."[59]

In spite of the assertions to the contrary, the sectarian nature of the enterprise is quite transparent. Reviews of the curriculum confirm this impression. For example, the Texas Freedom Coalition (an advocacy group for religious freedom) released a study that characterized the course as "an error-riddled Bible curriculum that attempts to persuade students and teachers to adopt views that are held primarily within conservative Protestant circles."[60] The author of this report is Biblical scholar Mark Chancey who is on the faculty of Southern Methodist University in Dallas, Texas. Though he acknowledges that the curriculum urges teachers "not to impose religious beliefs upon their students" he offers the following assessment:

> In my professional judgment as a biblical scholar . . . this curriculum on the whole is a sectarian document, and I cannot recommend it for usage in a public school setting. It attempts to

> persuade students to adopt views that are held primarily within certain conservative Protestant circles but not within the scholarly community, and it presents Christian faith claims as history:
>
> - The Bible is explicitly characterized as inspired by God.
> - Discussions of science are based on the claims of biblical creationists.
> - Jesus is presented as fulfilling "Old Testament" prophecy.
> - Archaeological findings are cited as support for claims of the Bible's complete historical accuracy.
>
> Furthermore, much of the course appears designed to persuade students and teachers that America is a distinctively Christian nation—an agenda publicly embraced by many of the members of NCBCPS's Board of Advisors and endorsers.[61]

The NCBCPS claims that its curriculum has been adopted by 312 school districts in 37 states and that 175,000 students have already taken the course. They also claim that 92 percent of school boards that they have approached have voted to implement it.[62]

Though it is true that the introduction of intelligent design into biology classes and the adoption of a sectarian course on the Bible "as history or literature"[63] would introduce students to new worldviews that they might not otherwise encounter, these initiatives violate the principle of nonrepression because serious engagement of these perspectives requires adherence to a religious premise that is itself a form of repression. Gutmann makes a parallel claim in relation to teaching about creationism:

> The distinctly democratic problem with teaching creationism stems from the fact that it . . . is believable only on the basis of a sectarian religious faith. Teaching creationism as science—even as one among several reasonable scientific theories—violates the principle of nonrepression in indirectly imposing a sectarian religious view on all children in the guise of science. Teaching creationism as a scientific theory entails teaching children to accept a religious view that takes the words of the Bible to be the literal god-given truth as a scientific explanation of the origins of species.[64]

Though the focus of her remarks is on creationism, the same critique is applicable to teaching about intelligent design and sanctioning a sectarian course on the Bible in a public school context. Both require that students accept the religious premises that provide the foundation for the exploration itself and this would constitute a violation of both nonrepression and the Establishment Clause of the First Amendment that prohibits state sponsorship of religion.[65]

At this point in the conversation, one could legitimately ask why the same standard does not apply in the reverse: that is, why is it not considered a form of "repression" when secular theories of interpretation are required to be adopted by, for example, Christians who believe in creationism when they study evolution? A similar question could be raised regarding the "repression" that conservative Christians feel when homosexuality is presented in a positive light. These are important questions that reside at the heart of the culture wars. Many conservatives make precisely this claim when they challenge the legitimacy of what they perceive to be the imposition of secularism and secular values in public schools. Gutmann addresses this issue and her comments are instructive:

> In a religiously diverse society, secular standards of reasoning accommodate greater agreement upon a common education than religious faith. The case for teaching secular but not religious standards of reasoning does not rest on the claim that secular standards are neutral among all religious beliefs. The case rests instead on the claim that secular standards constitute a better basis upon which to build a common education for citizenship than any set of sectarian religious beliefs—better because secular standards are both a fairer and a firmer basis for peacefully reconciling our differences.[66]

If we return to an understanding of democracy as that which promotes the conditions for the conscious social reproduction of society in its most inclusive form, then this articulation makes good sense. Gutmann believes that "The indirect—if not the direct—result of establishing religion in public schools would be to restrict rational deliberation among competing ways of life."

> If democratic majorities in a religiously diverse society refuse to differentiate between a sectarian and a secular curriculum, they will unintentionally thwart the development of shared intellectual standards among citizens, and discredit public schools in the eyes of citizens whose religious beliefs are not reflected in the established curriculum.[67]

Though teaching creationism and intelligent design in biology classes as alternative "scientific" theories to evolution are examples of *teaching religion* and are therefore unconstitutional and educationally unsound, teaching *about* these perspectives in a social science course that might, for example, focus on understanding the culture wars would be very appropriate and timely.[68] Similarly, it would be appropriate to teach a course (or a section of a course) that focused on comparative methods of Biblical interpretation that could include both sectarian and nonsectarian approaches. In this way, Biblical literalism would be presented as one method among many, rather than as the only foundation for exploration. I realize that this approach is not without controversy and I will elaborate upon it more fully in the next chapter. I mention it here, however, to underscore the fact that public schools need to help future citizens develop the tools to deliberate about these controversies from a more informed perspective and in a context aimed at deepening understanding rather than fueling antagonism. The culture wars are predicated on ignorance and fueled by misrepresentation; both of which are at cross-purposes with deliberative democracy.

I agree with Gutmann's analysis and believe it is imperative to protect the secular framework of public education as the only foundation capable of promoting a shared set of values amidst our religious and cultural diversity. We simply must, however, do a better job of promoting the religious dimensions of multiculturalism in the schools as well as the cultivation of a more general religious literacy. The failure to do so promotes repression by perpetuating ignorance and limiting the exposure of students to rational considerations of religious worldviews as legitimate and widely held expressions of the good life.

Public schooling is the *only* venue where a majority of future citizens can learn about religion from a nonsectarian perspective. Neither of the current practices of virtually ignoring religion altogether or promoting sectarian assumptions is acceptable. Neither will help us responsibly address the deep cultural divides that plague us and neither will help promote democratic ideals within and beyond our current cultural crisis.

CHAPTER THREE

How to Teach About Religion in the Schools

> Congress shall make no law respecting an establishment of religion, or prohibiting the free exercise thereof;[1]

There were two important and related Supreme Court rulings in the 1960s that were pivotal in defining the role of religion in public education. In *Engel v. Vitale* (1962) it was decided that government should not sponsor prayers in public schools. In *Abington v. Schempp* (1963) the Supreme Court ruled that the government should not sponsor Bible reading and recitation of the Lord's Prayer in public schools. The banned activities were symbols of the lingering Protestant Christian hegemony in public education and these decisions were thus met with both scorn and praise for what they represented. While many hailed these rulings as a strong endorsement of the separation of church and state and thus an affirmation of pluralism, others felt that they signaled the demise of a common moral foundation that served to unite all Americans amidst our diversity. These same tensions persist today and many trace the roots of the current culture wars to these rulings.[2]

Though the heart of these decisions addressed what was not permissible in public education, there was an important affirmation in *Abington v. Schempp* regarding what *was* allowed in the intersection of religion and the schools that I cited in the "Introduction" and that bears repeating here:

> It might well be said that one's education is not complete without a study of comparative religion or the history of religion and its

> relationship to the advancement of civilization. It certainly may be said that the Bible is worthy of study for its literary and historic qualities. Nothing we have said here indicates that such study of the Bible or of religion, when presented objectively as part of a secular program of education, may not be effected consistently with the First Amendment.[3]

This important articulation has been overlooked in the history of how the separation of church and state in the schools has been interpreted. Though there has been a slight shift over the past decade, most Americans since the 1960s believe that the separation of church and state that is affirmed in the rulings cited above meant that religion in all forms was banned. As Justice Clark's comments above clearly indicate, this is not at all the case. Indeed, some have argued that it may be a violation of the First Amendment when the study of religion is *not* included in public school curricula.[4] Though it is clear that teaching about religion is acceptable, how to do so is a more complex undertaking. This is the challenge I engage in this chapter.

I will begin by reviewing the guidelines regarding religion and education that have come to be widely accepted in our contemporary U.S. context. I will then articulate my formulation of what constitutes religious literacy as a comparative guidepost of sorts for evaluating the five commonly practiced approaches to teaching about religion in the schools today: the intentionally and unintentionally sectarian; the phenomenological; the literary; and the historical. I will then consider different representations of multiculturalism and will close with an articulation of a seventh method that I call the cultural studies approach. This approach situates the study of religion within the broader discourses of multiculturalism and democratic education. I will argue that this is the best vehicle through which to promote religious literacy because 1) it is the most accurate in depicting the complexity of religion and its influences in historical and contemporary contexts; 2) it emphasizes the diversity within traditions as well as between them; and 3) it represents a method of inquiry rather than content knowledge alone.

Guidelines for Teaching About Religion

I draw first on the important work of the First Amendment Center[5] which has been pivotal in helping to promote the study of religion in the schools in the United States. It has published useful guidebooks for educators regarding the distinction between an academic and devotional approach to religion. An especially relevant resource for our study is one entitled *A Teacher's Guide to Religion in the Public Schools* that contains some pedagogical guidelines regarding how to teach about religion within the parameters of the First Amendment.[6] These guidelines have been distributed to all public schools by the U.S. Department of Education:

> The school's approach to religion is *academic*, not *devotional.*
>
> The school strives for student *awareness* of religions, but does not press for student *acceptance* of any religion.
>
> The school sponsors *study* about religion, not the *practice* of religion.
>
> The school may *expose* students to a diversity of religious views, but may not *impose* any particular view.
>
> The school *educates* about all religions, it does not *promote* or *denigrate* religion.
>
> The school informs students about various beliefs; it does not seek to conform students to any particular belief.[7]

These guidelines appropriately assume the distinction between teaching *about* religion from an academic perspective versus teaching religion from a devotional lens. As such, they provide a useful thumbnail sketch to guide educators in the public school context. Indeed, they have been very helpful in alerting teachers and administrators to the fact that there *is* a distinction between an academic and devotional approach. One of the manifestations of widespread religious illiteracy is the equation of religion with devotional practice.

The guidelines are, however, limited in that they assume a certain neutral objectivity that an *academic* approach supposedly represents. Education is never neutral, and neither are the tools of academic inquiry that are employed in all educational contexts. This observation does not undermine the validity of the distinctions articulated above. There is, for example, a significant difference between learning about the Bible from a particular sectarian belief and studying the Bible from the perspective of a secular history, religious studies, or linguistics. My point is that it would be wrong to assume that the secular historical approach is somehow "objective" in contrast to the seemingly more "subjective" approach of the believer. All knowledge claims are subjective in that they inevitably represent particular perspectives that are shaped by myriad personal, social, cultural, intellectual, and historical factors too complex to (ever) fully name. Historian of science Donna Haraway calls these "situated knowledges" and contrasts this understanding of epistemology to the "god-trick" of presumed objective universality.[8] I will elaborate upon the implications of this insight more fully later, but for now it is important to note that recognizing the subjective nature of all knowledge claims gives credence to conservatives who rightly identify "secularism" as a value-laden ideology. Conservatives and secularists are also right to recognize that the academic approach to teaching about religion in the schools is not neutral. Secularists recognize that the approach gives credibility to religion itself as a valid field of inquiry while conservatives note that the study of religion assumes the legitimacy of multiple religious perspectives that by definition challenge those who believe that their convictions represent an exclusive truth.

As noted in the previous chapter, the argument for why public schools should be secular is not because a secular foundation is neutral. It is because a secular approach is the strongest philosophical foundation to promote nonrepression and nondiscrimination in the service of democracy: the conscious social reproduction of society in its most inclusive form. This understanding, in turn, complicates the relationship between religion and education in light of the guidelines outlined above. The very enterprise is predicated upon assumptions that promote certain religious perspectives over others (e.g., acceptance of pluralism over exclusivity.) This does not mean that the enterprise itself is flawed, but it does mean that the pretense of neutrality must be abandoned so that the values that are being promoted will be more transparent and given the justification they need in the context of our multicultural democracy.

The Goal: Achieving Religious Literacy

The following definition constitutes what I believe is the minimal standard necessary for achieving religious literacy:

> Religious literacy entails the ability to discern and analyze the fundamental intersections of religion and social/political/cultural life through multiple lenses. Specifically, a religiously literate person will possess 1) a basic understanding of the history, central texts, beliefs, practices and contemporary manifestations of several of the world's religious traditions as they arose out of and continue to be shaped by particular social, historical and cultural contexts; and 2) the ability to

> discern and explore the religious dimensions of political, social and cultural expressions across time and place.[9]

In our own context, citizens should be well versed in a cultural studies approach to Christianity and its specific manifestations in the United States as well as the complex role that religion has played in the cultural, intellectual, and political life of the continent from before colonization to the present.

This understanding of religious literacy emphasizes a method of inquiry more than specific content knowledge, though familiarity with the world's religious traditions and their central texts in their social/historical manifestations is an important foundation for understanding the intersections of religion with other dimensions of human social life. It is this form of religious literacy that I believe is best suited to promote the aims of democratic education in ways that I will further elaborate upon below when I discuss the cultural studies approach. Before doing so, however, it is important to review how religion is currently being taught in the nation's schools.

Common Approaches to Teaching About Religion in the Schools

Intentional Sectarianism

In Chapter Two I already addressed why intentionally sectarian approaches to the study of religion in the schools are problematic from the perspective of democratic education, so my analytic comments here will be brief. It is important to note, however, that many who promote this approach are not acting out of historical ignorance or overt defiance of the First Amendment as many progressives assume. Rather, their interpretation of the relationship between religion and education represents an accurate view of the historical foundations of public schooling.

To illustrate, educational theorist James Carper frames the history of the relationship between church and state as one comprised of competing and even antithetical foundations: "biblical Christianity with its emphasis on revelation and transcendent authority and the Enlightenment tradition with its emphasis on rationalism and human experience."[10] James Fraser offers an excellent analysis of this tension and the ways that Enlightenment rationalism was a minority view for most of the early history of public education in the United States.[11] Though each author emphasizes different dimensions of this history leading them to different interpretations, both rightly illustrate how most white Protestants favored the "common school" movement from the late eighteenth through most of the nineteenth centuries because it reflected a Protestant ecumenism that Fraser calls "comfortably familiar."[12] Carper characterizes the time period in the following way:

> As Alexis de Tocqueville recognized in the 1830s, and several generations of historians have confirmed, public schooling was nurtured by a robust evangelical Protestant culture that emerged from the Great Awakening of the 1730s and 1740s and was nourished by the Second Great Awakening—a series of religious revivals stretching from 1795 through the Civil War. With few exceptions, notably several Lutheran and Reformed bodies, which opted for schools designed to preserve cultural and/or confessional purity, Protestants were generally supportive of common schooling. Indeed, many were in the vanguard of the reform movement. They approved of early public schooling because it reflected Protestant beliefs and was viewed as an integral part of a crusade to fashion a Christian—which to the dismay of Roman Catholics, meant Protestant—America. (Kaestle, 1983; Neuhaus, 1984; Noll, 1992; Smith, 1967; Tocqueville, 1835/1966). According to church historian Robert T. Handy (1971), elementary schools hardly had to be under the control of particular denominations because "their role was to prepare young Americans for participating in the broadly Christian civilization toward which all evangelicals were working."[13]

According to Fraser, there was more internal diversity (and controversy) within Protestant circles than Carper acknowledges here, but both accurately represent the Protestant nature of public schooling from the early years of the Republic through the nineteenth century and beyond.[14] While the schools nurtured a broad Protestant ecumenism, the specific denominations were responsible for teaching a more particular sectarian set of beliefs and for "saving souls." This complementarity was widely supported for it gave a "common" language for the nation as a whole while also providing purposeful support for particular denominations to promote their own "sectarian" beliefs. The ubiquitous *McGuffey's Reader* and the practice of reading the King James translation of the Bible without comment were two representations of how Protestant values and assumptions were foundational to the early public school enterprise.[15]

There was also a strong link between Protestantism and nationalism that this history represents. Fraser cites education historian David Tyack who documents how Protestant belief served as a point of unification against "foreign" elements that were threatening the "Christian" (read "white Protestant early settlers and their descendents") nature of the nation. Those who were at the forefront of promoting public education in the nineteenth century were confident that "Schools and churches were allies in the quest to create the Kingdom of God in America . . . From the Alleghenies to the Pacific . . . evangelical clergymen spread the gospel of the common school in their united battle against Romanism, barbarism and skepticism."[16] Fraser also quotes Calvin Stowe, a professor of Bible at Lyman Beecher's Lane Seminary in Ohio: "It is not merely from the ignorant and vicious foreigner that danger is to be apprehended. To sustain an extended republic like our own, there must be a national feeling, a national assimilation; and nothing could be more fatal to our prospects of future national prosperity than to have our population become congeries of clans, congregating without coalescing, and condemned to contiguity without sympathy."[17] The national feeling and source of assimilation was, of course, a broadly defined Protestant ecumenism.

As previously noted, this "common" foundation was not without controversy and several challenges emerged that led to the steady erosion of the longstanding Protestant hegemony that characterized the early years of public schooling. The Industrial Revolution, Darwin's *Origin of the Species*, rising immigration (especially among Roman Catholics), and the effective protests of many others who were marginalized began to erode public support for schools that represented Protestantism under the guise of nonsectarianism. This shift was difficult for many white Protestants who self-confidently conceived of Protestantism as the unifying ideology of America and therefore believed it was appropriately emphasized in the public schools. Fraser insightfully characterizes the challenge associated with this shift.

> [A]s the country changed—and it began to do so very dramatically by the middle of the nineteenth century and even more throughout the next hundred years—this self-confidence turned to discomfort and fear. There seemed to have been a golden age when all agreed on faith, morals, and the right institutions to carry them out. Now more and more people disagreed. More and more of those who had been left out joined new immigrants with their own faiths and concerns to demand change. For many in Protestant

> America, the result has been more than a century of uncertainty about their place in the culture and the role of their religion in its educational enterprises.[18]

Carper cites sociologist James Davison Hunter's more dramatic characterization of this shift:

> [I]n the course of roughly thirty-five years (ca. 1895–1930), Protestantism had been moved from cultural domination to cognitive marginality and political impotence. The worldview of modernity [often termed secular humanism or civil humanism] had gained ascendancy in American culture.[19]

Carper defines the modern worldview as that which "posits an evolutionary view of the cosmos, touts science and reason as the keys to human progress, denies the relevance of the deity to human affairs, and claims that moral values derive from human experience." He argues that since the 1950s these values have also had a considerable influence in culture itself, including the "entertainment industry, the news media, government, and certain parts of the educational enterprise." From his perspective, the shift away from the dominance of Protestant influences in the schools was more gradual than Hunter's quote represents, though no less profound. Prior to the 1963 decision, Carper claims that 11 states had already banned Bible reading in the schools and that "Bible reading in some form was practiced in less than half of the nation's public school districts."[20] Yet for progressives, the fact that Bible reading was this widespread will likely come as a great surprise.

Given this historical context, it is easier to understand how many conservatives interpreted the Supreme Court rulings in the 1960s as a devastating blow to their understanding of the nature and purpose of schooling as a vehicle to transmit "common" Christian values. Carper summarizes this perspective succinctly:

> Although the Supreme Court's decisions on prayer and Bible reading . . . merely marked the culmination of better than a half-century-long process of "de-Protestantization" of public education (Nord, 1995), many conservative Protestants have interpreted the official removal of these symbols of the evangelical strain of the American civic faith as "yanking" God out of the public schools. Rather than making the schools "neutral" on matters related to religion, they have concluded that these decisions contributed to

> the establishment of secular humanism as the official creed of American public education. This belief has, in turn, led them to scrutinize public education to a greater extent than ever before. Once crusaders for the establishment of public education, conservative Protestants are now, ironically, among the most vociferous critics of public schooling.[21]

This historical context is important to understand when considering the current debates. Indeed, as I stated in my definition of what constitutes religious literacy, this history should be common knowledge for U.S. citizens. The secular nature of public education is a relatively new phenomenon in the history of schooling and needs to be clearly defended rather than simply presumed as self-evident truth. Furthermore, the fact that the serious study of religion has not been included in secular education is also problematic from the perspective of multiculturalism and needs to be addressed. Conversely, those who are promoting a more explicitly religious agenda need to respond to concerns regarding how their proposals appear to thwart democratic education in a multicultural society. As Fraser clearly demonstrates, the white Protestant hegemony over public education for the better part of its history was predicated upon either the exclusion or oppression of marginalized groups, including Roman Catholics, other white Protestants, blacks, immigrants, Native Americans, those from other religious traditions, and "secularists." This is hardly a model for advancing respect for diversity and multiculturalism.[22]

One final issue is worthy of consideration and clarification before moving on. Conservative Christians have responded to the shift from a Protestant-influenced public education system to one that is more explicitly secular in a variety of ways, but the three most typical responses have been to 1) influence the curricular and extracurricular dimensions of public education; 2) establish both affiliated and independent private Christian schools; and 3) homeschool their children. We have already addressed the growing influence of conservative voices in pubic education in the previous chapter. Even though the primary focus of this book is on public education, it is important to note here that the numbers of conservative Christian private schools and children who are homeschooled in conservative Christian households have both increased over the past few years.[23] Given that there is little, if any, uniform regulation of these forms of education,[24] it is difficult to determine whether children and young people in these settings are being exposed to the information and skills required to function as participating members of a deliberative, multicultural democracy. Religiously based education is not by definition antidemocratic, but it can be. (Similarly, secular approaches to education are not necessarily democratic in the ways outlined in Chapter One but they are more regulated and therefore accountable.[25]) I make a distinction here between what I call inclusive and exclusive forms of sectarianism to distinguish between those types that promote democratic education and those that do not. I will briefly define the distinction below.

Inclusive sectarianism is defined as education that overtly privileges a particular theological worldview but also exposes students to a diversity of other worldviews from a nonsectarian perspective. For example, a Roman Catholic school in the Jesuit tradition might divide its Religion Department into two subsections: one might be called "Religious Education" and teach Roman Catholic doctrines, history, and theology from the perspective of the Church. The other side of the divided department might be called "Religious Studies" where students are exposed to the study of Roman Catholicism and other traditions from an academic versus devotional perspective. In the rest of the curriculum (history, literature, etc.) students could be exposed to a nonsectarian interpretation of the intersections of religion, history, and culture that might mirror the cultural studies approach outlined below.

Inclusive sectarianism would require subjecting one's own faith tradition to the same historical/cultural representation and therefore scrutiny that the other traditions receive. The difference between this approach and a nonsectarian one is that clearly defined aspects of the school and curriculum are intentionally devoted to promoting a particular sectarian worldview. In the Roman Catholic example, students might be required to take Religious Education courses and abide by school rules that are formulated in keeping with the theological tenets being promoted, for example, mandatory community service, abstinence education, required attendance at Mass, and so on. The strength of this approach from the perspective of democratic education is that it honors the principles of nonrepression and nondiscrimination while still promoting a particular worldview that is not predicated on either ignorance or misrepresentation of competing claims.

Exclusive sectarianism is defined as education that restricts exposure to and accurate information about competing claims and/or worldviews that differ from the religious worldview being promoted. The dangers of this form of education from the vantage point of democratic education have already been addressed in the previous chapter but they bear repeating. In this model, students are neither exposed to accurate depictions of the diversity of worldviews represented in a multicultural society nor are they practiced in the skills of deliberative discourse required of citizens in a healthy democracy. To the extent that such students also live in relatively "closed" communities whereby their familial, social, religious, and educational circles overlap and reflect the same minimal exposure to accurate and positive depictions of conflicting claims, their ability to function as informed participants in a multicultural democracy is significantly diminished. A further concern is the violation of autonomy that children and young people experience in such settings.[26] Though I raise these concerns in relationship to the growing numbers of students enrolled in conservative Christian private schools and those raised in Christian homeschool environments, they are applicable to any form of exclusive sectarian education regardless of the tradition.

Given the numbers of children and young adults who are being schooled in Christian and other sectarian contexts in the United States, it would be wise to raise questions about the relationship between sectarian education and democracy in the same ways that these questions need to be debated in the context of public schooling.

Unintentionally Sectarian Practices

Unintentional sectarianism happens quite frequently and it could be argued that it is the most common way that information and attitudes about religion is conveyed to students. For example, there are myriad ways that the Christian hegemony in the culture is represented in the schools. Specific examples include, but are not limited to, the following illustrations.

A first and obvious example is that the school calendar is based on Christian holidays. Though the origin of the long summer break relates to the agricultural nature of the early Republic, the schedule from August–June typically includes breaks for Thanksgiving and the "winter" and "spring" holidays that correspond to Christmas and Easter. Similarly, the weekly schedule is also based on Christian patterns of worship whereby sports events and other extracurricular activities are often scheduled for Friday evenings and Saturdays. Rarely will major school events fall on a Sunday morning.

Second, to the extent that the Western literary canon, European history, art and music are privileged in the curriculum, Christianity is also privileged. Christianity is woven into the very heart of Western European history and culture and cannot be separated. Until the recent (and still highly controversial) introduction of multiculturalism into school curricula, the intellectual and cultural traditions of Western Europe and their impact on the United States were nearly exclusively taught as "our" history. Indeed, the standards of what constitutes an "educated person" were and often still are based upon knowledge of the various facets of this tradition.[27] Finally, this tradition has been used to establish the very criteria for how literature, art, music, and so on is defined. Consequently, distinctions were and still are drawn between "the classics" and "world literature"; "language" and "dialects"; "art" and "craft"; "classical" music and "folk" traditions; "history" and "ethnographic studies"; "Christianity" and "primitive" (e.g., African and Native American) religions.

In another example related to the above, the valorization of Western European history, culture, and traditions is also a valorization of Christianity. The nearly exclusive post-Enlightenment historical equation of Western European influences (including Christianity) with "civilization" and its people as "civilized" is still widespread. These associations are predicated upon valorized representations of Western European history that omit, for example, the brutalities of colonialism. The Thanksgiving story of how the pilgrims and the indigenous peoples (their tribes are often nameless) joined together for a common feast of thanksgiving is a betrayal of the historical record of what historian David Stannard calls the "American Holocaust" that resulted from European contact with the Western Hemisphere.[28] Similarly, the Western European colonization of Africa was justified by an ideology of superiority that gave sanction to all manner of horrendous crimes against Africans, their culture, and their continent.[29] Indeed, one of the reasons that the twentieth-century Holocaust targeting Jews is sometimes singled out as unique is not because of its horror or even its relative scope (though both were significant) but rather because it was overtly perpetuated by a self-perceived "civilized" nation against its own people. It is instructive to note in this context that much of the Nazi propaganda was aimed at presenting Jews as "foreign" and "dirty" in comparison to "Aryans."[30] The pervasive anti-Semitism that runs throughout much of Christian history (including contemporary expressions) also played an important role in the ideologies that led to genocide in the Holocaust.[31]

Another related form of valorization is represented in texts or perspectives that reproduce an "orientalist" view of history and culture that reached its height in nineteenth- and early twentieth-century Western Europe and (some argue) is still employed by prominent scholars today.[32] It represents a particular attitude toward how "the other" is characterized in comparison to an unreflective "self" which is considered normative. Edward Said is the one credited most for exposing the problematic assumptions of this worldview in his now classic study entitled *Orientalism*.[33] In this work, he presents a critique of how the "East" and the global South have been characterized by "Western" scholars in "sometimes sympathetic but always dominating" ways.[34] "Orientalist" biases in a variety of forms are common in texts that indirectly (or sometimes directly) valorize Christianity as an imbedded dimension of Western civilizations. This represents a widespread and often unacknowledged form of Christian sectarianism.

Another form of unintentional sectarianism that is the direct result of the intellectual and historical legacy cited above is when non-Christian beliefs, people, and institutions are characterized as (or made to feel) "foreign" in the United States. We already encountered the stories in Chapter Two of Kentucky-born Samieh Shalash who wore hijab and was assumed to be "foreign" born and of Amandeep Singh who was suspended from school for wearing his kirpan. Many might and do argue that the United States *is* an overwhelmingly Christian nation and has been since its founding. They conclude, therefore, that other religious traditions are "foreign" and it is appropriate to designate them as such. The historical truth, of course, is that Christianity is itself "foreign" to the indigenous inhabitants of this soil, but the point I wish to emphasize here is that the "default" assumption about religion in our culture in general (and our schools in particular) is that of Christianity. I wish to make this widely unconscious assumption more explicit so that it can be evaluated regarding its appropriateness in the context of secular, multicultural schools. For example, indicative of the school schedule and calendar illustrations cited above, Christian students encounter few if any obstacles in the schools when they seek to practice their faith in constitutionally protected ways. Individual prayers have never been forbidden and symbols of their faith such as wearing a cross or reading the Bible in their free time have also always been allowed. Similarly, their weekly services of worship rarely conflict with school activities.[35] Non-Christian practices and symbols that are equally protected under the Constitution, however, will often require special accommodations that may or may not be granted. For example, many schools forbid the wearing of "headgear" while in classes to discourage wearing caps. This common rule is often passed without recognition that the religious dress of Sikhs, Orthodox Jewish boys, and some Muslim girls will place them in violation of this rule.[36] My point is that, contrary to popular beliefs across the ideological spectrum, Christianity is still deeply imbedded in "secular" schools in ways that subtly promote unintentional Christian sectarianism.

Other common practices that represent unintentional sectarianism are ones that are not exclusively Christian. For example, educators will often invite a local religious leader or cleric into class as an expert in her or his religious tradition. Though some religious leaders may also be trained in the academic study of religion and therefore qualified to represent the diversity of religious views within the tradition itself, this is not often the case. Religious leaders are (appropriately) trained within the context of their own particular sectarian perspective and will often unwittingly privilege that perspective over others when asked to present an overview of the tradition as a whole. What local Imam could adequately represent Islam in all of its diverse complexity? Obviously no single speaker could ever fully represent the diversity of Muslim expressions of the faith, but someone trained in the academic study of Islam could help represent the diversity of expressions as a central dimension to understanding Islam itself. Religious leaders and clerics from any tradition are not usually trained in this way. This is not a comment about their capacity, but rather one about their vocation as religious leaders, an appropriately sectarian pursuit. There is a different kind of training involved in learning about religion from a nonsectarian perspective, and classroom speakers should be well versed in the study of religion itself to minimize the reproduction of unintentional sectarian biases.

A final example that I will discuss is the unintended sectarian beliefs of the teacher her/himself. As was already acknowledged in the first chapter, all teachers come into the classroom with a host of imbedded assumptions about everything related to their vocation as educators. The assumptions that teachers bring about their students, their subject matter, and what they believe regarding the purpose of education all heavily influence the nature of how they will function in the classroom. Good teachers are reflective practitioners who consciously attempt to name their underlying assumptions and to reflect upon how those assumptions promote, hinder, and/or thwart their aspirations as educators.

An often unexamined arena of assumption relates to the personal religious (or nonreligious) views of teachers and the ways that these views will impact curriculum decisions, classroom practices, and behaviors. This is not unlike assumptions that teachers bring about issues related to race, class, gender, sexuality, and ethnicity. Though it is relatively common for in-service and preservice teachers to be exposed to multicultural studies in ways that help them be self-reflective about the identity categories listed above, it is quite uncommon for religion to be included as a category for analysis. Individual experiences and assumptions regarding all of these categories are complex and informed by a host of social, historical, cultural, and personal contexts. Like the other categories, the religious beliefs (or none) that educators hold will inevitably play themselves out in the classroom in conscious and unconscious ways. The aim is for educators to be as vigilantly aware as possible about their own assumptions while simultaneously interrogating their practices to minimize unconscious behaviors.

For example, I have already discussed common forms of unintentional sectarianism related to teachers in the form of choosing texts and or approaches that valorize particular religious traditions and denigrate and/or ignore others. It is also easy for teachers to unintentionally reinforce stereotypes. One world history teacher in Texas reflected upon how he used to teach about Islam solely as a "religion of conquest." It was not until he participated in a continuing education seminar on Islam that he realized his error. "There were lots of factors that supported this interpretation, including textbook depictions. But what really surprised me was my personal resistance to learning anything positive about Islam. My own Christian faith was getting in the way."[37] Another example comes from a self-described atheist who realized that she was underestimating the intellectual capacity of her students who self-defined as "religious." She was especially biased against those who represented themselves as Christians and whom she believed were participants in an extracurricular conservative Christian club.[38] A converse example in this category is when teachers represent religious traditions as uniformly positive. Assertions such as "Islam is a religion of peace" or "Christianity promotes love, not hate" are often made to counter widespread negative associations or representations. As well meaning as these assertions may be, they are actually theological statements that represent particular versus universally held assertions about whatever tradition is being characterized. More accurate and appropriate comments would be ones that were explicitly qualified, such as "Many Muslims abhor the violence being perpetuated in the name of Islam" or "Christians are themselves divided on the controversial issues of our time," and the like.

These are just some of the ways that imbedded assumptions about religion can promote unintentional expressions of sectarianism. Religious literacy as outlined above would give educators the tools to better discern these expressions and to assess them on their merits. Though textual, cultural, and individual biases will always be present, the hope is for educators to develop the tools to recognize them more readily and to help minimize their unconscious reproduction.

Intentional and unintentional forms of sectarianism promote particular religious beliefs and worldviews over others. Though the remaining four approaches that I discuss can also be used and/or interpreted to promote sectarian aims, they are most widely employed in the service of learning about religion from a nonsectarian perspective. It is this latter understanding that I will present here.

The Phenomenological Approach

Another approach that is frequently used in teaching about religion is a form of phenomenology that can best be characterized as a nonsectarian, descriptive study of the beliefs, symbols, practices, and structures of religion and religious expression. This approach assumes that religious experience is a unique category that cannot be accurately represented when analyzed through nonreligious frameworks (e.g., psychology, history, sociology, etc.) It seeks to expose students to the uniquely religious dimensions of human experience without critique in an effort to foster deeper understanding of religious life and practice. The aim of a phenomenological approach is for the student to suspend judgment and approach the study of religion in a spirit of empathy. This approach also allows for a type of comparative methodology whereby different traditions can be compared through the lens of certain categories, such as sacred spaces, rites of passage, and so on.[39]

A popular text in secondary school departments of religion or where comparative religion courses are offered is Huston Smith's *The World's Religions*.[40] Smith's approach can be characterized as a popular form of phenomenology in that he presents an overview of several of the world's religious traditions in about 25–30 pages each by introducing readers to basic beliefs, practices, rituals, sacred texts, and leaders of each tradition. It is a readable volume that is often used as the foundation for introductory courses and supplemented with relevant translated "sacred" texts such as the Bible, the *Bhagavad Gita*, and the *Tao Te Ching*.[41]

The strength of this approach is that it provides a sympathetic introduction to religious traditions that is accessible to the novice. Smith's text in particular is popular because it provides information in a succinct, readable format. To many, another strength is that the method itself aims to promote deeper understanding about religion and different religious traditions by encouraging students to "bracket" their own beliefs in order to empathize with the tradition under investigation. Finally, this method offers a framework for comparison between different traditions.

As compelling as this approach may seem, there are significant weaknesses that need to be addressed. This method has come under considerable scrutiny among religious studies scholars over the past few decades and the critiques are numerous and significant. For our purposes, they can all be summarized under the broad umbrella of the ahistorical nature of the method itself. Traditions are often presented as timeless, uniform, and unchanging systems of belief that betray the social/historical dimensions that define all religious expressions and interpretations. Subcategories of this same critique include the following: Religions are often presented as 1) essentialized expressions that are uniform as opposed to internally diverse and 2) idealized in that they are represented in an uncritical light. This method also assumes that the researcher is both "objective" and capable of accurately representing the meaning of the symbols and practices under investigation. Finally, the comparative dimension of this method is also problematic in that the similarities represented between traditions are also devoid of historical/cultural context. This can lead students to make inaccurate assumptions about commonalities between traditions that are misleading.

In summary, while this method serves some useful purposes in the context of secondary school education about religion, its major flaw is that it serves to reinforce the common and deeply problematic assumption that religions somehow exist outside of their social/historical contexts. The approach fails to expose students to the diversity within traditions while also failing to give them the tools to understand how religion has always and continues to function in the service of a full range of often competing ideological convictions. These are critical dimensions of religion that students need to know if they are to become religiously literate. It is not enough to know the Five Pillars of Islam, the Four Noble Truths of Buddhism, or the Ten Commandments of Judaism and Christianity. How these doctrines arose and how they have been modified and interpreted in different social/historical contexts is the essence of literacy in the context of democratic education.

The Literary Approach

Religion and religious themes are often broached in literature classes across America. Though there are some courses in secondary schools that study the Bible from a literary perspective, most students encounter religion in literature courses through novels, short stories, and poems. Religious allusions in texts are common and the religious influences of authors are often quite salient in their work. The aim of this perspective is to apply the tools of literary analysis to enter into and understand the world created within a given text, including its religious dimensions. Though this approach rarely includes an historical analysis of these dimensions, it is an excellent way to introduce students to the ways that religion and culture are deeply entwined. It is also a good source for exposing students to representations of religious expression in defined contexts. Secondary school English teacher Karen Russell recognizes the importance of religious literacy for teachers as exemplified in the following comment: "Religion is not beside the point of literature, it's the crucial point of literature: What is behind that symbol and what does it mean? Recognizing a symbol's religious significance opens the door to literary insight."[42]

In spite of how common it is for religious themes to emerge in literature courses, many teachers report feeling inadequate when it comes to engaging these themes in depth.[43] This is not a commentary about their competence but rather about their lack of adequate training. While a few articulate feeling confident in their knowledge, many others report that they either avoid the religious dimensions of texts altogether or rely on their own self-study or previous knowledge derived from their own faith practices. It is important to offer teachers opportunities to enhance their knowledge in these areas and I will suggest particular methods to do so in the follow chapter.

In addition to providing teachers with better training, it is also appropriate to include a broader range of texts for investigation in literature courses, including those that are considered "sacred" in the world's religious traditions. As I mentioned in Chapter Two, many classic texts such as the *Qur'an*, the *Mahabharata*, and the *Tao Te Ching* are rich literary resources in their own right as well as profoundly influential in larger cultural and political spheres.

The Historical Approach

This approach uses the tools of historical research to understand a religion within the wider political context out of which it emerged and developed. While it is true that the historical study of religion has always been included in school history texts (some more accurately than others), most of these depictions are limited to the origins of the traditions and significant moments in political history where religion played a major political role (e.g., the Crusades, the witch trials in Europe, and the early U.S. colonies, the founding of the State of Israel, etc.). It is rare, however, for texts to address the religious dimensions of political, intellectual, and cultural life in a sustained way outside of those pivotal defining moments that are interpreted as overtly religious. This, too, reinforces the belief that religion is fundamentally separate from other dimensions of human life except in premodern times and in exceptional modern expressions that are often negative or portrayed in a negative light (e.g., religious forms of terrorism, the Islamic revolution in Iran, etc.).

As Warren Nord demonstrates in his text *Religion and American Education*, commentators from across the ideological spectrum agree that the treatment of religion in American school history texts is inadequate even though they disagree regarding what is needed to remedy the situation.[44] The reasons for this deficiency are numerous, but the two most salient for our purposes are 1) that religion tends to be controversial and textbook publishers are notoriously eager to avoid controversy and 2) texts tend to emphasize political and social history as opposed to a more inclusive approach that would also address the cultural, intellectual, and religious dimensions of historical understanding. This more inclusive approach to history is a significant aspect of the cultural studies approach I develop below. First, however, I will turn to a consideration of multicultural theories of education and their relevance for teaching about religion in the schools.

Multicultural and Cultural Studies Approaches

Multicultural Education

Multicultural education has emerged as an umbrella term to encompass decades of research related to how teachers can best engage the rich diversity of students who fill our nation's classrooms. Differences related to race, culture, ethnicity, language, gender, social class, and disability have traditionally been included under the concept of multiculturalism.[45] Though religion is sometimes addressed, it is surprisingly absent from most of the literature and discourses in the field.[46] I suspect that the major reason for this omission relates to the broader illiteracy about religion as an important dimension of culture coupled with a general lack of exposure by multicultural theorists to study about the religions of the world in their social historical contexts. Another reason may be uncertainty on the part of scholars and practitioners regarding the legal and political dimensions of teaching about religion in the schools. Whatever the reasons for the scant attention to religion in multicultural theory, many of the tools developed in the field of multicultural education are quite relevant for teaching about religion responsibly. Indeed, the cultural studies approach that I promote below has a great deal in common with one of the models of multicultural education that Christine Sleeter and Carl Grant have identified in their now classic text *Making Choices for Multicultural Education: Five Approaches to Race, Class, and Gender.*[47] In order to highlight both the strengths and limitations of a multicultural approach to teaching about religion in the schools, I will briefly outline the typology of multicultural approaches that Sleeter and Grant have identified and illustrate how the study of religion could be incorporated within each framework.

The first approach that they outline is called "Teaching the Exceptional and the Culturally Different."[48] This approach developed in the 1960s in the context of desegregation and focuses on "adapting instruction to student differences for the purpose of helping students succeed more effectively in the mainstream."[49] It promotes the assimilation of students with different racial, ethnic, and class backgrounds into mainstream culture. It does not invite the critique or interrogation of the underlying norms, values, and assumptions that define "mainstream" in any given context, but instead assumes the legitimacy and goodness of status quo practices. In regard to religion in America, this approach may recognize those who are overtly religious as different, and attempt to assimilate them into the "mainstream" culture that promotes either a veiled Protestant Christian worldview or secular humanism, depending on both context and interpretation. The difference is how "mainstream" is defined and by whom. Assimilation and academic achievement are the major goals emphasized in this approach.

The second framework is one that Sleeter and Grant define as the "Human Relations Approach" and this developed at about the same period in the 1960s as the approach defined above.[50] It emphasizes individual relationships and helps to foster respect and more effective communication between students from diverse backgrounds and/or abilities. It also emphasizes reducing stereotypes through experience and exposing students to knowledge and information about diverse peoples and cultures. In relationship to religion, this approach is widely practiced and employed when students learn about religions other than their own (usually from a phenomenological perspective) and when they are encouraged to change negative views or impressions. According to Sleeter and Grant, this approach to multiculturalism in a broad sense is the most widely practiced by educators, especially white elementary school teachers.[51] This approach fails to address the underlying social dimensions of how negative stereotypes develop in the first place and how they are structurally reinforced and perpetuated. It also tends to represent different groups as internally uniform, which can lead students to believe, for example, that all Koreans or all Jews are alike.

The third model is called the "Single-Group Studies Approach" that developed in the 1960s and 1970s out of the civil rights struggles of African Americans, other racial/ethnic minorities, and women.[52] Ethnic studies and women's studies programs emerged at this time to address the specific plight of particular identity groups and to empower members of those groups to challenge their oppression and raise their social status. Unlike the first two models, the Single-Group Studies Approach does address the underlying structural dimensions that give rise to oppression and which serve to perpetuate it. Goals are to promote structural equality and to uncover and teach about the "lost" or manipulated histories of the group in order to challenge negative representations and stereotypes. This approach could be applied to religious minorities in America such as Jews, Muslims, Roman Catholics, and Sikhs. Critiques of this method center on the failure to recognize intra-group diversity that can inadvertently lead to promoting particular forms of oppression while attempting to overcome others. A classic example is the way in which both the first and second waves of the women's movement in America were led by and addressed the needs of white, economically advantaged women in ways that promoted the marginalization of poor whites and all women of color. Similarly, women's voices and experiences are often excluded or inadequately addressed in other representations of Single-Group Studies.

The fourth approach that Sleeter and Grant outline is entitled "Multicultural Studies."[53] This approach emerged in the late 1960s and early 1970s and attempts to address the shortcomings of the Single-Group Approach by recognizing identity as multifaceted and by linking the oppression of specific groups to a more encompassing understanding of the structural dimensions of power and powerlessness. This approach also emphasizes diversity as a positive value to be promoted. Educational theorist D.M. Gollnick summarized the goals of this approach as follows:

1. Promoting the strength and value of cultural diversity;
2. Promoting human rights and respect for those who are different from oneself;
3. Promoting alternative life choices for people;

4. Promoting social justice and equal opportunity for all people;
5. Promoting equity in the distribution of power among groups.[54]

The pedagogical goals that accompany this approach are very similar to those I outlined in Chapter One: critical thinking, analysis of alternative viewpoints, and cooperative models of learning. Like the Single-Group Approach, this model addresses issues of structural inequality but does so with an emphasis that addresses the complexities of identity and the positive dimensions of diversity. This approach could incorporate religion as an important dimension of identity that would further enrich the complex understanding of identity that it attempts to foster. Multicultural Studies has been the target of significant critique from those advocating for an assimilationist approach to education in the interests of promoting an "American" identity. These critics fear that multiculturalism will serve to further fragment our already diverse society.[55] Other critics fear that educators are not adequately trained to represent the sophisticated synthesis that the method requires, thus reducing it to a series of Single-Group representations rather than a truly integrated model. Finally, some critics argue that multicultural education thus defined does not explicitly address the issue of social transformation beyond knowledge acquisition. These critics advocate that students should not only learn about cultural diversity, structural forms of inequality, and strategies for change but that they should also have the opportunity to develop their skills as activists able to effect positive change toward the goals represented in the multicultural approach. This leads us the fifth and final model that Sleeter and Grant outline.

The "Multicultural and Social Reconstructionist" method encompasses the goals outlined in the Multicultural Studies Approach but extends them to include active social engagement with these issues both within and outside of the school community. Sleeter and Grant summarize the goals and methods associated with this approach in the following way:

Goals

Societal goal: Promote social structural equality and cultural pluralism.

School goals: Prepare citizens to work actively toward social structural equality; promote cultural pluralism and alternative life styles; promote equal opportunity in the school.

Practices

Curriculum: Organize content around current social issues involving racism, classism, sexism, handicapism; organize concepts around experiences and perspectives of several different American groups; use students' life experiences as starting point for analyzing oppression; teach critical thinking skills, analysis of alternative viewpoints; teach social action skills, empowerment skills.

Instruction: Involve students actively in democratic decision making; build on students' learning styles; adapt to students skill levels; use cooperative learning.

Other: Decorate room to reflect social action themes, cultural diversity, students interests; avoid testing and grouping procedures that designate some students as failures.

Support: Help regular classroom adapt to as much diversity [re: special needs] as possible.

Schoolwide: Involve students in democratic decision making about substantive schoolwide concerns; involve lower-class and minority parents actively in the school;[56] involve school in local community action projects; make sure that staffing patterns include diverse racial, gender, and disability groups in nontraditional roles; use decorations, special events, school menus to reflect and include diverse groups; use library materials that portray diverse groups in diverse roles; make sure that extracurricular activities include all student groups and do not reinforce stereotypes; use discipline procedures that do not penalize any one group; make sure building is accessible to disabled people.[57]

This approach is the most comprehensive and addresses the issues I raised in Chapter One regarding the role of public education to promote the ideals of democracy and the skills required to participate as active and informed citizens in our multicultural society. This advocacy approach takes students seriously as moral agents and helps them develop the tools of discernment, accountability, and negotiation needed to engage in positive social change. In relationship to religion, this approach affords the opportunity to represent the ways that religion intersects with culture and how it can serve as a culturally defined resource for cultivating hope, vision, and moral imagination regarding human agency and capacity. For example, Martin Luther King, Jr. and other civil rights leaders drew upon representations of Christianity that were developed in the Black Church tradition to inspire and sustain their long fight for emancipation. King was especially skilled in translating dimensions of that tradition into language that was meaningful and inspiring to a broader and more diverse audience.[58] King was a student of Mohandas Gandhi, another deeply religious leader who was inspired by his faith to challenge the dehumanizing structures imposed by British colonialism. Like King, Gandhi was able to translate insights derived from his own Hindu tradition into an articulation that many outside of that tradition also found meaningful and inspiring.[59] Finally, many Christian, Jewish, and Muslim women have found inspiration within their traditions to challenge the patriarchal interpretations of those traditions that have historically prevailed.[60] This approach to multiculturalism provides the methodological structures whereby the religious dimensions of culture and experience can be discerned and represented as a resource for emancipatory social change.

The only critiques of this position that Sleeter and Grant offer are related to doubts regarding its feasibility and the difficulty of defining it as a single approach given that it represents several different types of studies articulated in different disciplines.[61]

They find this approach the most compelling and effective in promoting the ideals of democracy that they wish to support. I am also drawn to this model and find the methods and values articulated to be very much in keeping with those I advocate in Chapter One. I am left wondering, however, about what mechanisms are in place in the approach itself to avoid the dangers of valorizing the perspectives of the marginalized and/or demonizing those of the privileged. Put differently, what will ensure that all perspectives will be scrutinized and evaluated in relation to whether they promote or hinder the ideals of democracy in multicultural America? For example, in our current cultural context it is entirely feasible to imagine a scenario where marginalized members of society might join forces with privileged constituencies to oppose the formation of a GLBT caucus at the local high school. As Sleeter and Grant have noted, the multicultural approach itself developed out of Single-Group Studies as a result of recognizing how marginalization alone is no guarantee against the active promotion of discrimination.

Conversely, privilege may initially hinder consciousness regarding how structural forms of oppression exist, but the theory itself has to offer more than guilt as a motivation for people of privilege to participate in emancipatory social change. The social locations identified through structural analysis are not themselves determinative of individual or collective agency. Structural analysis simply identifies both the resources as well as the obstacles to forms of consciousness that can lead to emancipatory action. As historian of science Donna Haraway states, "The standpoints of the subjugated are not 'innocent' positions. On the contrary, they are preferred because in principle they are least likely to allow denial of the critical interpretive core of all knowledge."[62] In a similar vein, the standpoints of the privileged are not inevitably "tainted." They are, however, experientially hindered from recognizing how values and the subsequent privileging of some representations of truth and goodness over others are socially constructed. Elaborating upon an illustration I offered in Chapter One may be helpful at this juncture.

As a white person who has grown up in a society that values whiteness, it is difficult for me to recognize the ways that social norms, customs, and values privilege whiteness in our culture as normative. On the other hand, as a lesbian mother I experience how heterosexual norms and assumptions are deeply imbedded in culture and privileged in ways that heterosexual individuals and couples have difficulty identifying because those norms and assumptions mirror their own experiences. Being a lesbian who is conscious of heterosexism does not, however, grant me moral superiority over heterosexual men and women. Similarly my white skin does not, by definition, render me morally deficient in relationship to people of color. Though few would overtly defend such essentialist characterizations, I fear that Multicultural Studies and Multicultural and Reconstructionist approaches inadvertently promote such views because there are no built in mechanisms in the theoretical formulations themselves to challenge such essentialized interpretations.

In the case of religion, the problems associated with such essentializing tendencies are especially apparent. No religious tradition can be accurately represented as a singular worldview nor can any religion be characterized as either promoting or hindering the democratic ideals outlined above. As history proves, religion can be used in the service of either promoting or denigrating human dignity and well-being. There is nothing "essential" about religion that lends itself to an accurate portrayal of any given tradition as ideologically or epistemologically "uniform." In the context of multicultural education, being a Muslim or Jew or Sikh in America does not necessarily mean that your worldview will be consistent with democratic ideals. It *will* mean, however, that you will be in a better position to understand how imbedded cultural assumptions promote both Christian and secular values that often thwart your ability to fully express yourself as a religious person in multicultural America. A cultural studies method will help identify these cultural assumptions while also providing the tools to interrogate all value claims and assess them in light of whether they will serve to promote or hinder human agency and well-being in the context of our multicultural democracy.

I believe that the cultural studies approach mitigates these dangers of essentialism while retaining the critical and emancipatory dimensions of the multicultural and reconstructionist theory outlined here. It is to the cultural studies model that I now turn.

The Cultural Studies Approach to Teaching About Religion

The field of cultural studies can be best defined as an amalgam of disciplines that combines sociology, social theory, literary theory, film/video studies, the creative and fine arts, and cultural anthropology to study cultural phenomena in historical and contemporary societies. Cultural studies researchers often concentrate on how a particular phenomenon is ideologically interpreted in relation to race, social class, and/or gender and thus its affinity with multicultural studies is clear and well established. More broadly, cultural studies theorists aim to examine their subject matter in terms of cultural practices and their relation to power. The objective is to understand culture in all its complex forms as expressions of the social and political contexts in which culture manifests itself.[63]

In the following section I will outline my own conception of cultural studies as it pertains to the study of religion in schools. Though much of what follows has been deeply informed by cultural studies theorists, my articulations may or may not be fully in keeping with various self-definitions of the field in its current iterations. Indeed, cultural studies is notoriously difficult to define due to its multivalent representations. In spite of this definitional ambiguity I have chosen to retain the descriptor cultural studies because it best represents the multiple dimensions of my project here. In addition, one of the field's earliest proponents describes the inception of cultural studies in ways that are very much in keeping with my approach. Raymond Williams states,

> When I moved into internal University Teaching . . . we started teaching in ways that . . . [related] history to art and literature, including contemporary culture, and suddenly so strange was this to the Universities that they said "My God, here is a new subject called Cultural Studies." . . . The true position . . . was not only a

matter of remedying deficit, making up for inadequate educational resources in the wider society, nor only a case of meeting new needs of the society, though those things contributed. The deepest impulse was the desire to make learning part of the process of social change itself.[64]

The essential features of my definition of cultural studies include but are by no means limited to the following:

1. A cultural studies approach to teaching about religion is multidisciplinary in that it assumes that religion is deeply imbedded in all dimensions of human experience and therefore requires multiple lenses through which to understand its multivalent social/cultural influences.

2. Cultural studies challenges the legitimacy of the assumption that human experience can be studied accurately through discrete disciplinary lenses (e.g., political, economic, cultural, social, etc.) and instead posits an approach that recognizes how these lenses are fundamentally entwined. Cultural studies is also inclusive of other forms of expression heretofore ignored in academic discourse, such as "popular" culture and media. Specifically, this approach would assume, for example, that political dimensions of human experience cannot be adequately understood without considering the religious and other influences that define the cultural context out of which political actions and motivations arise. Similarly, cultural expressions (including popular and religious ones) are influenced by and, in turn, influence political life. In this way, the term "cultural" is widely inclusive of all dimensions of human experience.

3. Cultural studies recognizes that all knowledge claims are "situated" claims in that they arise out of certain social/historical/cultural/personal contexts and therefore represent particular and necessarily partial perspectives. This assertion is represented in contrast to claims that "objective" forms of knowledge exist that are equated with "unbiased" perspectives that are considered universally credible. Donna Haraway calls the latter presumption a "god-trick" that assumes the ability to "see everything from nowhere" as opposed to the "situated knowledges" that more accurately define the human endeavor of interpretation. This recognition of partial or situated knowledges is not, however, a form of relativism where all positions are considered equally credible. Indeed, Haraway asserts that relativism is the mirror-twin of totalizing theories and is therefore another representation of the god-trick. Instead, she posits that the recognition of all knowledge claims as "situated" offers the firmest ground upon which to make objective claims that are defined

not by their detachment but rather by their specificity, transparency, and capacity for accountability.

> . . . the alternative to relativism is not totalization and single vision, which is always finally the unmarked category whose power depends on systematic narrowing and obscuring. The alternative to relativism is partial, locatable, critical knowledges sustaining the possibility of webs of connections called solidarity in politics and shared conversations in epistemology. Relativism is a way of being nowhere while claiming to be everywhere equally. The "equality" of positioning is a denial of responsibility and critical enquiry. Relativism is the perfect mirror twin of totalization in the ideologies of objectivity; both deny the stakes in location, embodiment, and partial perspective; both make it impossible to see well. Relativism and totalization are both "god-tricks" promising vision from everywhere and nowhere equally and fully, common myths in rhetorics surrounding science. But it is precisely in the politics and epistemology of partial perspectives that the possibility of sustained, rational, objective enquiry rests.[65]

This assertion that all knowledge claims are "situated" will be familiar to students of history, the social sciences, languages and literature, but less so for students new to science and theology. For all their differences, the latter two fields are associated with providing "totalizing" theories of "truth" from their respective foundations. (This is, of course, one reason why the debates regarding creationism, intelligent design and evolution remain so heated.) It is no accident that Haraway employs the language of the god-trick in her endeavor to challenge the supposedly objective (read unbiased, impartial, universal) nature of the scientific enterprise.

Contrary to popular belief, it is important to note here that most practicing scientists and theologians are also comfortable with the notion of situated knowledges. Haraway, for example, claims that "no practitioner of the high scientific arts would be caught dead acting on the textbook versions [of unbiased objectivity] . . . The only people who end up actually *believing* and . . . acting on the ideological doctrines of disembodied scientific objectivity enshrined in elementary textbooks and technoscience booster literature are non-scientists, including a few very trusting philosophers."[66] Similarly, I would argue that most theologians also recognize the "situated knowledges" of their own perspectives and, indeed, most world religions have internal "checks" against the temptations for humans to claim understanding of "God" or ultimacy such as this expression: "A god understood, a god comprehended is no God."[67] In spite of these acknowledgments by scientists and theologians regarding the situated knowledges that define their respective enterprises, science and theology are still associated with totalizing theories of representation that are exploited in the marketplace of social discourse. A sophisticated understanding of how all knowledge claims are situated should be a focus of the educational enterprise as one way to challenge any claims that are aimed at closing further legitimate democratic inquiry.

Before moving on, it is important to reiterate that the acknowledgment that all knowledge claims are situated (including scientific and theological ones) does neither undermine their credibility nor the larger credibility of the intellectual enterprise itself. Indeed, as Haraway persuasively argues, by locating knowledge claims in their particularity they are more transparent, accountable, and therefore potentially credible when evaluated in relationship to the larger value claims being promoted. This is why Haraway rightly argues that epistemological claims are ultimately claims about particular ethical, political (and I would add religious) ideologies that need to be exposed and defended.

In relationship to the study of religion itself, a cultural studies approach that affirms all knowledge claims as situated provides an especially useful foundation upon which to study religion in a way that exposes both the internal complexity of any given tradition as well as the multiple ways that religion is woven into the fabric of human experience and utilized to justify a full range of ideological convictions. For example, god-tricks that claim there is one legitimate interpretation of Christianity or Islam or any religious worldview will be exposed as particular or situated representations that arise out of specific historical/cultural contexts. In this way, such depictions will more accurately be represented as one set of interpretations/representations among many others that are all recognized as "legitimate" theological expressions from an academic lens. A cultural studies approach provides the mechanism for studying the diversity of theological expressions within a tradition by locating them within the historical/cultural contexts out of which they arise. This also allows for competing claims to be represented and acknowledged, even if those claims are not the most politically prominent or persuasive.

4. Fourth, a cultural studies approach recognizes that the lens of the interpreter is also one that is situated and therefore partial, biased, and

particular. This is always the case, so the aim is to become as conscious as possible regarding the assumptions that inform and define one's perspective. We have already encountered examples of how uninterrogated conscious assumptions (and unacknowledged unconscious ones) can thwart learning. Troublesome conscious and unconscious assumptions about religion in our culture are especially prevalent and deeply rooted. Awareness alone will not overcome biases, but it will help the interpreter negotiate the terrain of inquiry from a more informed and transparent understanding.

5. Fifth, a cultural studies approach explicitly addresses issues related to power and powerlessness. It provides a framework to ask the following types of questions: What worldviews or perspectives are prominent in particular contexts and what social mechanisms are in place that give legitimacy to certain views over others? What perspectives are missing or marginalized and why? In relationship to any perspective, who benefits from the adoption of particular representations over others? By asking these and other similar types of questions, the complexity of the cultural construction of value claims can be understood more fully and positions scrutinized in light of the democratic values being promoted.

6. Finally, as indicated in the opening paragraphs of this section, a cultural studies approach self-consciously affirms the political dimensions of the educational enterprise. Learning is never a neutral activity and all knowledges are formed in the service of (sometimes multiple) ideological claims. Again, this acknowledgment is not an indictment against the legitimacy of the educational enterprise as hopelessly biased and therefore suspect (as various critics of education have claimed over the decades). It is, rather, an overt recognition that neutrality in education is an impossible and (I would argue) ultimately undesirable goal. Issues as broad as how the educational enterprise is structured and as focused as how an individual teacher assesses a particular student's assignment are all rooted in certain sets of assumptions that are ideologically laden. In relation to our subject, whether (and if so how) one teaches about religion has ideological implications. A cultural studies approach recognizes this and requires that these implications be transparent and defensible.

In summary, the key to a cultural studies approach is the employment of multiple lenses to understand the subject at hand, including an awareness of the lenses of the interpreters (authors, writers, artists who are being studied) inquirers (students), and teachers who set the larger context for the inquiry itself.

An illustration may be helpful at this juncture to clarify the differences between the seven approaches to the study of religion in public schools outlined above. Consider the Ten Commandments. A conservative Christian sectarian approach might promote teaching about the Ten Commandments in schools from the perspective of a literal reading of the Biblical account as represented in either the King James or the New Living translations of the Bible. From this perspective, the account of Moses receiving the tablets directly from God is interpreted as historic fact. This viewpoint would most likely also promote the belief that the Ten Commandments served as a foundational influence in the founding documents of the nation. This assertion is represented by the ADF in their support of displaying the Ten Commandments in government buildings (including schools) and for promoting the view that the Ten Commandments should be a central component in public school curricula. "The Ten Commandments are the basis for much of our current legal system, and the role of faith and providence was recognized in our public buildings, historical documents and institutions. The attempt to remove this heritage more than 200 years later is nothing more than an attempt to 'sterilize' our nation's history."[68] What is at stake for the ADF and others who support this view is the formal recognition of the religious (read Protestant Christian) nature of the Republic.

An unacknowledged sectarian assumption related to the illustration cited above is the way that the Ten Commandments are interpreted in the current cultural debate through the lens of a particular representation of Protestant Christianity. There are unacknowledged theological claims that are represented in this debate that should be more transparent. Another way that unacknowledged sectarianism is often promoted in relation to the Ten Commandments in schools is when they are represented as general moral codes of conduct devoid of any explicit reference to their religious roots and contemporary associations.

A phenomenological approach would not address the debate about displaying the Commandments on government property at all but would instead represent the Ten Commandments theologically as central to Judaism and secondary to Christianity.

A literary approach might focus on the Biblical account of the Ten Commandments from a literary standpoint while also referencing sample allusions to the Commandments in other literary sources.

An historical approach in the schools to the Ten Commandments would entail introducing them in the context of their relevance to Judaism and as an example of how Christianity retained dimensions of

Jewish thought in its own historical formulation. If the contemporary debate regarding the display of the Commandments in government buildings would be covered at all, it would most likely be presented as a debate between broadly defined "religious" and "secular" interests and unrelated to the historical and theological origins of the Commandments themselves. Such a discussion would probably also be unrelated to an informed view of the religious dimensions of American political history.

A multicultural approach might interpret the Commandments as central to Judaism and may overtly or more subtly support the notion that Jewish interpretations of the Commandments should be privileged over other views by virtue of the historic marginalization of Jews throughout history and their unique historical and theological relationship to the Commandments themselves.

In contrast, a cultural studies approach would provide students with a more situated understanding than those outlined above. This approach would cultivate the intellectual and methodological tools that would enable students to explore how the Ten Commandments must be understood through the intersecting lenses of religion, history, politics, and culture that would include but expand upon the other approaches. It would also include a more broadly understood awareness of the context of inquiry itself (what the teacher hopes to achieve in assigning and designing the lesson, unit, class) as well as an awareness of the student's own lens of analysis. It is important to clarify, however, that the aim is *not* to produce a thoroughly comprehensive cultural studies history of the Ten Commandments! Such an endeavor would be impossible and unnecessary. Rather, the aim is to provide students with the tools to gain a more comprehensive understanding of the Ten Commandments (or any other subject for that matter) in *particular cultural and historical contexts* whereby the multivalent dimensions of interpretation are recognized, explored, and interrogated.

For example, in the context of a course on U.S. history, a cultural studies approach would broadly include the religious and other cultural dimensions of political life from precolonial times to the present. Though it would be impossible to engage in an investigation of every subject of inquiry from the multiple lenses required of a cultural studies approach, it is not unrealistic to consistently recognize that multiple perspectives are always present and to judiciously choose to illustrate this understanding by carefully selected case studies at various intervals of the course. In this way, a cultural studies approach is as much about a method of inquiry as it is about content coverage itself. In relationship to our topic, an excellent case study would be one that focused on any of the pivotal founding documents of the Republic in an effort to better understand the role that religion played in the shaping the ideological foundations of the nation. A teacher could intentionally frame the investigation in light of the current debates as a way of naming the larger context and making the investigation relevant to students. (e.g., "The Ten Commandments are the basis for much of our current legal system, and the role of faith and providence was recognized in our public buildings, historical documents and institutions."[69]) There are several legitimate ways that such an investigation could be framed and organized, but essential features must include 1) transparency regarding the teacher's aims; 2) an awareness on the part of students that all knowledge claims are situated, including their own; 3) an investigation of multiple sources of information (e.g., political writings, literature, popular print media, etc.); 4) an accurate portrayal of competing ideological perspectives in both contemporary and historical contexts; 5) a critical investigation of the various implications inherent in differing positions; and 6) an understanding of why this (or any) investigation is relevant in relationship to cultivating the articulated aims of the purpose of education.

Such an investigation would reveal the competing ideological beliefs (including religious ones) of the founding fathers while providing the methodological tools to understand how those beliefs were formulated, altered, challenged, and institutionalized. It also provides a methodology of interpretation that recognizes multiple perspectives and the role of the interpreter her/himself. It is true, of course, that religion was an influential factor in the founding ideology of the nation, but how so? Which religious representations were influential and which were marginal and how was this determined? What criteria should we use to evaluate this legacy? Though religion is obviously not the only relevant dimension of cultural and political life worthy of understanding, it is certainly an important one that has unfortunately been consistently neglected. Even a cursory review of the religious history of the United States reveals the profound intersections between American religious, political, and cultural life. A cultural studies approach provides the method to study the religion in its social/historical contexts thereby promoting religious literacy while simultaneously challenging the assumption that religion is an ahistorical phenomenon that resides outside of everyday social/political and cultural experience.

Implications for Pedagogy and the Issue of Accommodations

I hope it is apparent at this juncture that a cultural studies approach is consistent with the learner-centered model I outlined in Chapter One. Indeed, I would argue that a cultural studies approach requires a learner-centered method if it is to be internally consistent. If a central tenet of cultural studies is the recognition of multiple perspectives and interpretations (including the perspectives and interpretations of the inquirer) then the method must facilitate the possibilities for multiple perspectives to emerge. If all information is mediated through the lens of the instructor, then multiple perspectives are diminished. Even if the teacher represents a variety of viewpoints, the interpretive lens remains consistent whereas if students participate in selecting and representing the viewpoints explored then a greater variety of perspectives is represented. Furthermore, the importance of the interpretive voice of individual students is emphasized and highlighted in an overt fashion rather than in the more limited ways offered through teacher-centered practices. Remember that the goal is not to attempt to achieve a comprehensive, objective truth regarding inquiry into a subject but rather to learn how to discern, identify, and interpret relevant multiple perspectives. This does not, of course, mean that all perspectives are equally valid and/or accurate. Universal claims or those that are irrelevant or based in false representations or assumptions need to be discouraged and challenged. The cultural studies approach itself, however, would be undermined if a multiplicity of interpretive and analytical perspectives were not considered central to its method.[70]

This approach is also consistent with the Multicultural and Reconstructionist method outlined above in that it can be employed in the service of actively promoting the values of democratic education both within and outside of the classroom. However, by encouraging self-criticism and open scrutiny of all perspectives (including one's own), cultural studies can help avoid the potential imbedded in the Multicultural and Reconstructivist model for valorizing marginalized perspectives and demonizing privileged ones. These practices ultimately thwart educational efforts to promote democratic ideals.

Another comment regarding pedagogy is in order here and it relates to the need to always respect the religious beliefs (or none) of the students themselves. I have already addressed the ways in which the study of religion is, by definition, a challenge to those who hold theological or secular beliefs predicated on the exclusivity of their own truth claims. There will inevitably be students in our classes who hold such beliefs and teachers need to be clear in their own minds about how it is possible to engage in the study of religion while still maintaining one's own belief system. This requires that teachers be intentional at the outset in creating classroom environments where respectful discourse amidst a full range of diversities can be engaged. In relationship to religion specifically, it is important to be clear about the distinction between an academic and devotional approach to religion and how an academic perspective appropriately studies a diverse range of belief systems within and between traditions. Students who hold particular beliefs should see their beliefs respectfully and accurately represented as one perspective among many, but decidedly not all equally promoted in the context of a secular school committed to the values advanced in a multicultural democracy. For example, a self-proclaimed secular humanist should see her/his perspective respectfully represented in the curriculum but not in ways that are predicated on the denigration, omission or false representation of religious worldviews. Similarly, an evangelical Christian should be able to see an accurate depiction of her/his faith as one of many religious narratives that comprise the American historical and contemporary landscape, but not as one that should be represented in the curriculum as privileged over others. Finally, based on the principle of nondiscrimination, neither should be allowed to act in discriminatory ways in the context of the school, even if those beliefs are religiously sanctioned or (in the context of nonreligious beliefs) firmly held and/or widely shared.

Finally, a brief note about accommodations is in order. As I mentioned in Chapter Two, I share Amy Gutmann's view that it is important to grant students special accommodations when their religious principles are at odds with school policies and/or practices, but not if the accommodations requested represent a form of discrimination. For example, it would not be appropriate for schools to grant an accommodation to exempt a student from reading literature or studying history by or about African Americans, evangelical Christians, or homosexuals. Exposure to diverse points of view that are represented in our multicultural society is not synonymous with adopting those views, and exposure to diversity is one important dimension of promoting the principle of nonrepression. It would, however, be appropriate to grant an accommodation for a request to wear a hijab, carry a kirpan, or be exempt from having to say the Pledge of Allegiance. The latter examples represent matters related to individual expression and conscience and do not discriminate against others in their execution.

Though the examples cited here can be used as a general rule of thumb, it is also important to address individual cases as they arise in order to take into account the specific circumstances of any given situation. There will always be exceptions but I believe that, in general, everyone benefits when religious literacy is promoted in the schools in ways that expose students to religious as well as other dimensions of diversity in our multicultural society.

Cultivating religious literacy through a cultural studies approach will help to deepen awareness of our diverse multiculturalism and enhance the ability to engage in responsible public discourse about matters of grave importance and urgency. In these ways it will also contribute to strengthening democracy. Though the terrain regarding how to teach about religion is a challenging one where even master teachers can and do stumble, it is important to note that there are no alternative paths. Nearly every teacher in America teaches about religion at least some of the time, and many do so much of the time. The question is whether they are doing so consciously and successfully. Given the costs associated with widespread religious illiteracy and the unconscious reproduction of troubling stereotypes and assumptions, it is critical that citizens take the challenge of cultivating religious literacy seriously. I have tremendous confidence that American educators are more than capable of negotiating this terrain with their consummate skill, passion, dexterity, and keen sense of discovery. All they need is the proper training and equipment for the journey. In the next chapter I will reflect upon what types of training teachers need to engage this challenge responsibly.

CHAPTER FOUR

Teacher Education: What Teachers Need to Know

In the following pages I will outline suggestions for ways that both in service and preservice teachers can gain the knowledge and skills required to responsibly and creatively promote religious literacy in the schools. Before doing so, however, I first want to articulate the underlying assumptions I hold regarding teachers and the teaching profession. These assumptions deeply inform the approach to teacher education that I outline below and are, therefore, important to explicate. These build upon and assume the more fundamental assertions I articulated in Chapter One regarding the purpose of public education itself. To reiterate, I believe that schools should provide students with the skills and experiences that will enable them to 1) function as active citizens who promote the ideals of democracy; 2) act as thoughtful and informed moral agents; and 3) lead fulfilling lives. This assumes that we need to train teachers who will also share these values and who will be equipped to inspire their students to achieve these goals.

Teachers and the Teaching Profession

Teachers are one of our nation's most valuable and, arguably, underappreciated resources. They shoulder the profound responsibility of helping to educate our children to be active and informed citizens, moral agents, and lifelong learners. We entrust them with our children for hours on end and we commend them to help cultivate the future of our multicultural democracy. In spite of their critical role in our personal and political lives, teachers are notoriously underpaid, their classrooms and projects underfunded, and their work widely undervalued.[1] This situation reflects the comparatively scarce resources that are allotted to public education in America in general as well as the disproportionate way that those resources are distributed.[2] Though I realize that there are some in the profession who do not belong there by virtue of disposition, skill, training, and/or heart, I contend that the vast majority of teachers are competent and dedicated educators who deserve our profound respect, active support, and ongoing gratitude. They should be treated as *professionals*, supported as *scholars*, recognized as *moral agents*, and given voice as *public intellectuals*.

As *professionals*, teachers need to be centrally involved in educational decisions at the school, district, state, and federal levels. Administrators and policymakers need to be guided by the knowledge and experiences of classroom teachers and be accountable to them for decisions taken. Too often classroom teachers are saddled with effecting policies that they had no voice in shaping and which they recognize as educationally unsound. When differences in strategies and/or priorities arise, justifications for the positions promoted need to be openly debated and negotiated in forums where there is public accountability. Teachers need to be treated as professionals with important insights and experiences to share regarding educational policies and priorities.

Teachers are rarely seen as *scholars*, yet their command of knowledge in their fields of expertise is often both wide and deep. The intellectual resources needed 1) to master the scope of information required of educators and 2) to master the practices to effectively inspire a love of learning in their students through the lenses of their fields are significant and need to be recognized and nurtured. Teachers should be given time to write about and opportunities to publish their insights as scholar-practitioners. If this were the case they could play a more prominent role in shaping the field of teacher education. In a related point, classroom teachers should play a more significant role in schools of education as professors of the practice to ensure that teacher training and research is geared toward addressing the real-life challenges and opportunities facing public school students and educators today.

As I have argued consistently throughout this book, education is a moral enterprise and educators are *moral agents*. The question is whether this dimension of the educational enterprise is explicit or implicit. A cultural studies approach requires that those of us who are teachers be explicit about the larger goals of education (e.g., what we are ultimately hoping to achieve), the values that underlie and support those goals (e.g., how goals are justified), and to endeavor to align classroom practices and priorities with those articulations. Making this moral dimension of education explicit and recognizing the significant role that teachers play as moral agents are important dimensions of democratic education.

The journal *Foreign Policy* defines a public intellectual in the following way: "Someone who has shown distinction in her or his own field along with the ability to communicate ideas and influence debate outside of it."[3] I believe that teachers serve as *public intellectuals* within the contexts of their classrooms when they effectively translate the contemporary relevance of what they are teaching to their students in a manner that inspires the students to think for themselves in new ways. By virtue of their expertise as educators, teachers are especially well equipped to contribute to and enhance public discourses regarding a variety of topics that concern citizens, including (and perhaps especially) those that are most contentious. Teachers should be encouraged to share those skills outside of the classroom as well as within it.

Programs that recognize and value teachers as professionals, scholars, moral agents, and public intellectuals will fashion their teacher training initiatives in ways that support, strengthen, and develop these dimensions of teacher identity in the methods employed in the training program or initiative itself. In addition, teacher training programs need to mirror the values and methods that are consistent with the articulation of the larger goals of the educational enterprise that a particular program aims to promote. Teacher training (like teaching itself) should never be focused on content transmission alone. As I argue throughout this text, *how* content is conveyed and engaged is at least as important as the content itself. This is certainly true regarding the study of religion in the schools.

In my remarks below, I will outline the basic knowledge and skills that teachers need to master to teach about religion responsibly. I will follow this outline with an illustration regarding how we in the Program in Religion and Secondary Education at Harvard Divinity School address these issues in our own preservice teacher training program. I will then suggest ways that other preservice education programs might incorporate these dimensions of training into their curriculum. I will close with suggestions regarding some innovative in-service teacher training approaches that I have piloted to offer current teachers the training they need while valuing the expertise they already bring. Comments in relationship to all three contexts assume that the following cultural studies methods will be adopted: 1) instructors will be transparent about what they are teaching and why; 2) educators/students will be engaged in an ongoing interrogation of their own assumptions and responses to the literature and/or topics under investigation; 3) the classroom or workshop pedagogy employed is learner-centered and focuses on problem-posing methods of inquiry; 4) religion is approached as a dimension of multicultural studies; and 5) the relevance of the literature/topic/issue to a broader understanding of the purpose of education itself needs to be articulated by the instructors and affirmed by the educators/students.

What Teachers Need to Know

The Historical and Contemporary Context: Religion, Democracy and Public Education

Educators need to be well versed in the evolving relationship between church and state in the United States from the early years of colonization and continuing through to the present day to include both majority and minority religious experiences. The history of schooling itself should be highlighted as the primary lens through which this evolution is introduced, and an important focus should be competing notions of how the purpose of education is defined and by whom to what ends. Educators should be exposed to the debates themselves including the differing definitions of democracy and opinions related to issues of diversity that underlie competing claims. They should be asked to engage these debates toward the goal of articulating their own understanding of what the purpose of education *should be* in our contemporary age and what role religion should play in this formulation. Finally, educators should be introduced to the policy as well as the curricular dimensions of these issues.

Personal Assumptions and Community Context

Educators should develop the tools of reflective practice that will enable them to interrogate their own assumptions about religion in order to minimize unconscious bias. In a related point, educators should be aware of the religious (or nonreligious) beliefs and practices of the larger community and of their own students in particular. They should seek to learn more about traditions and/or beliefs that they encounter in their students or community that are unfamiliar to them while also being careful to guard against assuming more familiarity with common experiences than is merited. Educators should also endeavor to recognize how unintentional sectarianism is promoted and to help minimize such practices.

Methods in the Study of Religion

Educators should be familiar with the diversity of approaches to the study of religion outlined in the previous chapter in order to 1) understand the methodological frameworks that have defined and continue to influence the field; 2) determine which approach or approaches are most suitable for them to employ in their own classes; and 3) be able to situate and better evaluate scholarship in religious and/or theological studies that they may wish to incorporate. Readers know that I promote a cultural studies method but teachers need to be well versed in a variety of approaches in order to make their own determinations regarding which one or ones will best suit their own contexts and articulations regarding the aims they wish to achieve.

Learning About Religion from a Cultural Studies Framework

Educators should learn about at least two religious traditions from a cultural studies framework in order to learn how religion intersects with other dimensions of human experience and to establish a strong foundation of knowledge about the diversity within and between specific traditions. Methods learned in the study of particular traditions can be applied to others. Also, it is in the process of studying specific traditions that one's own (often unconscious) assumptions about religion itself begin to emerge.

Such initial exposure to the study of religious traditions will naturally be introductory, but it will provide a strong foundation upon which to build.

Implementation in the Classroom: Content, Method, and Integration

Regarding content, teachers should know how to incorporate the study of religion into their own disciplines by 1) recognizing and illuminating the religious dimensions of curricula that are already being taught and 2) discerning where religious themes and/or topics should be added.

Like race, gender, ethnicity, and sexuality, religion and religious assumptions are imbedded in most curricula and a cultural studies approach will help discern how this is so. Teachers should learn why teaching about religion as a discrete unit in a history course, for example, is problematic in the same way that adding a separate unit on women or African Americans would be. It sends the message that religion was absent or irrelevant in the other units studied and it promotes the idea that religion can be separated from other cultural phenomena.

Regarding method, teachers should learn how to think about religion as a dimension of multiculturalism and to apply the methodological tools of cultural studies to teaching about religion responsibly.

There are also legal dimensions to teaching about religion in the schools that need to be understood and respected. Educators will become familiar with the debates that have shaped current policies when they learn about religion, democracy, and education in the U.S. context, but they will also need to have experience integrating all the dimensions of teaching about religion in actual classroom practice.

Educators and future educators should be well versed in these areas as a minimal standard of competence regarding teaching about religion in the schools. Like knowledge and understanding in all subjects, their strengths in these areas will continue to develop and mature with experience. These are minimal standards that will supply a firm foundation upon which to build.

Teacher Training for Preservice Educators

One Approach: The Program in Religion and Secondary Education at Harvard Divinity School

The Program in Religion and Secondary Education (PRSE) was founded in 1972 as a unique teacher-training program designed for those who wish to pursue a middle or secondary school teaching career in conjunction with their graduate work in the study of religion. In addition to earning either a Master of Theological Studies or a Master of Divinity degree, PRSE students earn middle or secondary school teacher licensure in one of several disciplines in the fields of the humanities, social sciences, or natural sciences. In the context of their education toward licensure, students are specifically prepared to teach about religion from a nonsectarian perspective and to develop curriculum resources that incorporate religion and religious worldviews within their field(s) of expertise. They also learn about constitutional and public policy issues that arise when considering the complex relationship between religion and public education. In this regard, the PRSE is a specialized training program in that it provides the explicit opportunity for teachers to explore the ways that the academic study of religion can contribute to and enhance policy and content discourses across the educational spectrum.[4]

In my tenure as Director, I have worked with colleagues to strengthen the intellectual core of the program while also being more explicit about the goal of educating for democratic citizenship in multicultural and multireligious America. Integrating the study of religion into the curriculum cannot be done in a vacuum and needs to be understood within the larger context of the purpose of education itself. As I noted in Chapter One of this volume, students in the program are expected to formulate their own understanding of that purpose and to be prepared to articulate how all dimensions of their practice align with their stated philosophy. This is an ongoing endeavor and not one that ends at graduation. Thus a central feature of the PRSE is the cultivation of skills in reflective practice.

Requirements for licensure in the PRSE are fulfilled by completing five education-related courses, serving as a student teaching intern at a local middle or secondary school in partnership with a master teacher, passing the two Massachusetts state-sponsored licensing exams, and completing the requirements for either the M.Div or MTS degree. The five courses are as follows:

Religion, Democracy and Public Education

The focus of this course is to develop an understanding of the complex intersection between religion, public education, and democracy in multicultural America. The exploration includes 1) an overview of the historical context of public schooling in the United States that informs current debates; 2) a review of pivotal Supreme Court cases related to religion and education and their social/political ramifications; and 3) an investigation into the contemporary "culture wars" in education and the competing assumptions regarding religion and democracy that inform them. Throughout the term students have the opportunity to develop their own articulations of what the purpose of education should be and the proper role of religion in their conceptions.

Colloquium in Religion and Secondary Education

This is a theory and methods course that focuses on teaching as a vocation. Participants have an opportunity to explore the social and ethical assumptions that inform both their choice of vocation and their approach to education. The course methodology includes a combination of field-based experiences, class presentations, and readings in educational theory and method. For final projects, students construct unit plans within their field of licensure that will 1) consciously reflect their own developing theory of education; 2) incorporate varied and innovative methods appropriate to their disciplines; and 3) represent a multicultural and cultural studies approach to curriculum design that includes the academic study of religion. In addition to the class, participants reserve several hours per week for school visits.

PRSE Teaching Practicum

This is a double credit course. Participants are assigned to a master teacher at one of the training schools in and around the Boston area for a minimum of 150 hours of teaching experience in their field of licensure. Weekly seminar meetings provide an opportunity for shared reflection on the practicum experience through research, focused inquiries into specific relevant areas of education and skill development in reflective practice. In addition to seminar meetings, participants are observed in their internship settings on a weekly basis by a PRSE learning facilitator and they have weekly meetings with a cohort of their peers for reflection and feedback. Mentor teachers join the practicum for at least four meetings for shared reflection. A consistent (but not exclusive) focus throughout the practicum experience is on the intersection of religion in the curriculum and culture of the schools as well as in larger public policy debates.

PRSE Research Seminar

PRSE students are required to write a major paper during their last term that focuses on some dimension of the intersection of religion and education. It is intended as a capstone project in the program and an opportunity to contribute to scholarship in the field.

In addition to the four course sequence outlined above, students in the program are also required to take a course in adolescent psychology. They must also pass the two tests administered by the Massachusetts Department of Education that are required for all licensure candidates prior to their student teaching experience in the fall of their second year.

Students in the program gain knowledge and experience regarding how to teach about religion in the schools from a multicultural and cultural studies perspective in the courses outlined above. They also develop their own theoretical and methodological approaches to education more generally. Students learn about religious traditions and methods in the study of religion in other coursework taken to fulfill the requirements for their master's degree in religious studies. They gain a solid background in the academic study of at least two religious traditions that are especially relevant for their teaching.

Though the PRSE is unique due to its explicit focus on training teachers in the content and methodological dimensions required to teach about religion responsibly, the fundamental aspects of the program could be replicated in other teacher training programs. Below are suggestions for how schools of education can incorporate the theories, methods, and content knowledge regarding the study of religion outlined above.

Suggestions for Other Preservice Teacher Training Programs

Schools of education could take the following relatively modest steps to enhance their own teacher training programs to better equip preservice teachers to negotiate the complex issues regarding religion and education in America today: 1) develop their multicultural studies offerings to include religion as a consistent category of analysis; 2) partner with their campus religious studies department or program to offer religious studies courses geared toward educators; and 3) include the requirement that preservice teachers demonstrate competency in integrating the nonsectarian study of religion into their field in constitutionally sound and educationally innovative ways.

For the first and third suggestion, programs need to simply include religion as a category into courses and methods of evaluation that are already offered or practiced. The second suggestion does require additional course work but classes in this category could count toward content area requirements, especially if they are taught from a cultural studies approach that many religious studies scholars already adopt. I would suggest that schools require preservice educators to take a minimum of two religious studies classes: one that would address the social context of education and religion in America and a second that would focus on a cultural studies approach to particular traditions.

In-Service Teacher Education

In-service teacher education programs could offer a sequence of four courses for teachers that would 1) introduce teachers to the historical context regarding religion, values, and public education in the United States; 2) address the content and methods required to include religion as a category of multicultural studies; and 3) introduce teachers to the study of religion through a cultural studies approach that could focus on particular traditions or religion as it is manifested in the context of particular geopolitical regions. Issues related to methods in the study of religion, integration of the study of religion into the curriculum, and the opportunity for reflection regarding personal assumptions and the cultural context of the school could be incorporated into the above classes to form a comprehensive sequence of courses that would provide educators with the range of skills and content knowledge required. Though it may be possible to acquire this foundation through discrete courses and workshops, I strongly urge programs to offer opportunities for a more synthesized and integrated sequence of offerings. Given the widespread religious illiteracy in our culture coupled with the contentious and complex issues related to religion and education, teachers need to be able to develop the skills and knowledge base required to negotiate this challenging arena in the context of a comprehensive program. In this regard, I encourage the establishment of certificate programs for in-service teachers that will address these dimensions of training and formally recognize teachers who have gained competency in these foundational arenas. The suggested sequence of seminar offerings is as follows: *Religion, Democracy, and Public Education*; an introduction to a religious tradition from a cultural studies approach, *Religion and Multicultural Studies*, and another introductory course from a cultural studies perspective. Teachers who successfully complete all four seminars would have established some basic competencies in religious literacy for educators.

In keeping with the assertion that teachers are professionals and scholars who should be recognized as such, I introduce below a method of training for in-service teachers that takes their already established competence seriously and which also mirrors the learner centered pedagogy that I promote throughout this book. I call this the *Peer Scholar Method* and it offers an opportunity for teachers to gain new content knowledge in partnership with other teaching colleagues in a learner-centered, seminar format. Though this method could be applied to any subject, I will introduce it through the lens of a professional development program aimed at training teachers in the foundations required to teach about religion in the schools responsibly. I have piloted individual teacher training seminars of this type on Islam in Kenya and the United States, which were deemed highly effective in both settings by participants and evaluators alike.

The Peer Scholar Teacher Education Method in Religion

The Peer Scholar Method in Religion is for in-service teachers who wish to deepen their competence in the areas required to teach about religion in the schools in constitutionally sound, intellectually accurate, and educationally innovative ways. The method is based upon the assumption that teachers are already capable scholars and skilled professionals who are motivated to develop their own religious literacy in ways that will enhance their teaching. Teachers work in partnership with each other and resource scholars from a participating university in a learner-centered format aimed at deepening content understanding and retention while simultaneously allowing educators to shape their own explorations in ways that are relevant for their teaching contexts.

The method can best be utilized in the context of a core sequence of graduate level seminar offerings that reflect the competency areas outlined above: *Religion, Democracy, and Public Education*; an introductory class on a religious tradition or religion within a geopolitical region organized through a cultural studies lens; *Religion and Multicultural Studies*; and a second introductory class as outlined above (e.g., *Islamic Cultural Studies, Christian Cultural Studies, Religion in Southeast Asia, Religion in the United States*, etc.) Ideally, educators will be in residence for the first two courses of the sequence (*Religion, Democracy, and Public Education*, and an introductory class to a tradition itself) that will be taught by university-based scholars from a cultural studies perspective with a learner-centered emphasis. Once these foundational content *and* methodological competencies are established, educators can join with peers to deepen their understanding through engaging in seminars employing the Peer Scholar Method.

Each Peer Scholar Seminar has a syllabus that is constructed for educators by a university scholar in the relevant area along with an education scholar who specializes in the study of religion. The syllabus is comprised of assigned and recommended readings and/or other resources for each seminar gathering, a series of central questions addressing the theme or topic assigned and suggested activities for participants to engage. The content and education professors who construct the syllabus serve as the resource scholars for the relevant seminar. Seminar participants are comprised of teams of educators from individual schools and/or districts (6–12 people for each team) and each team has a designated lead facilitator who has been specially trained in both the content and method of this approach and who participates as an active member of the group. Each seminar is aimed at strengthening the content and skill base for educators who will then incorporate their learning into their own classes.

The unique feature of this method is that the seminars are peer led and facilitated, which recognizes educators as scholars and accomplished professionals. Seminar participants gather for four meetings with designated resource scholars and are in regular contact with them through an online discussion board, but the seminar sessions themselves are conducted within teams and members share facilitation on a rotating basis. This learner-centered method enhances content understanding, allows educators to shape their learning through their own analytical and disciplinary frameworks, and affords teachers the opportunity to work in collaboration with peers. Teams can also be formed across disciplines, which affords the opportunity to enhance interdisciplinary and multidisciplinary thinking and resource development.

The following outline provides a more detailed articulation of the structure of each Peer Scholar Seminar.

- Introduction: All teams join together for a two-day introductory workshop that is facilitated by the resource scholars. In this workshop participants are introduced to the method and structure of the seminar as well as the relevant content information required to give educators a strong foundation upon which to build.
- Part I: Teams meet separately in their school or district locations to discuss and engage the scheduled syllabus assignments as peers without the presence of the resource scholars. A teacher who has been specially trained in the method and content of the seminar will serve as the lead facilitator to help organize the sessions, keep the calendar, and to help make sure the conversations stay on course while maintaining the learner-centered focus of the gatherings. S/he participates as a member of the group and does not presume the role of "expert." Team members share facilitation of the discussion for each session on a rotating basis and the designated facilitator for each meeting determines how to structure the seminar based on the assigned readings and/or resources. Participants are in regular contact with resource scholars and members from other team or teams (if relevant) via an online discussion board. Participants also keep personal reading journals.
- Mid-Term: At the mid-point of the seminar, participants join together with the resource scholars for another one or two-day workshop to further enhance content and pedagogical understanding.

- Part II: Participants continue to meet in their individual teams to complete the seminar sessions. They remain in contact with resource scholars and participants from other teams via the online discussion board.
- Final Synthesis Workshop: Following completion of the seminar sessions, teams gather with resource scholars for a final two-day workshop to further clarify issues related to content and to engage in a series of discussions and activities aimed at helping them to synthesize their learning.
- Curriculum Development Phase: Participants continue to meet on a regular basis as they read through vetted resources related to the content of the seminar for possible use in their own middle or secondary schools classrooms. They develop lesson and unit plans aimed at incorporating religious studies resources into their curricula that they share with one another for comment and feedback. Ideally they will visit one another's classes when the lessons are taught providing additional opportunities for feedback and evaluation.
- Curriculum Development Conference: Educators join together with resource scholars for a final conference whereby lesson and unit plans are presented and evaluated by peers and resource scholars. Effective lessons and units are posted online as resources for other educators who have completed similar training.

To summarize, this method recognizes the expertise that teachers already possess while providing an opportunity to enhance their knowledge and skill development in a complex new arena of understanding that is increasingly relevant in schools across the nation. The focus on peer learning allows educators to experience and practice learner-centered pedagogies while also providing the opportunity for collegiality that is all too rare in our nation's schools. Finally, this method encourages interdisciplinary collegiality that can invigorate scholarly imagination and enhance curricular offerings within and between departments.

Bringing the Pieces Together: Mentor Teachers and the Internship Experience

Before closing, I want to say a brief word about how preservice and in service teacher training programs regarding religious literacy come together in the internship experience. As all mentors and student teachers know, the relationship between mentor and intern is a complex one. Negotiating terrain that often involves different personalities, different styles of teaching, and perhaps different philosophical and political views regarding the purpose of education itself can lead to a mutually enriching experience or one that is profoundly frustrating. Often it is both. Like all teacher education programs, we in the PRSE try to find mentor teachers who are both exemplary educators and skilled mentors. The two are not synonymous, but we have been fortunate to have the opportunity to work with many educators who are deeply competent in both arenas. Over the years we have also come to realize the importance for our mentors to undergo training in religious literacy. Without this training they are unable to help our preservice teachers learn how to negotiate the complex challenges that arise when religion is employed as a lens in the process of educating students for democratic citizenship in multicultural America. Though our preservice teachers possess the intellectual and theoretical tools to engage religion as a dimension of multiculturalism, they need the help of seasoned educators who can guide them through the complexities of implementation in the same way that mentors provide guidance in other dimensions of the internship experience. For mentors to fulfill this function, they obviously need to gain the same foundations in religious literacy as their interns possess. The following example illustrates this requirement in a vivid fashion.

An intern in our program who was earning his licensure in biology was working with a dedicated and extremely competent master biology teacher who was a new mentor to our program. The school where the mentor and teacher were working experienced encounters with conservative religious groups the year before regarding issues related to support for GLBT students, so the community as a whole was highly sensitive to the debates surrounding religion and education. This was also a time when the intelligent design/evolution controversies were in the forefront of the news. It is additionally important to note that, with the exception of the incident described below, the mentor was very impressed with our intern and found him to be an especially knowledgeable, creative, and gifted young teacher. The mentor's final evaluation of the intern was glowing.

The following incident took place two months into the student teaching experience. Our intern was teaching a lesson on the molecular structure of water to a standard ninth grade biology class and was attempting to help his students relate to the subject more holistically. As part of one very short introductory exercise, he asked students to jot down their "associations" with water and suggested a number of categories that they might consider, including (but not limited to) the following: physical, emotional, and/or spiritual.

The mentor teacher became extremely anxious about the inclusion of "spiritual" in the description of categories for consideration and later told the intern that it was completely inappropriate to include it given the "separation of church and state." The mentor shared this incident with other secondary school biology teachers from out of state who were also adamant in their assertion that this was inappropriate in any public school context but especially so in a biology class given the possible ways that such an exercise might be interpreted by students, parents, or both in the highly charged national political climate. (The mentor teacher knew that the intern was not trying to promote a religious "agenda" and shared this information with his peer teachers who initially assumed that our intern was on a stealth campaign aimed at challenging the legitimacy of the scientific method.) All of the science teachers believed that the inclusion of this category represented a clear violation of the separation of church and state, and the mentor was firm in his insistence that this as well as any exercise that would be similar to it should not be repeated. Our intern attempted to defend his choice but found that there was no common language or foundation of assumption upon which to build a fruitful discussion. After many conversations with his Learning Facilitator from the PRSE, who witnessed both the lesson and the mentor's response, they decided together that it was best to honor the mentor's request. They noted, however, that there was much more to this issue than the mentor and intern were able to address given time constraints and the lack of a shared foundation of analysis.

This incident was a catalyst for us to work with our mentors to provide opportunities for them to undergo special training in religious literacy so that mentors and interns would have a shared foundation to negotiate these and similar types of questions more fruitfully. It is important to note that given the climate of the school in the illustration above and the particular controversies regarding biology and religion that were so prominent at the time, it is entirely conceivable that the mentor would have come to the same decision even if he had undergone training in religious literacy. The nature of the discussion itself would have been dramatically different, however, and the mentor could have helped the intern consider issues of context and interpretation even though the lesson itself was constitutionally sound. These are the complexities that arise when attempting to integrate the study of religion into the schools, and we need master teachers who are well versed in these issues to help our students integrate theory with practice.

In conclusion, the challenges related to the intersection of religion and education are profound ones, and they are especially pronounced in this historical moment when sectarian religious ideologies have gained political prominence in a cultural climate defined by widespread religious illiteracy. There is an urgent need for informed, skilled, and dedicated educators who can help students negotiate this complex terrain. It is incumbent upon schools of education and in-service teacher training programs to provide educators with the tools needed to confront this challenge in the service of promoting the democratic ideals that unite us as American citizens. I know that our educators are more than capable of meeting this challenge and of nurturing future generations in the skills required to avoid the deep cultural divides that currently plague us. We need only to give them the opportunities, time, and resources required. If given proper support, I have every confidence that our nation's teachers will not fail us.

PART TWO

Implementation

Introduction to Part Two

In this section, I will offer reflections from my own teaching practice to demonstrate some examples of how to implement the approach and methodology outlined in Part One. There are many ways to incorporate a cultural studies methodology in the classroom, so what follows represents one of a myriad of options. As in all other dimensions of the educational enterprise, teachers need to shape their own classroom practices in response to the combination of 1) their own strengths; 2) the expectations generated by the discipline, school, district, and state that educators need to meet; 3) the personalities, interests, skills, and passions of their students. It is this rich and unique dynamic that makes teaching a form of creative artistry that cannot simply be transferred from one teacher or classroom to the next. Teachers know this, but it bears repeating at a time when the mass production of "teacher-proof" curricula is on the rise. I offer these reflections, then, in a spirit of collaboration with other educators who also wrestle with the constant challenges of what it means to integrate theory with practice in ways that are personally authentic and attentive to our unique contexts and ever changing student populations.

The chapters that follow reflect the cultural studies method outlined in Chapter Three. To reiterate, I posit that a cultural studies approach needs to incorporate the following characteristics:

1. The inquiry must be multidisciplinary and interdisciplinary with an emphasis on the ways that religion is deeply imbedded in all dimensions of human experience. The investigation must also incorporate "popular" forms of expression as well as those forms traditionally deemed worthy of scholarship.
2. The inquiry must include the recognition that all knowledge claims are situated and therefore represent particular rather than

universally applicable claims. This notion of situatedness applies to the texts and materials being investigated, the scholarly interpreters of those materials, student inquirers, and teachers themselves. Analysis includes an understanding of the social and cultural contexts out of which particular perspectives arise.

3. The inquiry must include an analysis of power and powerlessness related to the subject at hand. Which perspectives are politically and socially prominent and why? Which are marginalized or silenced and why?
4. The inquiry must include reflection regarding the relevance and implications of the investigation itself. In other words, it must recognize that the educational enterprise is never neutral and so educators must be transparent regarding their aims.

Given the climate of religious illiteracy that I review in Part One, it is inevitable that most students will harbor problematic assumptions about religion. I know that many of these assumptions will only be challenged by exposure to issues and information that contradict those deeply held views in ways that are relevant and meaningful. In this way, the acquisition of religious literacy is a process rather than an event. This is a critical distinction and one that has profound implications for how we educate about religion effectively.

A final comment is required regarding the relevance of the following commentary for public school educators. My classroom practices are drawn from my experiences teaching secondary school students at Phillips Andover Academy. Phillips Andover is a nonsectarian, independent, coeducational, boarding school with a diverse student body. Grades range from 9–12 and there are approximately 1,000 students. Class sizes are typically much smaller than most public schools (14–17 as opposed to 20–30 or higher). There is also more freedom in curricular design than is often the case in public schools. For example, it is rare (but not unprecedented) to offer an entire class on religion in a public school context but quite common in nonsectarian independent schools.[1] Another significant difference is that there is typically a much wider range of established learning competencies in the public school arena than we encounter in our classrooms at Phillips. These differences are significant and I do not mean to minimize or dismiss them. My work with both preservice and in-service public school educators through the Program in Religion and Secondary Education at Harvard has made me acutely aware of the particular challenges that public school educators face as well as the rewards they enjoy. In spite of these differences,

I hope that educators from a variety of contexts will find the examples in Part Two helpful and relevant because of the emphasis on methodology. I have used the same methods that I outline in Chapters Five and Six with classes of up to 40 people. I also know that several of my former students from Harvard and many other master teachers that I have met over the years have employed similar methods in a full range of public school settings. The method itself requires adaptation to particular learning contexts and is not restricted to the one I reference here.

In order to offer an in-depth example of how to integrate theory with practice, I have decided to focus the bulk of Chapters Five and Six on a course I teach at Phillips entitled *Islamic Cultural Studies* as a type of case study.[2] In Chapter Five I offer a detailed description of the first two days of the *Islamic Cultural Studies* course as an example of how I construct a learning community that is learner centered and reflective of a cultural studies model. I end this chapter with a general discussion of how to construct a learning community with these same goals in courses where religion is *not* the main content focus. For this latter part of the chapter I use illustrations from a course I teach about the Holocaust. In Chapter Six I advance the discussion by continuing to focus on the *Islamic Cultural Studies* course where I comment on syllabus construction, discuss common issues that arise when teaching about religion, and share student evaluations and reflections regarding their own learning. In Chapter Seven I broaden the discussion to address how to integrate the study of religion responsibly into courses that are typically taught at the secondary school level with a focus on American history, economics, biology, and literature. I end the book with a brief Epilogue.

My aim in focusing the bulk of Part Two on my own teaching practice as represented through a particular case study is to offer a concrete example of how theory and practice merge in a specific classroom context. This goal, however, is a bit more challenging to meet than it may at first appear. When employing a cultural studies method, the relational dynamics of a given class are much more prominent and central than they are in contexts where the methods employed are teacher-centered and the content itself more narrowly defined. These relational dimensions have many components that include dynamics between students, between students and the instructor, and between the students, the instructor and the content material engaged in the course itself. Given this complexity, it is difficult to discuss in general terms how to go about implementing a cultural studies method because these relational dynamics always take shape in specific manifestations. At the same time, these specific manifestations are unique and therefore cannot be simply observed and replicated.

In light of these realities, I address all of the relational components outlined above in my case study commentary and include information about specific dimensions of content where applicable. This level of specificity is included so that readers can more fully understand the intricate dimensions of a cultural studies framework. I offer the following case study, then, as a glimpse into the dynamic nature of a cultural studies method rather that as a course template to be specifically followed or adapted.

The rich relational dynamic that is central to the cultural studies model makes teaching and learning marvelously unpredictable and potentially transformative for students and teachers alike. Sadly, this notion of unpredictability is anathema to many current "reform" efforts in education aimed at creating ever more definitive "measurable outcomes" as determined by performance on high-stakes standardized tests. Measurable outcomes in themselves are potentially valuable tools in reform efforts, but not when they are employed at the expense of spontaneity, relevance, creativity, and the simple joy of a surprising discovery. Teachers know this, and I hope the chapters that follow provide some helpful tools to further support their ongoing efforts to keep their classrooms vital, engaging and, yes, marvelously unpredictable.

CHAPTER FIVE

Constructing a Learning Community

Every educator knows how important the first few days are for a new class. Along with information about the course content and expectations, a classroom culture is established during these early meetings either by design or default. For educators wishing to create an intentional learning community that is student-centered and where participants are equipped to engage a cultural studies model, the construction of a sound foundation during these early class sessions is essential.

Though each class is unique, there are some consistent dimensions of classroom culture that I try to cultivate in all of my courses. They are as follows:

- A learner-centered, inquiry based methodology whereby discussions are generated by students and are not channeled through me.
- A syllabus that is (in part) responsive to and reflective of the particular interests of the students in the course.
- Assignments that focus on both an accurate representation of the content topics *and* student interpretation/response to the ideas and themes addressed.
- An opportunity for students to explore their own particular interests in depth through a final project and/or other activities that are built into the syllabus.
- Clear links established and continually reinforced regarding how the topic of inquiry is relevant to the lives of the students and why it is worthy of their (our) considered attention.
- A genuine respect for and interest in student contributions, ideas, and perspectives. Also, a genuine belief that students are partners

in the learning enterprise and not problems who need to be managed.

When these components are in place, a cultural studies methodology serves as a consistent extension of the philosophy and pedagogy represented by this approach to teaching and learning. The interpretive nature of the educational enterprise is built into the methodologies employed and (in relationship to our topic) the inclusion of religion as one lens of analysis can be incorporated by those trained in the study of religion and able to recognize the intersections of religion and political/social/historical life.

Because the successful implementation of a cultural studies method is so dependent on the establishment of a strong classroom culture within the first class meetings, I have decided to devote this entire chapter to a presentation of the early days of representative samples of two different types of courses that I teach: those that overtly focus on religion or religious texts (e.g., Islamic Cultural Studies, Introduction to Asian Religions, Introduction to the Hebrew Bible, etc.) and those that focus on a different topic but where religion is introduced as a lens of analysis (e.g., Understanding the Holocaust, Views of Human Nature, American History, Literature, etc.).

After careful deliberation, I have chosen to focus on specific courses to outline (*Islamic Cultural Studies* and *Responses to the Holocaust*) rather than provide a more general narrative because, as I note in the introduction to Part Two, the specific contexts matter. What the topic is, who the students are, the instructor's own interests and strengths, and the particular constraints of a given context (i.e., departmental requirements, coverage requirements, etc.) combine to make each situation unique. By offering a detailed introduction to my own practices, I hope this information will prove helpful for educators as they think through how to construct their own learning communities in ways that align with their particular courses, values, contexts, and goals.

In the examples below, I offer a detailed description of the first two days of a particular iteration of the *Islamic Cultural Studies* course that includes information about the students enrolled (via pseudonym) and some of their specific comments and responses. Given that my general approach to all my classes is the same, my discussion of the course on the Holocaust is much shorter and focuses on how I introduce religion as a lens of analysis in a course that is not itself focused on religion per se. My discussion of how I introduce the Holocaust course is also more general and does not reflect a particular class.

Islamic Cultural Studies

Islamic Cultural Studies is a course offered through the Philosophy and Religious Studies Department at Phillips Academy. My colleague in the department Susan McCaslin and I constructed the course originally and I taught it for the first three years before she took it over for the following two. I recently returned to it with fresh ideas, new materials, and a deepened understanding of Islam and Muslim civilizations as a result my work on this topic with my Harvard colleague Professor Ali Asani and public secondary school educators. The course is an elective.

I revised the course description to read as follows:[1]

> Islamic Cultural Studies is an introduction to Islam with an emphasis on its diverse political, cultural, religious and social expressions. Consideration will be given to origins and formative developments but the focus of the course will be on contemporary manifestations from a variety of geopolitical regions. Topics for investigation will be based on student interest and may include gender, modern political conflicts and expressions, art, literature, music, architecture, science, philosophy and religious practices. Students will engage in a final research project and presentation that will be constructed in consultation with the instructor. This is an advanced course open to Uppers [11th grade] with permission and Seniors.[2]

This revision represents my desire to be more explicit about the ways that student interests will inform the course content and to emphasize the focus on modern issues and representations.

Eleven students enrolled in the course during one of our trimesters that meets for approximately nine weeks. Some of the characteristics of the students who enrolled are as follows:

Ten Seniors and one Junior (an "Upper" in PA nomenclature).
Seven males, four females.
Five Caucasians, two African Americans, two Asian Americans, one South Asian American, one from a country in the Middle East.
One Sunni Muslim, one Reformed Jew, one "conservative" Christian, two other Protestant Christians, one "raised Christian and now questioning," one Roman Catholic, one atheist, one agnostic, two undisclosed.

The course met three times a week (T, W, F) for two 45 minute periods and one 75 minute period on Wednesdays. The classroom was equipped with a circular table large enough for all of us to sit around, which was perfect for the discussion-based pedagogy that I employ in all my classes. (If the course met in a classroom with desks we would have arranged them in a circle.) I emphasize this circular structure because it is an extremely important dimension of a learner-centered classroom.

Day One: Constructing a Learning Environment and Becoming Conscious of Assumptions

My aim in these first few days was to establish a learning community that was student-centered, inquiry based, and respectful of diverse views and opinions. I was explicit with the students about these hopes and attempted to structure comments and activities that would represent these goals. On the first day, I opened class with a greeting and a few introductory remarks but then moved directly into the following activity:

Word Association

I asked everyone to take a piece of paper and pen and write down their immediate word associations corresponding to a series of prompts. I asked them not to think, but just write whatever came to mind and to do so quickly for they would only have a few seconds between categories. I gave them the following four prompts at 20-second intervals: Islam, religion, Christianity, and Iran. I then asked them to share their lists with a neighbor and reflect upon similarities and differences and to speculate regarding the source or sources of their associations. I listened in on their small group discussions while also taking attendance and learning their names.

After about 5 minutes, I asked everyone to wind down their individual conversations and to share their lists and reflections with the larger group. I explained that I wanted them to have a conversation with each other about this exercise and asked them to speak to everyone around the table *except* me to break the habit of having conversations volleyed through the instructor. I shared a hand signal that I give when students revert to speaking only to me that reminds them to speak to their peers. I had to use this signal 3–4 times, but then the conversation began to flow.

I asked one student to list the associations that people shared on the board and to mark those that were repeated. Here is the compiled list:

Islam	*Religion*	*Christianity*	*Iran*
terrorist or terrorism 7x	Creationism 2x	Jesus 4x	nuclear weapons 2x
veils 7x	spirituality	Pope 2x	oppression of women
mosque 2x	God	Bible	axis of evil?
Muhammad 2x	prayer	against homosexuality and abortion	Persia
9/11 2x	Heaven and Hell	love	Ayatollah Khomeini
Qur'an	church	belief	Rushdie
prayer	Bible	hope	rugs
suicide bombs	violence	religious right	
oppression of women	not science	sex abuse scandal	
Jihad			
peace			

After everyone shared their associations, I asked them to offer their reflections on the list as a whole. They noted how many negative characteristics were attributed to Islam and Iran compared to religion and Christianity. When I asked them to ponder the source of their negative associations (in all categories), the media (especially news) was the most prominent, with other influences taking a distant second (i.e., family, friends, 9/11, etc.). When I asked about the more positive associations listed in all categories, the most prominent response was personal experience followed by the media. I then asked whether there were any associations that they thought were inaccurate. After a lot of discussion about all categories, they decided that the lists were accurate but not adequately representative.

Why I Teach This Course and Attendant Goals and Assumptions

I used this exercise as a catalyst to talk about why I teach the course. I spoke about my concern regarding religious illiteracy among U.S. citizens in general and especially in relationship to Islam given current world events and the problematic representation of Islam through the rhetoric of politicians and the contemporary media. I was very explicit about the need for citizens to have better tools to understand the role of religion in society so that they can help strengthen public discourse around contentious issues from a more informed position. Specifically, I was eager for them to learn about how religion is deeply imbedded in all arenas of public life in both contemporary and historical contexts and how it has been and continues to be used to inspire and justify the full range of human agency. I also spoke about the difference between an academic study of religion and religion as devotional practice to further explain the religious studies approach we would be employing throughout the term. I closed this portion of my remarks by sharing my goals for the course:

1. To learn more about Islam with an emphasis on its diverse political, cultural and religious expressions;
2. To learn more about the role of religion in historic and contemporary life through the lens of Islam;

3a. To recognize multiple perspectives of understanding and interpretation; and

3b. To analyze the social-historical contexts out of which diverse perspectives and understandings arise;

4. To apply the knowledge gained through the course by formulating informed and well-considered opinions about course materials and related contemporary issues;
5. To strengthen critical reading, writing, and thinking skills;
6. To strengthen listening and oral communication skills;
7. To cultivate an appreciation for and comfort with complexity;
8. To encourage the reflective integration of beliefs with practices in one's personal, social and political life.

I shared my belief that knowledge is never neutral, nor is the educational enterprise through which some forms of knowledge are transmitted. I stated that I wanted to be transparent with them by articulating my overarching goals as an educator: First, to foster the knowledge and skills that will enable people to be responsible and self-reflective participants in our multicultural, multireligious democracy. Second, to inspire students to take themselves seriously as moral agents who can effect positive change in the world, and third, to enhance one's personal life. I explained that the goals outlined for the course were intended to serve those ends.

Syllabus Review

I then turned to the syllabus to review the course content and expectations. I highlighted the learner-centered nature of the course and the importance of each voice in the term-long conversation. I also commented that I would never speak as much in subsequent classes because the discussion would be generated by them and directed by their interests. I explained that they would all be engaged in shared readings and other materials and that they needed to understand those readings and materials and interpret them accurately. That, however, was not the endpoint of the assignment but the foundation for an exploration regarding the implications of what they were discovering. I told them that I was most interested in their responses, ideas, and reflections on the challenging issues we would be addressing.

Given that the classes would be focused on their responses to the material engaged, I told them that I assumed they would each be regularly prepared for class but knew that there would be some days when they would not be due to other commitments or unexpected issues that might arise. On those occasions, I asked them to please let me know before class that they were not prepared so that I could 1) shape the discussion groups accordingly, and 2) avoid embarrassing them inadvertently by asking them to comment on a text that they had not yet read.

We then reviewed the specific assignments which I will not detail here except to say that the assignments were constructed in an attempt to reflect the cultural studies model with a learner-centered emphasis. For example, one of the forms of assessment was a series of one to two page reflection papers on the daily reading assignments that students were to prepare prior to class. The papers were not intended to represent a comprehensive overview of the readings but were assigned as a focused reflection on a particular aspect of the reading that students found compelling and/or problematic. They were instructed to offer a text-based synthesis of the selection along with a personal commentary/analysis. There were twelve papers due out of a possible twenty assignments so students could choose which readings to respond to in this way. This assignment served as a vehicle for individual response and interpretation of a shared reading while also giving students the opportunity to choose which assignments to write about which reinforced their personal ownership of their learning. The papers also gave me insight into the ways that students approach the literature of the course and the particular narratives they were constructing. Finally, they also served as a helpful vehicle to focus class discussion and to further develop critical thinking and writing skills.

Introductions and Articulation of Students' Interests

Finally, I stated that the syllabus was incomplete because I wanted to hear about what topics they wished to focus upon. What did they want to learn about? What questions did they have? What issues were they most interested in exploring? I asked them to write down one to three topics that they wished to learn more about this term. I then asked them to introduce themselves to me and to each other by sharing the following information with the group: their name and articulated topic or topics of interest along with other basic information such as any previous study of Islam and/or religion more generally, hometown, and reasons for taking this class. (While sharing their answers, I again reminded them to speak to each other and not to me.) I told them I would finish constructing the syllabus based on their interests and present a working draft at our next meeting, noting that even the final version would remain flexible and responsive to their interests as the term progressed.

The following is a brief description of each student (listed in alphabetical order by pseudonym). Here, also, are the diverse interests that they already expressed at the beginning of the course.

Benjamin is a Caucasian male who identified himself as Jewish raised in the Reformed tradition. He wanted to explore the role of Islam in contemporary global conflicts.

Carrie is a Caucasian female who identified herself as an atheist. She wanted to learn more about religion and thought Islam was a good focus given its prominence in world affairs. She was interested in exploring women's oppression in Islam.

Charles is an African American Roman Catholic male. He stated that he has friends who are Muslim and wanted to learn more about the faith. He was especially interested in learning more about the Nation of Islam and differences between Sunnis and Shi'is.

Farid is a Sunni Muslim male from the Middle East. He wanted to take this course to learn more about his own faith.

Hope is an Asian American female who identified herself as a "conservative" Christian. She commented about how she did not know very much about Islam and was eager to learn.

Jason is a Caucasian male who expressed interest in exploring contemporary political events in the Middle East with special attention to anti-American sentiments among Muslims.

Peter is a Caucasian male who identified as a Protestant Christian. He wanted to explore the role of Islam in contemporary politics. He specifically mentioned his interest in learning more about Islam in Turkey.

Rebecca is a South Asian American female who wanted to explore issues related to women's oppression as well as Islam in South Asia.

Richard is a Caucasian male who was "raised as a Christian" and was currently "questioning" his religious identity. He was especially interested in investigating issues related to current political events.

Sharon is an Asian American female who identified herself as an agnostic. She was interested in pursuing questions regarding women in Islam and terrorism.

Timothy is an African American male who identified himself as "Christian." He wanted to learn about the basic tenets of the faith with particular attention to the role of women and Islamic justifications for terrorism.

Most people shared that they took the class because they wanted to learn more about Islam in general and professed that they had little to no knowledge beyond what they remembered from their history classes ("snippets") and what they could glean from the news. Three others had more exposure to Islam through personal experience and/or more extended study. It was during these initial introductions that some students shared information about their religious background and/or beliefs that are represented above.

Following the introductions, I collected their written topics and announced that I wanted to use the remaining few minutes to participate in some preliminary reflections on questions related to the larger themes of the course.

Point of Departure Exercise

I wrote the following question on the board: *Does essence precede existence or does existence precede essence?* I explained that it was the French existentialist philosopher Jean Paul Sartre who posed this formulation and then gave them a brief overview of Sartre's historical context and an explanation regarding what he meant by "existence" (physical, material existence) and "essence" (one's unique individuality). Were humans born as a "blank slate" upon which our individual "essence" was created through experiences in the world or did one's "essence" precede our physical manifestation in the form of a soul or similar conceptualization? I did not say what Sartre's answer was yet because I wanted them to formulate their own responses first. I asked them to do so and to then share their answers along with a brief rationale with their neighbor opposite to the one they spoke to during the first exercise. I emphasized that there was no "right" answer and that the question offered an opportunity to reflect upon fundamental assumptions that can quite legitimately differ.

I listened in on these conversations to try to pick up themes and to assess the level of engagement. Students were eager to share their reflections and the discussions were animated. After a few minutes, I gave a two-minute warning and encouraged them to finish their current thoughts before continuing the discussion with the whole group.

For the full group discussion I reminded everyone that there were no right or wrong answers and to be respectful of differing opinions. I also reminded students to speak to each other and *not* to me and requested that everyone be attentive to the dynamics of the group discussion to help make sure that everyone had a chance to speak. I had to use the hand signal reminding individuals to speak to the whole group a few times but eventually the conversation was flowing across the table in all directions. I interjected when someone was trying to speak but had a difficult time breaking in. At that point I made another brief comment encouraging everyone to help monitor the discussion and the conversation continued in a more inclusive way.

Their responses were varied and thoughtful. They were almost equally divided between whether essence precedes existence or existence precedes essence. Those who believed that essence precedes existence offered both religious and scientific (usually genetic) reasons for their responses while those who believed that existence precedes essence posited that social and cultural influences (including religion) were determinative factors in shaping one's essence. Everyone agreed that both social and physical/scientific factors played an important role in determining essence and the discussion centered around how much weight these and other factors carried. There was also an interesting conversation regarding how "precedes" should be defined.

The discussion was quite involved and could have continued much longer but the end of the class was drawing near. I closed with an explanation of Sartre's answer (existence precedes essence) and the atheist existentialism that served as the basis for his claims.[3] I explained that differing views regarding such fundamental questions of meaning would be the subtext of our explorations this term and that I wanted them to begin to identify their own beliefs and assumptions in preparation for their encounters with the views of others via the literature of the course and further discussions with their peers in the class.

I ended the session with a review of the homework assignment for the next session which was the preface of Carl Ernst's text *Following Muhammad*. I told them that the preface related to our initial word association exercise in that Ernst outlines an explanation for why many in the United States have such a negative and (he argues) inaccurate view of Islam. He also talks about how to study a religious tradition from an academic lens and the importance for Americans to learn more about Islam. I asked them each to choose a quote that they found compelling and/or problematic (with page number reference) and to write a paragraph outlining their response. I also asked them to pay special attention to the biographical information that Ernst provides and his reasons for writing the text itself.

Reflections and Commentary

In regard to specific activities, I often use the Sartre question as one way for students to articulate what I call their own "point of departure" regarding existential assumptions. It provides an accessible vehicle for self-conscious reflection about beliefs and a framework for shared discussion of these assumptions among peers where a variety of viewpoints are always in evidence. In the small and large group discussions, I encourage students to ask each other questions to further clarify the opinions expressed and to ponder the implications that their views hold for how they act in the world and the values they wish to promote. It is also a good exercise to help establish a learner-centered classroom atmosphere. Everyone has an opinion that is interesting and worthy of attention. Students can choose how much they wish to disclose and still actively participate. Since there are no "right" or "wrong" answers, it is easier to generate a discussion between themselves rather than one channeled through me. In short, the exercise provides an opportunity for self-conscious reflection regarding one's own assumptions, a framework for recognizing and appreciating the legitimacy of differing worldviews, and a vehicle to promote peer learning and a student-centered classroom culture. All of these are foundations for the cultural studies model I outline in Chapter Three.

Another exercise that serves the same purpose but that is a bit more involved is to invite their reflections on Kant's four fundamental questions:[4]

What can I know?
What ought I to do?
For what may I hope?
What is a human being?

Sometimes I modify these to the following: Who am I? Why am I here? Where am I going? (e.g., Is there life after death?) and For what may I hope? I always introduce either set with a brief overview of Kant himself and why he posed these questions. I explain that there are no "correct" answers and that they are not expected to provide comprehensive responses. I usually ask them to prepare a paragraph on each question as homework for the second session of the course. I have them share their responses first in small groups (two to three participants) and then open the discussion to the large group with the same discussion-related skill prompts that I outline above in the exercise on Sartre's question (i.e., to respect diverse views, to speak to the entire group, etc.). Depending on what course I am teaching, I sometimes return to these questions at the end of the term and ask students whether their answers have changed as a result of their work in the class.

There are countless ways to help students identify and reflect upon their own basic assumptions about the fundamental questions that will be engaged in any given course. I offer these two suggestions as examples of ones that my students have found helpful and compelling to ponder. Readers will note that both are rooted in the Western philosophical tradition, but I often draw from other sources as well, depending on the course content, what I am hoping to accomplish, and how much time I have to devote to these preliminary reflections. I have learned, however, to always include some exercise of this type to illustrate the interpretive nature of any study that relates to fundamental questions of meaning and especially those that include religion. Readers may remember my commentary in Chapter Two regarding the negative consequences that ensued when I failed to give adequate attention to these foundations.

The word association exercise is a good way to reveal general assumptions and culturally imbedded stereotypes in a nonthreatening manner. Thoughtful students are always more hesitant to reveal negative associations with any category if they are asked to do so in an intentional and measured way. By asking them not to think and to write their initial associations in rapid succession, common stereotypes usually emerge from several sources and reveal how certain assumptions are culturally rooted. Once a list is established, the group can reflect on it in a more thoughtful way and discuss both the sources of assumption and their perception of the accuracy of the articulated characteristics.

During this phase of the discussion in the class outlined above, there was an interesting interchange regarding whether terrorism was a perversion of Islam or not. A similar set of questions arose regarding Christianity and the Religious Right. These reflections provided an excellent foundation for me to discuss religious illiteracy as a cultural phenomenon and the differences between the academic study of religion and religion as devotional practice. They had already wrestled with these distinctions themselves through the exercise though they did not have the language to help them do so directly. The homework assignment on Ernst reinforced and further elucidated how religious expressions are culturally influenced and how the academic study of religion can help develop the tools to analyze different manifestations responsibly.

Finally, I wanted to include different types of categories for the word association to help reveal assumptions about religion more broadly. In my remarks following the exercise, I highlighted the fact that "Creationism" and "not science" were included under the category of religion and asked the class to think again about the accuracy of these associations. I had to point out that the Creationism debates emerged out of a particular representation of Protestant Christianity and did not represent all Christian views let alone those of other faith traditions. In a similar vein, I articulated how the assumption that science and religion were antithetical by definition was also flawed as they would soon discover in our exploration of Islam and science. Through this discussion they were then able to recognize how "religion" was often equated with a particular representation of Christianity and commented on how surprised they were that they did not notice this initially. When I asked them to reflect about why they did not "see" this sooner, someone noted that "Except for negative news about Islam, almost everything you hear about religion in the media is about Christianity."[5] Though there was some disagreement with this assertion, there was a general consensus at the end of the discussion that their sources of information about religion were extremely limited and rarely (if ever) sufficient.

Regarding the overall learning culture and atmosphere, I tried to effectively convey the following through my affect as well as through my comments and exercises: that 1) I genuinely liked them and looked forward to getting to know them better; 2) I respected them as individuals with interesting ideas versus a group of kids who had to be managed; 3) I was personally excited about engaging in this exploration with them and assumed I would learn a lot through their comments and reflections; 4) I was confident in my role as the instructor and interpreted that role as one of facilitation versus content delivery; 5) I assumed their competence, interest in the subject matter, and maturity; 6) my desire to shape the class in relationship to their interests was genuine; and 7) their individual contributions mattered to the overall success of the course.

In my experience, students always respond positively when taken this seriously. This includes younger students as well as seniors. It is important to note, however, that learner-centered environments require intention to construct and maintain. Because most students will have little to no experience in this form of learning, they will need support to develop the skills required to be active participants as well as encouragement to take themselves seriously as individuals with important contributions to share. In a vast majority of schools, the default reality is that classrooms are teacher-centered in ways that (often unwittingly) reproduce banking models of education and assume that students need to be managed rather than engaged.

For example, new secondary school teachers are sometimes advised "not to smile until Thanksgiving" and to "set the bar high" as two examples of many strategies to employ to ensure that they establish and are able to maintain their intellectual and disciplinary authority in the classroom. Even if the strategies adopted are less severe, there is an "us versus them" dynamic assumed in this posture that I believe is both unnecessary and unfortunate. Though I am certainly not advocating for the other extreme where teachers try to be their students' peer, I do hope that we as educators will choose to exercise our authority and responsibility in ways that enhance rather than diminish the authority and responsibility of our students. At the very least, it is good educational practice for us all to engage in ongoing self-refection regarding our assumptions and to strive to align our beliefs with our practices in ways that are authentic, transparent, effective, and consistent with our own educational philosophies. This form of collaborative, self-conscious reflection can help mitigate unconscious acquiescence to a school culture that may not reflect our most cherished beliefs about our students and the possibilities inherent in the educational enterprise.

Day Two: Context, Assumptions, and the Religious Studies Approach

Short Video

While students arrived to the second class meeting I played a short film clip that a graduate student at Harvard created to visually depict the diversity of Muslims and varied expressions of Islam.[6] Dozens of colorful images flashed across the screen set to music by the Pakistani rock band *Junoon*. The images included men, women, and children from a variety of different cultural contexts with clothes that ranged from traditional garb representing a variety of different cultures to modern "Western" fashion; famous individual Muslims representing religious, political, artistic, and human rights arenas; and group scenes depicting Friday prayer services, peaceful marches, scenes from the *Hajj*, and angry mobs burning the American flag. There were also scenes from nature; scenes depicting a variety of different styles of mosques; representations of calligraphy; and the twin towers in flames.

Once everyone arrived and had viewed the three-minute video at least twice I told them about the origin of the film and how it was designed for another introduction to Islam course at Harvard. I asked them to write down one or two images that stood out to them and any reflections they had pertaining to the video as a whole. After a few minutes, I asked them to share their reflections with the class, reminding them to speak to the whole group and to make sure everyone who wanted to speak had a chance to do so. I only had to use the hand signal a couple times before they settled into a full group discussion without being channeled through me.

They liked the video and everyone spoke about at least one image that captured their attention. They had some questions about who certain figures were and I answered those. They moved into commentary about their overarching impressions without being prompted. Most of them spoke about the range of images and their familiarity with some (the towers, angry mobs, veiled women, praying men) versus others ("ordinary" people who are Muslims, the architectural diversity of mosques). Someone stated how the video reminded them of Ernst's comment in the homework assignment about how there is a uniform depiction of Islam and Muslims that does not begin to represent the full diversity of people and practices. I used this comment to segue into the discussion on the Ernst text.

Following Muhammad

I asked them to partner with a neighbor to:

1. articulate what they learned about the author and why he wrote this text (Ernst is very explicit about this in his preface);
2. share their overall responses to the reading;
3. share the quote they each selected and why they chose it; and
4. choose one quote between them to talk about in more depth and to share with the class during the full group discussion.

(These directions were also written on the board.)

I sat in on each of the small group discussions to see if there were themes that were emerging. I answered clarifying questions but if the discussions started to be directed to me I asked them to share their reflections with each other.

They began the large group discussion by correctly identifying Ernst as a scholar of Islam writing to a U.S. audience. His aim is to inform readers about the diversity of Islam and to challenge the legitimacy of biased media and scholarly portrayals of Islam that cast Muslims and their tradition in a consistently negative light.

Following this overview, I asked a member from each team to read their quote aloud accompanied by a brief commentary regarding why they chose it.

Here are the quotes they chose along with their comments. One team chose the following:

> There exists, on one hand, a tremendous ignorance and suspicion about Islam in much of Europe and America, now considerably enhanced by recent tragedy. [9–11] On the other hand, there are extremists from Muslim countries who have used the language of Islam to justify horrific acts of mass violence.[7]

"We chose this quote because that's how we feel. We know that the 'suspicions' we hold aren't completely valid but they keep getting reinforced by the behavior of extremists."

The second team chose this quote:

> Those of us who have studied the text of the Qur'an, the writings of the great poets, and the history of Islamic civilization feel very keenly the distortion and perversion of Islamic symbols and

> authority perpetrated by these modern extremists. How much more anguish is felt by the vast majority of Muslims, who loathe acts of terrorism at the same time that they deeply resent the continued imposition of neocolonial influence over their countries?[8]

Farid was one of the members of this three-person team and he served as the spokesperson. "We chose this quote because it really captures how I and many of my friends and family feel. (Turning to the first team) "I don't blame you for being confused and for equating Islam with terrorism. It makes sense why you would, but it's so frustrating!"

The third team engaged a different theme. Ernst was commenting about how the educational goal of a workshop on Islam that he was involved in was to

> convince Americans that Muslims are human beings. This might sound like an absurdly simple point, but the Islamic religion is perhaps the one remaining subject about which educated people are content to demonstrate outright prejudice and bias.[9]

"We chose this comment because we don't really agree that Islam is the only acceptable subject of prejudice. Racism is still alive and well."

The fourth team had a similar response.

> It still amazes me that intelligent people can believe that all Muslims are violent or that all Muslim women are oppressed, when they would never dream of uttering slurs stereotyping much smaller groups such as Jews or blacks.[10]

(Directed at members of the third team.) "We agree with you. That's why we chose this one, too. There are a lot of people who think that all black men are violent criminals."

Hope and Sharon addressed the larger questions related to religion.

> Approaching religion from the perspective of history also reveals that behind the apparently seamless unity of religious concepts lie major debates and differences, signs of irrevocable pluralism, and multiple perspectives within every religious tradition. Although it is tempting to listen to voices that claim undisputed authority pronouncing blanket approvals or condemnations on all kinds of subjects, that deduction is open to charges of prejudice and bias.[11]

"We chose a different kind of quote than the rest of you. We were both struck with how this is such an obvious statement but really hard to understand. Isn't religion about absolute Truth?"

I then opened the discussion to the large group to respond to anything they heard or to ask clarifying questions. Farid was the first person to respond and he directed his comments exclusively to me. When I started to give the hand signal for him to speak to the whole group he put up his hands in mock protection. (It was a perfect response, and very funny!)

Farid then directed his comments to Hope and Sharon who raised the question about religion as absolute Truth. He agreed with them, but said that the extremists were not representing Islam even though they claim they are. He said that Islam does not condone killing innocent people. Others agreed but the conversation moved into how Truth is defined and who has authority in Islam to adjudicate between competing claims. Someone referred to the video from the beginning of class as an illustration of the diversity in Islam, and then asked if there was a Muslim "Pope."

I responded that there is not a Muslim Pope, but even if there were it would not resolve their question. I explained that there are disputes even among Roman Catholics who do have a Pope and that a religious studies approach recognizes and seeks to analyze (as Ernst states) the "multiple perspectives within every religious tradition."

I asked them to remember my comments from the first class regarding the distinction between an academic and devotional approach to a religious tradition. With those comments in mind I asked them if they thought that a religious studies approach was incompatible with a devotional one. A rich discussion ensued as they tried to sort all this out. (It is instructive to note that I basically "told" them the answer to this question during the first class meeting but they either did not remember or did not care.)

I would have intervened again if need be, but they came to the conclusion that the two approaches were compatible because studying about different perspectives of Truth in a tradition was different than proclaiming Truth. Proclaiming Truth fell within the arena of the devotional approach. They still had not resolved the issue of how different absolute Truth claims could arise out of a single tradition (Islam in this case) and how the disputes should be settled, but they felt that studying the differences was both legitimate and important.

I asked the class if there were any other responses they wanted to offer regarding the other quotes. There was a brief discussion about whether

Islam was the only "acceptable" prejudice and there was a consensus that it was not but that it was certainly a prominent and widespread one.

At the end of the discussion I spent a few minutes reviewing the reflection paper assignments for the course. I explained that the exercise they just completed contained all the components of a reflection paper in that they each chose a particular quote from the reading that they found compelling and/or problematic and then offered their focused reflections explaining their reaction. I reminded them that the reflection papers were not supposed to provide a comprehensive overview of the reading assignment, but were instead intended as a vehicle for students to respond to particular ideas in the article that captured their attention.

In the remaining few moments I handed out a copy of the completed syllabus with their interests incorporated and asked them to look it over announcing that we would review it during the next class. The homework assignment was listed and I explained that the next two readings comprised a basic overview of Islam to give everyone a comprehensive picture of the tradition before delving into specific dimensions in more depth. The author of the introduction I chose is Azim Nanji and I told them to look him up to learn more about him before reading the assignment. Finally, I reminded them that they could write one of their twelve reflection papers on the reading and encouraged them to do so. If they chose not to write a reflection paper, I told them that they should still come to class prepared to comment on a particular portion of the text that they wished to discuss and/or learn more about.

Reflections and Commentary

Though I did not address this in the narrative sequence above, I also had the students engage in an exercise to learn the names of their peers in the class. There are several exercises that instructors can employ, but being intentional about learning names is an important component of establishing a learner-centered classroom environment.

The short video that I showed at the beginning of this class session provided both a visual and aural depiction of the diversity of Islamic representation that complemented and enhanced their learning thus far. It also introduced elements of contemporary popular culture that shapes, in part, their own assumptions and the larger context of inquiry that Ernst spoke about in his preface. We could have spent more time discussing their responses, but a short conversation was sufficient and provided a good platform for the themes engaged during the rest of the class.

By the end of this second class, the group began to form its own identity. They felt comfortable speaking to one another and were generally good at making sure no one dominated the discussion and that quieter individuals had "space" to speak. In subsequent classes I still occasionally needed to intervene to help someone comment who was having trouble getting into a conversation. I also spoke to two people, separately, outside of class who tended to dominate discussions. I expressed appreciation for their contributions (both of them were always very articulate and thoughtful) but asked them to please try to monitor themselves to make sure others felt welcome to participate. I spoke to one other person who was active in small group discussions but relatively quiet in the larger group. I did not want him to feel pressured to speak but wanted to make sure he felt comfortable doing so. He said that he was generally shy but that there were a couple times when he had things to say and did not know how to "break in." I encouraged him to give me a nonverbal cue next time he wanted to participate and I would help him by interceding to give him the floor. I did so on two occasions over the next few weeks and this seemed to give him the confidence he needed to participate on his own after that.

This group gelled pretty quickly and the discussion dynamic was a good one. I suspect that this had to do with the relatively small class size coupled with the fact that they were mostly seniors and knew one another. The 11th grade member of the class fit in well. It often takes more time and outside conversations with individual students before discussions are consistently fluid, respectful, and balanced. There are always some students who are quieter than others in the large group conversations, but I do not believe that this is a problem so long as they feel able to participate when they want to do so.

With rare exception, I begin almost every class with a small group discussion to ensure that every student has an opportunity to both speak and be heard. In my opinion, this is one of the most essential features of a successful student-centered class because it regularly highlights the importance of individual voices while simultaneously developing both oral communication and listening skills. These small group discussions also give me another opportunity to monitor how individual students are doing on a daily basis. (For example, are they prepared? Engaged? Sluggish? Confused? Ill? Anxious? Excited?) When an individual student seems out of character I can approach her/him after class or during a break to check in. I learn a tremendous amount about my students in these brief exchanges that helps me better understand their lives outside of the classroom.

The Ernst preface is a really helpful reading to begin to examine the larger social/historical context that shapes an inquiry about Islam in the contemporary United States. It worked well to give students language to examine their own negative associations with Islam (as evidenced in the word association exercise during the first class) and to learn more about the religious studies approach. It is also a valuable resource for students to think about the perspective of authors. Ernst is very explicit about his own point of view, his audience, and what he hopes to achieve by writing this text. Authors are rarely this transparent, but through Ernst, students learned how important it is to try to discern for themselves what perspective an author is representing and to whom s/he is writing.

Whenever I assign a text I have my own notes regarding the central themes that I want to make sure are covered during classroom discussions. More often than not, the students themselves highlight these themes on their own without need of my intervention. For example, the three topics that I thought were most important from the Ernst reading were: 1) his own perspective and reason for writing the text (which I explicitly asked them to recognize); 2) his assertions regarding the challenges of studying Islam in a context where widespread and deeply imbedded negative associations of Islam and Muslims were regularly enforced in the daily news by the prevalence of extremist representations; and 3) how to study religion from a religious studies lens. I was prepared to raise these issues if no one else did, but the class addressed all three through their choice of quotations and their subsequent discussions. They also highlighted other themes that were both relevant and significant for them personally (i.e., the notion that racism is also still a form of "acceptable" prejudice and the identification that the Muslim student felt with Ernst's speculation regarding how difficult it must be for Muslims to see their religious tradition represented through the lens of either extremists or non-Muslims). In this way, content coverage is enhanced rather than sacrificed when discussions are student generated. There are always relevant dimensions of a text that will capture the attention of individual students that I would not highlight as central. If I always generated discussion topics then these dimensions would rarely surface. The contributions of individual students would thus be curtailed and the interpretive nature of the scholarly endeavor diminished. Classes would always be predictable.

In learner-centered discussions, students also have a greater investment in the process of learning as well as deeper knowledge retention. The inquiry arises out of their own questions and thus has an "anchor" of relevance that is often bypassed when the same material is presented externally. For example, remember the rich discussion that ensued when I asked whether a religious studies approach to religion is compatible with a devotional approach. This conversation transpired in spite of the fact that I had already "answered" the question in my remarks during the first class session.

Finally, I want to say a word about the significance of a learner-centered method as it specifically pertains to teaching about religion. As I highlight in the cultural studies model that I outline in Chapter Three, I believe that it is imperative to adopt a classroom pedagogy that allows for the expression of diverse views and interpretations in addition to learning about diverse views and interpretations through the material covered in the course itself. This combination reinforces and exemplifies the interpretive nature of all inquiries. With regards to learning about religion specifically, it is especially important that students are able to engage the material in ways that are relevant for them. Even the most astute instructors are never able to fully anticipate how a text, comment, or insight will be interpreted by a given individual, let alone the several individuals that comprise a class.

For example, I was prepared to highlight the same quote in Ernst that addressed the religious studies approach that Hope and Sharon selected to focus on for our discussion. The way they approached the quote, however, was different than the way I would have introduced it and their comments were extremely instructive to me regarding their point of view and the issues they wanted to discuss. Hope had previously identified herself as a conservative Christian. She first raised her questions about the quote in the initial discussion with Sharon who identified herself as agnostic. They were able to use the platform of their one-on-one discussion to articulate their shared struggle to fully understand what a religious studies approach looked like in practice, in light of their shared association of religion with absolute Truth (albeit from differing personal perspectives). The way they framed their response to the quote sparked a very different discussion than one I would have structured, which would have been a more straightforward review of the differences between a devotional and religious studies lens. It is likely that my way of framing the discussion would not have addressed either of the personal questions that inspired them to choose this quote for discussion. As it turned out, however, the issues that I wanted addressed were still covered but in a more meaningful and relevant way because they were generated by the students themselves. It is important, therefore, to create several opportunities for students to respond to the material in the course through student initiated discussions and reflective writing assignments as well as through an open invitation to discuss issues that arise in the course with the instructor. Though these strategies will not eliminate inadvertent offence or irrelevance, they will certainly minimize them.

I have offered a very detailed description of these first two class sessions of the *Islamic Cultural Studies* course in an attempt to give the reader an intimate view of the class and the subtle as well as overt dynamics that congeal to establish a classroom "culture." I chose a particular class to highlight in order to represent how individual voices contribute to the construction of a unique learning community that has tremendous resources to make the educational experience relevant, meaningful, and ever fresh for teachers and students alike. I turn now to a more general overview of how I construct a learning community for my course entitled *Responses to the Holocaust* as an example of a class that is not explicitly devoted to religion but that incorporates the study of religion as one lens of analysis.

Responses to the Holocaust

I teach this course at Phillips Academy as an elective and offer it least once and sometimes twice each year. The course description reads as follows:

> An exploration of the Holocaust through diaries, memoirs, films, works of fiction and later non-fiction reflections on the phenomenon. Questions to be engaged will include: What was it like for the victims? What was it like for the perpetrators? Who were the bystanders? How could it have happened? What elements from Jewish, Christian and secular tradition contributed to its possibility? What inspired and motivated resistance and how were resistance efforts sustained? How have various Jewish, Christian and secular thinkers responded to the challenge of this event? What have been some of its effects on our own feelings about life and human beings? Texts may include *Night*, *Between Dignity and Despair*, *The Sunflower*, *Tales of the Master Race*, *Ordinary Men*, *The White Rose*. Films may include *Night and Fog*, *One Survivor Remembers*, *Weapons of the Spirit*, *America and the Holocaust*.[12]

As I noted at the start of this chapter, the first few days of all my classes are quite similar in that my aim is the intentional construction of a learner-centered, problem posing learning community that is based on a cultural studies model whereby student voices are central. In this way, much of what I outlined in my detailed review of the *Islamic Cultural Studies* course pertains to the introductory sessions of almost all of my courses, including *Responses to the Holocaust.* Clearly the content examples differ, but the main components are essentially the same with the exception of how I introduce the study of religion. In courses where religion is itself the main topic of inquiry, there is a clear entrée into discussing how to approach the study of religion in that particular context. However, when religion is not the focus, it has to be introduced overtly and in ways that will not be misunderstood or misinterpreted.

I often introduce *Responses to the Holocaust* as a case study in human nature and capacity. As I noted in an earlier reference to the Holocaust course in Chapter Two, it is certainly possible to study this period in history as series of cause and effect phenomena that address the "what happened" dimensions of inquiry. I believe, however, that the "what happened" approach is ultimately a shallow and even dangerous way to study this material if "how" questions are not also engaged. It is shallow because it does not address the fundamental questions of meaning that such an encounter inevitably inspires us to ask if we take the topic seriously. It is dangerous because without asking "how" types of questions, there is an implicit assumption that historical events are somehow inevitable as opposed to contingent. Thus, in my mind, "how" questions in all forms of historical inquiry need to be central ones, and this is especially apparent in Holocaust and other types of genocide studies.

When considering "how" questions, issues regarding human nature and capacity inevitably arise. This leads us into an arena of study that is by definition interpretive. There are a variety of rationally legitimate, often competing claims about human nature that profoundly effect how one understands human agency in both historical and contemporary formulations. It is appropriate, therefore, to be cognizant of one's own assumptions as well as the assumptions of others when embarking upon an exploration of any phenomenon. This is one place where the study of religion is extremely relevant. Religious worldviews often inform assumptions about human nature and capacity and thus how history itself is understood and interpreted. For example, in returning to the question I mentioned above regarding whether historical events are interpreted as inevitable or contingent may, in part, be influenced by particular religious assumptions and interpretations of free will. Religious worldviews also often consciously affected how the subjects of historical inquiry themselves understood and interpreted their own circumstances and the decisions they made in response to them. For example, some religious individuals and/or communities may have interpreted positive experiences as a sign of divine favor and negative ones as a sign of disfavor. Their reactions to these experiences would have been profoundly affected by these sensibilities and thus difficult to understand from our contemporary lens without knowing this larger context. Finally, religious worldviews are also imbedded in cultural norms and assumptions in ways that are unconscious and which shape the parameters of what emerges as acceptable and unacceptable beliefs and behaviors for both the subjects and the interpreters of contemporary and historical events. For example, deeply imbedded forms of anti-Semitism clearly played a significant role in lending legitimacy to the social, cultural, and political marginalization and subsequent persecution of Jews in Nazi Germany. On the other hand, religious influences also profoundly shaped cultures of resistance to Nazism by Jews and Christians alike. In these and related ways, religion is a significant factor in many arenas of interpretation of human agency and students need to be equipped with the tools to recognize this dimension of human experience.

In my first two or three sessions of *Responses to the Holocaust*, I introduce religion in this way as one lens of analysis among others in our exploration of the "how" dimensions of our shared inquiry. First, however, it is important for me to be explicit about the underlying assumptions that inform my entire approach to the course itself. Chief among these are the following: 1) the Holocaust was not inevitable; 2) all of those involved (victims, bystanders/perpetrators, and rescuers/resistors) were human beings just like us as opposed to monstrous or saintly "others"; and 3) learning more about *how* it happened can better equip us to prevent other forms of violence and genocide in our own and future generations. These assumptions about human nature and capacity are not universally shared and some students may themselves hold different and perhaps even competing beliefs. It is important, therefore, for me to be explicit in the service of both transparency and the advancement of their own skills in critical reflection and analysis.

Again, there are several ways to put all of these components together in actual classroom practice. Below is a brief overview of one way to introduce students to the methodological and content dimensions of *Responses to the Holocaust*.

Implementation

During the first meeting of the Holocaust class I usually spend a significant amount of time introducing the course, method, and expectations to students before delving into a shared classroom activity. The gravity of the subject matter merits special care and sensitivity and I want students to understand this from the outset. It is during these initial remarks that I share the assumptions outlined above as a way to talk about why I teach the course and how I have organized our shared exploration. I always say explicitly that these are not universally shared assumptions and that some students may hold differing ones. I explain that I think this form of exploration is valuable for everyone to pursue regardless of their beliefs because it provides an opportunity to delve into the complexities of human agency and historical understanding that are valuable tools in critical thinking and reflection.

I explain that the course is organized to explore the experience of the Holocaust through a variety of different lenses: the victims, perpetrators/bystanders, and rescuers/resistors. It ends with a series of philosophical reflections regarding how to interpret this legacy and its implications for current and future generations. The emphasis throughout is what we can learn about ourselves through the lives of those in each of the three broad categories of exploration. As noted above, this approach assumes that victims, perpetrators/bystanders, and rescuers/resistors are human beings just like us; people with full, complex lives who cannot be accurately caricatured as one dimensional heroes or villains in ways that create a comfortable distance between their lives and ours.

This form of exploration allows for (and, I would argue, even *requires*) religion and religious influences to be included as one lens of analysis used in our attempts to understand the social/cultural contexts out of which these individuals emerged. Throughout the course it will become apparent that religion plays a profound role in relationship to all three categories in both overt and more imbedded ways. For example, religious influences are present in overt ways through socially sanctioned forms of anti-Semitism, the courage of many victims to resist dehumanization, and the activities of many rescuers. It is present more covertly in the way that religious influences shaped cultural norms and assumptions in contexts covering the full range of human relationships from small family, neighborhood, or township units to nation states and transnational entities and corporations. In this way, religion is an important lens of analysis that can accompany political, economic, and other social/cultural forms of understanding when attempting to answer the "how did this happen" questions related to genocide.

Included in this introduction is the same emphasis on the learner-centered and problem-posing methodologies that I outlined in the *Islamic Cultural Studies* case study above. I emphasize how classes will be shaped by student responses to the readings via small and large group discussions and how I will function as a facilitator. I review how course expectations also reflect this method. For example, students keep a reading journal that functions in a similar way to the more formal reflection papers assigned for the *Islamic Cultural Studies* course and more formal essays are constructed in a way that asks students to share their interpretations as well as to accurately synthesize readings or other course materials. For this class, the syllabus is already finalized without explicit student input but there is a great deal of latitude regarding how students engage the material.

Following this overview, I ask students to introduce themselves to me and to each other by sharing information about why they chose to take this course and what they are most eager to learn. I then often lead them in the same Sartre exercise I outline above and for many of the same reasons I use it in the *Islamic Cultural Studies* course; 1) it helps provide a framework for analysis; 2) it provides individuals with a conscious "point of departure" regarding their own existential assumptions; and 3) it provides a vehicle to establish a learner-centered, problem posing classroom dynamic. For the Holocaust course, it provides an additional resource for students to problematize the category of religion. Following the exercise and after I have shared Sartre's own philosophy and the atheistic existentialism that shapes his worldview, I speak about how Sartre served in the French resistance movement in opposition to the Nazis and how he spoke out in defense of Israel in 1967. I then share that Irving Greenberg calls Sartre a man of profound faith and more deserving of that title than many self-proclaimed "religious" people who did not act (as Sartre did) in the service of humanity in a time of crisis and need.[13]

These early classes provide a sound foundation for the exploration we engage in throughout the term and one whereby questions related to the influence of religion are imbedded in the methodology itself. Thus, when reading the texts of the course and viewing the films students are used to asking if religious influences are present and, if so, in what ways. Whether those influences are overt as in Marion Kaplan's *Between Dignity and Despair*, Viktor Frankl's *Man's Search for Meaning*, Simon Wiesenthal's *The Sunflower*, the PBS film *The Longest Hatred*, or Pierre Savage's film *Weapons of the Spirit* or whether they are more imbedded as they are in Fred Uhlman's *Reunion*, Marcie Hershman's *Tales of the Master Race*, Christopher Browning's *Ordinary Men*, Harold Flender's *Rescue in Denmark*, or the countless other individual accounts of rescuers and resistors, students learn to discern how religion is an important factor in understanding and interpreting human agency and capacity.

Conclusion

I have chosen to share reflections regarding my own classroom practices related to specific courses in the hope that by providing readers with concrete examples, they will be able to more clearly discern the methodological foundations that these examples illustrate. Regardless of the discipline or the topic of study, I believe that it is important for educators to be clear with their students regarding the underlying assumptions that inform their approach to education more broadly as well as their approach to the specific topic or topics at hand. I also think it is important for instructors to invite and encourage students to engage in the same process of self-conscious discernment and disclosure. Once the interpretive nature of the educational enterprise is established as foundational, there are myriad possibilities for how to shape particular explorations in ways that are academically sound, intellectually enlivening, and broadly relevant to fundamental questions of shared importance and urgency. Religion is one arena among many others that can be naturally incorporated when these foundations are established, and given the disturbing consequences of religious illiteracy, it is an area deserving of special attention and focus.

CHAPTER SIX

A Case Study: Teaching About Islam

In Chapter Five I outlined the importance of constructing a strong learning community as a foundation for a cultural studies model. I gave examples from my own classroom practices through the lens of two different types of courses: one that is explicitly focused on the study of religion (*Islamic Cultural Studies*) and one where religion is introduced as one lens of analysis among others (*Responses to the Holocaust*). Here I proceed with the discussion about how to teach about religion by continuing to focus upon the *Islamic Cultural Studies* course as a case study. In this chapter I will 1) briefly outline how I constructed the *Islamic Cultural Studies* syllabus as one rooted in a cultural studies framework; 2) identify and discuss my responses to five issues that emerged in the early days of the course that are common for students who are new to the study of religion; and 3) share reflections from student evaluations regarding their responses to both the method and content of the course. My aim is to help further illuminate how to implement a cultural studies model in an actual classroom and to include student reflections regarding their experiences.

As I have emphasized throughout this book, the specific school context, student personnel, and group dynamic that is formulated in a given class really matter in a cultural studies approach. My focus on a *particular* course, therefore, is to illustrate a method rather than model specific assignments and responses intended for replication. As all educators know, when the focus shifts from a teacher-centered to a learner-centered classroom, the dynamic is a deeply relational one. Each day is unique and possesses the potential for vitality, imagination, and meaningful encounter. In this way, it is certainly possible and appropriate to chart the contours of a given course, but educators need the freedom and support to be responsive to their students rather than merely directive. What follows here is a further glimpse into my own ongoing attempts to model the methods I outline in Part One. I hope these reflections will be helpful for educators who share similar aims.

Constructing the Islamic Cultural Studies Syllabus

I have already addressed the pedagogical dimensions of the *Islamic Cultural Studies* course in the previous chapter and will focus on the content dimensions of the syllabus here. Let me say at the outset that I am deeply indebted to my Harvard colleague Professor Ali Asani who teaches an introductory course at Harvard on Islam entitled *Understanding Islam and Muslim Civilizations*. He introduced me to many of the musical, literary, and artistic resources alluded to below, and his own course at Harvard is a model for the content dimensions of a cultural studies approach to teaching about religion.

Remember that a cultural studies model should include an array of cross-disciplinary and interdisciplinary resources that expose students to 1) the diversity of expression within a particular tradition; 2) the way that religion is profoundly shaped by and shapes other dimensions of human political and cultural expression across time and place; 3) the interpretative nature of the educational enterprise and, specifically, the interpretative nature of discourses regarding religion; and 4) the relevance of the study itself. The discussion below is organized in segments that represent units for the *Islamic Cultural Studies* course that I teach at Phillips Academy. I change the syllabus each time I teach the course, so the following discussion focuses on general categories rather than specific assignments. I do, however, usually adhere to the following unit sequence:

I. Introduction and Points of Departure (outlined in Chapter Five)
II. Overview of the Tradition
III. Foundations: Muhammad and the Qur'an
IV. Groups in Islam: Shi'a, Sunni, Sufi
V. The Expansion and Influence of Islam and Muslim Civilizations: Case Studies on Cordoba, Timbuktu, and Baghdad
VI. Islam, European Colonialism, and Modernity
VII. Contemporary Issue One (To be determined based on student interest)

VIII. Contemporary Issue Two (To be determined based on student interest)
IX. Final Projects (To be determined based on class progress and student interest)
X. Final Portfolios and Evaluations.

The discussion below references specific basic secondary sources that I use regularly and refers more generally to other types of resources. The intention is not to offer a detailed syllabus but rather to give readers an overview of the types of materials utilized in a cultural studies approach.

I) Introduction and Points of Departure

These first few days of class are so important for establishing a strong learning environment with clear expectations that I devoted the entire last chapter to this dimension of the syllabus. What follows assumes that readers will be familiar with these foundations.

II) Overview of the Tradition

Once a classroom culture is established as outlined in Chapter Five, I have found that students appreciate having an overview of the tradition that helps them understand the larger context before delving into specific dimensions of inquiry. It is always a challenge, however, to find an introduction that is sufficiently short to serve the purpose of an overview and one that also reflects the diversity inherent in the tradition in accessible and interesting prose. One such introduction that meets many of these needs is written by religious studies scholar Azim Nanji.[1]

III) Foundations: Muhammad and the Qur'an

When introducing students to foundational dimensions of the faith, it is important to represent a diversity of interpretations in order to underscore the interpretive nature of the enterprise itself and to challenge the common association that many students have of religion as uniform, timeless, and ahistorical. Following Nanji's general introduction, I spend a few days focusing on Muhammad as both a historical figure and one venerated by Muslims in diverse and varied ways for nearly 1,400 years. Carl Ernst's chapter on Muhammad in *Following Muhammad*[2] provides a good foundation for this section and I supplement his chapter with several different types of resources, including excerpts from anti-Muslim depictions of Muhammad's life and significance, songs in praise of the Prophet from several cultural contexts, poems from diverse cultural regions, different manifestations of festivals associated with Muhammad and representations of those Muslims who criticize such festivals as idolatrous, excerpts from *hadith*[3] collections and their interpretations, and so on.

In a similar way, I introduce the Qur'an through diverse lenses and interpretations. For example, Michael Sells' excellent volume *Approaching the Qur'an*[4] situates the Qur'an in its historical context. I then usually focus on Qur'anic recitations and calligraphic representations from a variety of diverse cultures and contexts. Finally, we often study diverse interpretations within Islamic tradition itself of specific Qur'anic passages related to issues of interest to the students (e.g., gender and the role of women, the relationship between Islam and other religions, the meaning of *jihad*, etc.). If there is time and interest, I sometimes include a section comparing the Joseph story in the Bible and the Yusef story in the Qur'an with accompanying artistic interpretations of each account.

IV) Groups in Islam: Shi'a, Sunni, Sufi

For this unit I often return to the Nanji overview and supplement his brief descriptions of these groups with concrete representations depicting the diversity within each designation as well as the differences between them. I often have students do focused research projects on different dimensions of these groups (e.g., how religious authority within each is demonstrated and recognized, depictions of contemporary communities and/or leaders, etc.). How do religious differences manifest themselves politically in different geographical regions and historic circumstances? What ritual practices are associated with each group and how do they manifest themselves in differing social historical contexts?

V) The Expansion and Influence of Islam and Muslim Civilizations: Case Studies on Cordoba, Timbuktu, and Baghdad

These three diverse yet highly influential examples of Muslim civilizations in the Middle Ages are wonderful topics for guided group research projects with a prescreened bank of resources representing a variety dynamic interactions in political, religious, cultural, and economic spheres. It is useful to have the class explore one civilization together as a group to offer a template for understanding the intersections of religion with other forms of human agency more generally. They can then work in groups on one of the other two case studies to prepare a class presentation. Fatehpur Sikri is another potential case study for this unit.

VI) Islam, European Colonialism, and Modernity

It is nearly impossible to understand contemporary global tensions within and between nation states without understanding the legacy of colonialism. This is especially true in the mislabeled tensions "between Islam and the West" which falsely implies that the two descriptors are discrete and somehow unrelated. There are many ways to approach this unit but minimally students need to be exposed to the impact of shifting world powers between the fifteenth and twentieth centuries when European forces associated with Christianity gained ascendancy and forces associated with Islam declined in influence. Muslims responded to both internal and external tensions through a series of revivalist and reform movements that formed the foundation for the diverse expressions of Islam in the contemporary world. John Esposito's overview of these developments in "Islam: The Many Faces of the Muslim Experience"[5] provides a useful foundation for this complex discussion. In class I often focus on specific examples of different reform and revivalist traditions and their contemporary influences so that students can understand these connections in a concrete way.

VII) Contemporary Issue One: Women and Islam in Contemporary Societies

Readers may recall that I try to leave the syllabus open in places in order to respond to student interests. I leave this flexibility for students to choose at least one and sometimes two contemporary issues for us to focus upon. For this case study, there was nearly unanimous interest in exploring issues related to women and gender more broadly. At this point in the course they had already been consistently exposed to forms of gender analysis in the other units, so I chose to focus this section on a series of case studies depicting a diverse range of Muslim women in their social and cultural contexts. Students worked in pairs to make presentations to the class on these differing representations.

VIII) Contemporary Issue Two: The Cartoon Controversy

In this particular iteration of the *Islamic Cultural Studies* course, students also expressed interest in exploring the issues surrounding the controversial cartoon depictions of the Prophet that were first published in the Danish newspaper *Jyllands-Posten* as part of an editorial on September 30, 2005. At the time, several Danish Muslims protested and, as the controversy grew, many media sources reprinted the cartoons and the debate became international in scope. Students researched and examined the full range of opinions expressed and engaged in a thoughtful and informed discussion about the tensions represented between freedom of expression and respectful public discourse. Issues of power and powerlessness were central categories of analysis.

IX) Final Projects

As noted earlier, it is important to leave as much room as possible for students to explore issues of interest and significance for them personally. Providing the opportunity for students to construct and implement individual final projects is one way to fulfill this aim. How much latitude there is for topic selection depends on the progress the class has made through the term. If students have really understood the issues addressed in the units of the course and therefore have a solid foundation in the study of Islam as well as sufficient tools for further exploration and analysis, then I will allow for a wide variety of different topics of exploration for the final projects. If students are still struggling with fundamental conceptual or analytical dimensions of the course, then I will be more directive in providing categories for their final projects that will help further their individual and collective grasp of the material.

X) Final Portfolios and Evaluations

As part of the requirements for the course students are expected to 1) complete an anonymous course evaluation; 2) complete a self-evaluation; and 3) submit a portfolio of all their work in the course for the term. These components provide the opportunity for students to assess themselves and the course and further emphasizes the learner-centered dimension of the course methodology. Course evaluations include questions regarding content, assignments, and pedagogy. Self-evaluations include questions related to what students learned, their individual effort and participation, personal assessments of performance on graded and ungraded assignments, personal assessment regarding development of critical thinking, writing, listening, and oral communication skills, and a proposed final grade. These self-assessments are submitted with their portfolios. I explain that if their proposed final grade differs by more than half a grade with my assessment of their work then I will contact them to schedule a conference to discuss the difference. In my experience of employing this method in many of my classes, I have only had to schedule five or six conferences of this nature over the past 13 years.

One final note is in order. I believe it is very important to have both a clear outline and course progression prepared and finalized within the first few days of a new course *and* to remain flexible regarding the schedule as the course progresses in order to be responsive to student progress, interests, and capabilities. It is important to have a clear outline so that students know what to expect, but flexibility and responsiveness are critical components of a cultural studies method.

Common Issues that Emerge When Teaching About Religion

Over the years I have seen some patterns emerge regarding the kinds of issues that students often raise in the early days of courses about religion or when religion is first engaged in the context of other disciplines. In this section I have highlighted five such issues as they arose in the early days of the *Islamic Cultural Studies* course. The five I have chosen to address are:

1. The treatment of religious practitioners as "experts" on their own tradition by virtue of their faith commitments;
2. An overly simplistic view of religious faith and practice;
3. Understanding how to reconcile competing interpretations of God;
4. The assumption that "other" religions are uniform and simple versus diverse and complex;
5. The potential for misunderstandings to become compounded.

This list is certainly not exhaustive, but it does capture a representative sample of the types of issues that commonly emerge when religion is overtly addressed. It is important to note, however, that even if the themes are similar, the issues themselves emerge in unique contexts that require particular rather than pat responses. My aim in this section is to highlight the significant role that individual student assumptions play in the learning process. Being attentive to these assumptions is especially important in relationship to complex topics like religion where illiteracy often couples with strong opinion to form a maze of presumptions that can distort information and thwart understanding. Many of these presumptions are unconscious and thus require an opportunity to surface in order for students to interrogate them and decide consciously whether they should be retained, modified, or discarded.

This individualized dimension of inquiry is also crucial to ensure that students' own beliefs and practices are honored and respected. This is true in relationship to all categories of identity, including those related to religion. Whether a student self-identifies as an atheist, devout Christian, agnostic, cultural Jew, humanist, Buddhist, Catholic, Muslim convert, or one of countless other self-understandings, the response to the literature and questions engaged will be informed by these and other dimensions of identity that need to be acknowledged and respected. A learner-centered, cultural studies approach to teaching about religion gives credence to the interpretive nature of the educational enterprise and thus recognizes the legitimacy of diverse approaches and lenses of analysis. For example, the questions and assumptions that an atheist, a devout Christian, and a Muslim bring to the literature of a course on Islam will often vary greatly, but all are legitimate perspectives that need to be acknowledged and engaged so long as the topic of inquiry is represented in an accurate light. Readers will encounter a diversity of perspectives represented in the continuation of the case study below.

Treating Religious Practitioners as Experts

This first issue emerged at the beginning of the third meeting of the class when we began to focus on Islam directly in response to the first half of the Nanji overview that I referenced above.

I asked students to form pairs to respond to the following general questions that served as a basic template for all discussions of assigned texts throughout the term:

1. Who is the author? What did you learn about his/her background? Who is his/her audience and what is s/he attempting to convey in this text?

2. What are your initial responses? Are there questions you have about the content that you do not understand and/or that need further clarification?
3. What did you learn that was new and/or surprising to you?
4. What did you find compelling and/or problematic in the text that you would like to discuss further?

Following the initial discussion of the Nanji reading, we moved into a full group conversation. After students discussed questions about Nanji himself and his audience, the focus shifted to the content of his article and the classroom dynamic changed immediately. Those who spoke began to direct all of their comments and questions about Nanji's commentary (and Islam more generally) to Farid because he was the only Muslim in the room. I immediately intervened to remind them that a practitioner of a faith should not be expected to know information about the tradition from a religious studies lens since that lens involves studying a diversity of expressions. I said that a practitioner might be familiar with a particular branch or representation of faith but that learning about a tradition through a devotional lens is a very different enterprise than learning about it through an academic one as we had already noted in previous class sessions. Though it is perfectly appropriate for practitioners of any faith tradition (or none) to refer to and speak out of their experiences during discussions and assignments, it is not appropriate to expect (or even to allow[6]) practitioners to act as "experts" on their tradition.[7]

Farid was appreciative of this intervention and reminded everyone that one of the reasons he enrolled in the course was to learn more about Islam just like everyone else there. "I don't even know as much as I want to about Sunni traditions, let alone other expressions," he said. I added that it was extremely common for people to turn to religious practitioners and/or to religious leaders as "experts" of the tradition as a whole. This failure to recognize the distinction between a devotional and religious studies approach to religion is one widespread manifestation of religious illiteracy.

An Overly Simplistic View of Religious Faith and Practice

The group conversation then returned to the text where the relationship between ritual and judgment day was the topical focus. In one section of the assigned reading, Nanji gives an overview of some of the ritual practices that many Muslims perform that include (but are not restricted to) what is sometimes referred to as the "five pillars" of Islam: the declaration of faith, daily prayer, fasting during the daylight hours of Ramadan, sharing one's assets through *zakat*, and the *Hajj* pilgrimage to Mecca.[8] The first topic that was raised for discussion (and originally directed toward Farid but then addressed more generally to the group) was "how Allah decides who should go to heaven or hell." Some felt as though the "requirements" for Muslims to pray regularly, to fast, to share their earnings through the practices of *zakat*, and so on were "excessive" and "imposed." They asked questions like the following: "If a Muslim doesn't practice these rituals consistently or in the right way, will s/he be punished with hell on judgment day?"

This understanding of ritual as "imposed" and practiced to avoid punishment in either this life (via reprimands from parents or religious leaders) or the next (eternal damnation in hell) is quite typical and the students in the class either agreed with these opinions or were struggling to articulate an adequate response. It was clear that several students were not satisfied with this understanding of ritual but they were unable to construct a coherent alternative.

After a few fits and starts, I asked members of the class to work in groups of three or four and return to the specific sections of the reading that would help them address the question regarding whether Allah will punish those who do not practice religious rituals in the "proper" way. I pointed out four different sections for their review[9] and posed the following specific question for them to respond to in their small groups: "Are there alternative answers besides fear of punishment for why Muslims engage in ritual practices?"

Students spent the next ten to fifteen minutes returning to the text selections that I suggested as well as others that they chose themselves. Their small group discussions were animated and engaged and I had to interrupt them to return to the large group conversation. In response to the question regarding why Muslims engage in ritual practices, each group agreed that there were alternative responses besides fear of punishment that they all found compelling and persuasive. For example, one group stated that ritual ideally served as a "tool" or a "vehicle" for Muslims to keep themselves "in harmony with God." Another spoke about regular prayer as a way to "keep perspective about what matters." There were other responses as well, but the main point was that they moved away from the idea of ritual *solely* as an imposition and/or a requirement to one that could be *also* be understood as a welcome and revitalizing opportunity for Muslims to align their beliefs with their actions in the world.

In returning to the original question regarding whether a believer would be "sent to hell" if he was not consistent in his ritual practices, the group realized that the issue was not the practice of the rituals themselves but that the rituals were often a way to keep one focused on the "straight" path rather than being "diverted" away from important priorities in pursuit of more superficial desires. Thus, they concluded, one would not be sent to hell for failing to pray regularly, but that such failure may lead to acting in "sinful" ways. When a particular believer is exposed to her own "record that will reveal all" on judgment day, she will become conscious of her own moral choices and their positive and/or negative consequences.

I encouraged the students to extend this understanding of ritual as a "tool" or "vehicle" rather than simply an "imposition" in relationship to other religious traditions besides Islam. There was an interesting conversation that ensued regarding ritual practices in the Roman Catholic and Orthodox Jewish traditions that enabled students to think about dimensions of those practices in a new and sometimes more empathetic light. Rebecca commented that this conversation helped her think about ritual practices in Hinduism in a new way.

By the end of this discussion, some still raised concerns about how ritual obligations in religion can be manipulated and abused by religious and other community leaders to enforce certain kinds of conformity. Examples such as the obligation to wear the veil in some Muslim contexts and social pressures within Christian communities to participate in public rituals were mentioned, among others. I was pleased that this perspective was voiced and would have raised it myself if it had not been. Students recognized this potential for abuse, but they also had a better understanding of the positive role that rituals *can* play in the lives of Muslims in particular and, by extension, other religious practitioners.

Understanding how to Reconcile Competing Claims About God

As I have emphasized throughout this book, when studying religion from a nonsectarian, cultural studies perspective, students are inevitably exposed to differing interpretations of God or the divine, both within and between religious traditions. Because so many students associate religion with devotional practice, initial exposure to diverse and sometime competing claims about God can be both conceptually and theologically challenging. In our study of Islam, this issue arose most explicitly when learning about theological disputes related to differing interpretations of the Qur'an and sectarian divisions between and among Sunnis and Shi'ites. (When I teach courses about Christianity these same issues arise regarding interpretation of the Bible and differing Christian sects.[10]) In my experience, students are eager to discuss the relevant issues that arise in the face of such encounters with diverse views but have limited tools to do so in thoughtful, respectful, and critically engaging ways. For example, when encountering different interpretations about specific passages in the Qur'an, many students initially wanted to know which interpretation was "right." The notion that there could be legitimate differing (and even competing) claims within and between religious traditions was a difficult concept for students to grasp. It took time for them to recognize that questions about the veracity of one interpretation over others arise out of a theological[11] as opposed to a religious studies framework. I reminded students regularly that the focus of inquiry from a cultural studies lens is to learn *about* differing interpretations of religious expression as opposed to asserting the truth of one interpretation over others. In other words, the focus needed to shift from "God" and/or the "divine" as subject to *interpretations about* "God" and the "divine."

A very rich and thoughtful discussion ensued throughout the course between those that believed in some form of God and those that challenged the legitimacy of such a belief precisely *because* there were so many differing and often competing claims. During the fourth class session these issues emerged in discussion as well as through reflection papers. Two papers were especially relevant. Both authors framed the question as one between an absolute Truth represented by God on the one hand, and human interpretation as purely relative and therefore highly suspect on the other. For example, Carrie (who identified herself as an atheist) offered the following reflection:

> This idea that the religious expression of a region depends more on its political situation than the long-held beliefs of its residents seems almost sacrilegious. The profound influence of human actions/situations on religion seems to point to theology as an outgrowth of human/regional conditions *rather than* as an otherwordly conception. (Emphasis added.)

Carrie's *concern* that theology might be a product of human interpretation *rather than* an "otherwordly" conception is typical. Similarly, her assertion that residents could possess "long-held beliefs" that somehow exist independent of a community's "political situation" is also common. Carrie goes on to ask the following:

> For if religion is an established truth and a god really does exist, shouldn't faith be universal and independent of time and place? Why did God instill his knowledge in multiple prophets? Did he change his mind somewhere along the way, or was it [people influenced by] regional circumstances that revised his original message? And, if our sociopolitical environment really is so intertwined with our religious beliefs, how can we separate the two?

The idea that reflections about God are human constructions that are necessarily subjective as opposed to objective was problematic for her and raised questions regarding the credibility of religion itself.

> In this vein, can we view Muhammad solely as an objective messenger of Allah? Certainly, he possessed strong social views of his own: he felt sympathy for the poor/disadvantaged and was disgusted by the materialism of Mecca. Not surprisingly, the revelation which Muhammad received from Allah is completely congruous with his social views. Did Allah choose Muhammad as a messenger because Muhammad possessed these views? Or did Muhammad distort Allah's message through his own opinionated lens? If the latter is the case, can we ever truly know God's message to humanity?[12]

The notion that the legitimacy of religious worldviews rests on whether religion can withstand "objective" scrutiny is a common one and informed by a host of often unacknowledged assumptions that include but are not restricted to the following: 1) that "God" can be known and discerned "objectively"; 2) that "objectivity" is the self-evident standard of judgment; and 3) that "objectivity" is itself possible to achieve. All of these assumptions are based on a misrepresentation of "scientific" ways of knowing that many accept as normative.[13]

Sharon (who identified herself as agnostic) raised a similar question in her reflection paper for the day. She, too, was interested in identifying the "right" interpretation and voiced concern regarding the implications of multiple views. She spoke of the dangers of how religion can be used to justify individual interests and desires and implied that multiple perspectives can invariably lead to a dangerous form of relativism.

> In attempting to understand religion and particularly Islam, which has so many different interpretations and adaptations to various cultures, is there a "right way" to interpret the word of God? Are we free to interpret and adapt it to fit our own lives? If that is true, then is religion more about the individual and how a particular religion can best serve the individual rather than ultimate truth or the "right way" to worship?[14]

Sharon and Carrie both shared their ideas during class and helped articulate common issues that many in the group were pondering and eager to engage.

In the ensuing discussion, my aim was to help students understand a third alternative between the assumption that God is able to be understood *independent* of human interpretation (i.e., "objectively") and the assumption that human interpretations of God, by definition, lack credibility because they are "subjective." An academic approach to the study of religion from a cultural studies framework provides the tools to give legitimacy to multiple perspectives without having to adopt a stance of relativity that is devoid of moral discernment. I asked the following question as a way to frame the discussion: "*If* one assumes that God exists, how are diverse (and sometimes even competing) opinions about God justified?" I reminded students that this *presumption of belief* is, itself, ultimately debatable. However, given that the aim of the course is to better understand Islam in particular and religion more generally, the intellectual acceptance of this premise is necessary in order to move beyond philosophical debates about belief per se. Such debates are important and appropriate for students to engage, but the study of any religious tradition will necessarily remain superficial if the question of the legitimacy of belief itself remains paramount. In this particular instance, the issues we were discussing in class were framed as a challenge to belief itself. I wanted to acknowledge the legitimacy of that perspective while also moving beyond it by reframing the question from the lens of assumption appropriate to our subject: *If* one assumes that God exists, how are diverse (and sometimes even competing) opinions about God justified?

In order to address this question, I explained that I wanted to introduce them to philosophical and theological resources from Islam as well as other monotheistic traditions that presume the existence of God.

I told them that I wanted to help them recognize how these existential questions regarding fundamental questions about belief and authority were widespread ones and not unique to Muslims.

I first introduced them to a saying attributed to Muhammad that values diverse opinions about God. "Difference of opinion in my community is a [result of divine] favour."[15] Second, I reminded them of Nanji's discussion about the rigorous monotheism of Islam expressed in the concept of *tawhid*, or the oneness of God. Idolatry is strictly forbidden and constitutes the sin of committing *shirk*, defined literally as "association" and understood as the association of anything with God. Third, I shared the quote by the eighteenth-century Christian mystic Tersteegan that I highlighted in Chapter Three: "A god understood, a god comprehended is no God." In a related point, I described the Jewish practice of writing G-d rather than spelling out the full name as a reminder that G-d cannot be fully represented in language or other human frames of reference.

Finally, I introduced them to Jewish philosopher Eric Fromm's suggestion that humans should dispense with the notion of theology (the study of God) and adopt, instead, the rigorous pursuit of "idology" which he defines as the study of human devotion to idols which are human constructs and, by definition, self limiting.[16] According to Fromm, study of God is impossible since God is ultimately unknowable. But studying human idol worship is a worthy pursuit because it helps people realize how common it is for individuals and entire communities to give ultimate allegiance to human constructions (idols). His claim is that when we do so, we hinder and perhaps even thwart our ability to be "open" to the revelations from God because our consciousness is cluttered and distracted with the self-limiting worship of idols. He offers examples that include giving ultimate allegiance to the pursuit of wealth and status, certain forms of patriotism, and even the idolatrous worship of god as an entity able to be clearly defined and fully comprehensible. Fromm's hope is that consciousness of "idol worship" will itself become a motivation to cease its practice and thus increase the possibility of fleeting encounters with the divine.

In light of these insights, I asked them to return to their original question: "If one assumes that God exists, how are diverse opinions justified and (according to the *hadith* quoted above) even valuable?"

I asked everyone to respond to this question first in small groups of two or three and then in a large group discussion. One pair believed that differences were justified because there were lots of ways that "Truth" could be expressed and manifested. Another group believed that diversity was good because it kept any one religion or perspective about religion from dominating and claiming to "own God." (They also commented on the fact that this did not actually work in practice because "all" religions claimed to be "right.") The third group was similar to the second in that they discussed how it is impossible to really know God because to do so would be to put humans on the same level as the divine.

By introducing students to the *hadith* (saying) of the Prophet regarding the legitimacy of multiple views in concert with a discussion of *tawhid*, *shirk*, Tersteegan, and Fromm, they were able to shift their lens of analysis away from God and onto human understandings of God in a more sophisticated way. Their responses to the question regarding how multiple perspectives of God could be considered valid provide evidence for this shift, and they clearly appreciated this new way to think about the dilemmas of multiple interpretations that they had been struggling with since the first class session. There were still lingering questions and related issues continued to arise throughout the term. This session, however, provided a helpful foundation upon which they could build.

The Assumption That "Other" Religions are Uniform and Simple versus Diverse and Complex

As the discussion progressed, I asked students to focus on the different expressions of Islam outlined in Nanji (Sunnis, Shi'is, and Sufi expressions) with the following question in mind: "How can these different expressions still fall within the same faith tradition?"

They struggled here with the difference between what someone called "the ideal and the reality." In practice, Sunnis and Shi'is seemed often to be at odds (as in Iraq) in spite of the fact that they were all Muslims. Then Peter speculated that he thought the reason there was so much tension between Muslims was because their beliefs constitute "more than a religion, they are a way of life." In that way, he asserted, there is more at stake if there are disagreements.

I was glad this point was raised because I wanted to make sure we addressed it and the underlying assumption that it represents. (This same assertion emerged in the previous class when a couple of students asserted that Islam was "more encompassing that Christianity.") I asked the class to ponder whether the assertion that Islam was "more than a religion" was accurate. Farid jumped right in to say no, it was not accurate at all. "Muslims are just like everybody else. Some are really,

really religious and some aren't so much. It's just the same for Christians or Jews or anybody else. It's crazy to say that all Muslims are more religious or even *more* than religious!" Hope agreed, saying she knows Christians who are "super devout" and others who are "Sunday Christians" or "even worse, Easter Christians!" Rebecca, however, defended the interpretation that Islam was more encompassing by pointing to the ritual practices that encourage more daily attention than the Christian practice of attending weekly services. Someone countered that claim by articulating how many Christians also practice their faith in "daily" ways and that Muslims are not alone in that way. "It seems that the issue is more about how devout someone is rather than about the religion itself."

Another student asked why Nanji represented Muslims as "different" in this way if it "wasn't true." No one was able to adequately respond, so I stated that Nanji was representing the fact that the traditions account for all aspects of life but that does not mean that all Muslims practice their faith in the same ways. Introductions to other religious traditions will often approach the topic in a similar fashion. I also pointed out that the reason it was easier for some people to make the assumption that all Muslims were more devout is because of a lack of experience with the diversity of Muslims themselves. In this way, familiarity breeds complexity. Sharon agreed, stating that it usually is not difficult for Americans to recognize the diversity within Christianity regarding issues of faith (Roman Catholic, Orthodox, different Protestant traditions) as well as different levels of devotion because Americans are more familiar with Christianity and Christians whether they are practitioners or not.

I returned to Rachel and Paul to hear their further thoughts given that many in the class were expressing disagreement with their assertions that Islam was more encompassing than Christianity. Paul said that he changed his mind and Rachel commented that it was wrong to assume that all Muslims were "the same" yet she still felt that there were more ritual opportunities for Muslims to integrate their faith in their lives than there were for many Christians. She also made the astute observation that when Muslims are in a minority (as they are in the United States) one common reaction is to adopt more uniform practices as a way to strengthen identity as a form of resistance. This is a theme we addressed directly later in the course.

One final reflection on this topic is worthy of note. Though I am still committed to the idea that it is important for students to have an overview of the tradition before delving into specific dimensions in more depth, there is also a danger that any basic introduction will reinforce the notion that broad generalities are acceptable. Nanji's introduction is still one of the best ones I have found in that he emphasizes the diversity within the tradition in the context of a relatively short and accessible narrative. Even then, the assertion that "Islam is not just a religion but a way of life" is an example of generalizations that students glean from the text in spite of Nanji's direct warnings against making such claims. I have tried to use more complex and qualified introductions (like Carl Ernst's text) but learned that they are confusing to those with little to no previous exposure to Islam. In the context of my experience teaching about other religious traditions in addition to Islam, I have come to realize that initially most students make sweeping generalizations about all categories of religious thought and expression and that this is, itself, a byproduct of widespread religious illiteracy that goes well beyond the particularities of studying a specific tradition. In this way, it is inevitable that most students will organize their initial experiences learning about any tradition in these broad categories that need to be problematized as the course progresses. As I stated earlier, the recognition that there is significant diversity within religious traditions becomes one of the foundations for developing religious literacy.

The Potential for Misunderstandings to be Compounded

In session five, the topic was Muhammad and the readings included a short passage from Carl Ernst's text *Following Muhammad*.[17] Charles wrote a reflection paper on Ernst that provides an example of how a reader's own lens of analysis will sometimes lead to overtly incorrect interpretations that need to be addressed directly before they get compounded. In this particular reflection, Charles responded negatively to a passing reference that Ernst made to how stories of Muhammad's "ascension"[18] were downplayed in some modern circles to diminish the mystical interpretations of the Prophet. Ernst refers to Muhammad's ascension in the following passage (that Charles quoted in his paper) *before* Ernst describes this event later in the chapter. Because Charles had no context to understand ascension in relationship to Muhammad, he automatically associated Ernst's articulation as an attack on the ascension of Jesus to Heaven.

> Supernatural events and miracles are de-emphasized to such an extent that the ascension of Muhammad to the presence of God,

> the subject of countless stories and commentaries in pre modern Muslim literature, recedes in the twentieth century to become for many a psychological event that in no way confers extraordinary status on the messenger of God.[19]

Charles misinterpreted Ernst's comments here as anti-Christian. Earlier in this section Ernst compared how Jesus and Muhammad were both venerated by their respective followers (albeit in very different ways), so this is where the comparison with Jesus probably originated in Charles's mind. I explained the context and the ascension story to Charles in my comments on his paper and followed up with him during the next class session. His reflection helped me realize that there are still passages in Ernst that assume knowledge that the novice simply does not have, even after reading the Nanji overview. It also helped reinforce how important it is for students to have frequent opportunities to respond to the literature in written and oral formulations in an ongoing way rather than only at designated pauses to test knowledge and comprehension. The chances for misunderstanding are legion and unless corrected they can easily compound. Charles was visibly relieved to hear that Ernst was not "attacking" Jesus in the way he had assumed. At the same time, Charles did realize that Christian interpretations of Jesus as divine were different than Muslim interpretations of Jesus as fully human and one of many in a long line of prophets that preceded Muhammad.

Summary

Again, these are five examples of common issues that emerge when students are first exposed to the study of religion. Though these issues can be broadly characterized, they always emerge within unique contexts that require unique responses if students are to be treated with respect and if their ideas are to be valued and affirmed.

As I stated in the Introduction to Part Two, given the climate of religious illiteracy that I review in Part One, it is inevitable that most students will harbor problematic assumptions about religion. Religious literacy includes cultivating a way to think about religion that students can develop through their own narratives. Simply being told that a particular perspective or assumption is problematic will not always address this wider theme. In many cases, students need to discover for themselves how to become self-reflective. Consequently, rather than always naming and attempting to overtly "correct" their unconscious assumptions, I often tried to raise questions that asked them to rethink assertions made in light of particular dimensions of the reading and/or class conversation. It is important to restate here that individual assumptions *always* shape the nature of inquiry and how students learn. Shifting the focus from a teacher-centered to a student-centered environment makes this process more transparent and reveals the complexity of engagement and comprehension. As I have emphasized throughout this book, I believe that tackling this complexity directly is an essential feature of effective teaching and is one that is especially important when trying to teach about religion, where unconscious and unstated assumptions are so widespread.

Student Evaluations and Reflections

One important dimension of a learner-centered methodology is to solicit explicit feedback from students at regular intervals regarding their responses to both pedagogy and content. Formal and informal evaluations provide invaluable feedback for instructors and underscore for students the fact that their voices and opinions really do matter. In my comments below, I focus first on anonymous student responses to both pedagogy and content via final course evaluations and close with commentaries from two different sets of student self-evaluations.

Anonymous Final Course Evaluations

Given that there is a full compilation of these evaluations included in the appendix of this book, I will limit my discussion here to providing an overview of results and selected significant findings. The evaluation form included questions that required short answers as well as categories where students were asked to provide a rating on a 1–5 point scale (1 = poor; 3 = average; 5 = excellent). The rated segments included room for comments and comprised the following categories: texts, the instructor, the organization of the course (including specific assignments), and overall rating for the class. The short answer segments included the following questions: Which section did you find most interesting and why? Which section did you find least interesting and why? What did you like most about this course? What did you find most problematic? What suggestions do you have to strengthen the course? What were the two most significant things you learned in this class? There were also a series of yes or no questions that related to whether writing and critical thinking skills improved and whether the evaluator would recommend the course and the instructor to a friend.

Ten students out of a possible eleven submitted anonymous course evaluations and students responses were very favorable across the board. Of the 23 categories that students rated from 1–5, only 2 received compiled ratings below 4.0 (one at 3.5 and one at 3.8) and 14 of the remaining 21 categories averaged ratings between 4.5 and 5.0. Every student gave the course an overall rating of either 4 or 5 and the compiled responses averaged 4.6. There were, however, 2 categories where at least one and up to four students offered ratings of 2 or 3 on a 5 point scale. These responses will be highlighted along with those in the section on course organization that averaged 4.7 or higher.

The first of the two compiled ratings in the 3 range is the 3.5 rating that students gave to Michael Sells' text *Approaching the Qur'an*. I have used this text in other *Islamic Cultural Studies* classes as this is the first time it has received a rating below 4.7. I attribute this uncharacteristically low rating with the fact that the Sells' readings were longer than normal and fell during an especially busy week in the term.

The other relatively low rating requires more attention, however, for it corresponds to a central dimension of my classroom pedagogy: small group discussions. The overall rating for this category was 3.8 and the specific breakdown is as follows:

1 (poor) = 0 responses
2 (fair) = 2 responses
3 (average) = 2 responses
4 (good) = 2 responses
5 (excellent) = 4 responses

Clearly there were two students who did not find this very central aspect of my learner-centered methodology to be helpful or rewarding and two others found it simply adequate. Unfortunately, there were no specific additional comments that accompanied these ratings so I was not sure how to interpret them. Though I certainly do not expect each student to find every dimension of the course compelling, the small group conversations are such a fundamental aspect of my approach that these numbers gave me pause. They prompted me to wonder if I had became overly confident regarding this aspect of my method and therefore not as attentive to the more subtle dynamics of individual engagement and participation. These numbers also prompted me to evaluate this dimension of my classroom practice at more regular intervals in subsequent classes.

Other aspects of the learner-centered method of the course faired much better in the evaluations. High ratings for the full class discussions (4.4), reflection papers (4.7), and final projects (4.7) were accompanied by several positive comments. The Qur'an essay and gender presentation were both rated at 4.1 each and student comments reveal that many found the assignments interesting and worthwhile. Six out of ten students claimed that the learner-centered, discussion based method is what they liked most about the class itself. The following comments were offered in response to the question "What did you like most about this course?"

- The classes. Discussion is effective.
- I enjoyed the discussion the most.
- I enjoyed class discussion. I felt like our class was very intelligent and most of the people contributed interesting things throughout the term.
- Exclusively based on class discussion.
- The emphasis on our views and ideas.
- The focus on discussion.

One student did, however, comment that the "large group discussion" was the most problematic dimension of the course and two others made more qualified critiques. One stated that "some of the class discussions seemed slow and circular" while another articulated that "some people had a tendency to talk a lot [which made it] hard to get in any word at times." These latter comments also deserve attention. Creating a classroom atmosphere that is dynamic and where everyone feels supported and encouraged to participate in both small and large group discussions is an ongoing challenge and one that requires constant vigilance. These evaluations reinforced the importance on ongoing attentiveness to these dynamics even after a class has "settled" into a conversational routine.

Though the concerns highlighted above and others expressed in the evaluations are important to consider and address, the overall responses were quite positive. All of the 10 students who submitted evaluations reported that 1) their critical thinking skills improved and 2) they would recommend this course to a friend.

Student Self-Reflections

I will close this section by focusing on how Farid (who self-identified as a Sunni Muslim), Hope (who self-identified as a conservative Christian), and Carrie (who self-identified as an atheist) responded to questions regarding what they learned in the course. I highlight these comments to demonstrate how the academic study of religion can complement and deepen rather than undermine a student's own beliefs and/or faith journey.

The following comments from Farid and Hope were made in response to a question that I assigned at the end of our full group class sessions and before their submission of a final project topic. "Name three things you have learned thus far in the term and three things you would like to learn more about." My hope was that this assignment would help them to synthesize their own learning and begin to formulate general topics for further exploration in their final projects.

Farid commented most extensively on what he learned about Shi'i and Sufi expressions of Islam from his perspective as a Sunni Muslim.

> Prior to taking this course, I simply equated Sufism [with] a mystical form of Islam. Due to my lack of knowledge, I even believed [that] Sufi Muslims [were] not "real" Muslims. The shortcomings of the "what is real Islam" mentality became more and more evident as the course progressed . . .
>
> As a Sunni Muslim, my experience with the Shi'a form of Islam was limited to my exposure to their different ways of praying . . . In taking this course, I was able to familiarize myself with the historical aspects of the split. Though our study also encompassed other differences between the two forms of Islam, I most appreciated the provided accounting of the dispute in leadership essential to the split.

Farid also spoke about his new understanding of some central tenets of Islam itself:

> I never before realized the centrality of social equality in Islam. My view of Islam, prior to taking this course, was very much deed based. In other words, I viewed Islam as a religion of submission by which one earns his or her place in either heaven or hell. Though this view is valid, I find the perspective that Islam is a means by which humanity can achieve its potential much more compelling.[20]

Hope also found our study helpful in relationship to her own faith journey.

> I am understanding why questions about God are not futile—they only lead to richer and more important questions and, if not conclusions, then understandings that leave a person better for them than without them. The questions help in dealing with the real fear—the fear of uncertainty. My appreciation for faith has grown with this course, and with the conversations I have had that have been sparked by questions from the material we have covered as well as questions I have had all along. I feel myself only more curious to learn about religion, Islam, and the ways people have tried to bring the apparent contradictions between their beliefs and their world to a more cohesive state.

She also commented on how much she learned specifically about Islam itself.

> This may seem a little ridiculous, but I now know what the difference is between "Muslim" and "Islam". In relation to the larger picture, I mean to say that I know more about Islam, the basic beliefs and rituals of its people, and the foundation from which it has become not only a religion but also a culture, a legislative guide, and an identity. This knowledge has already become so valuable, even when just listening to the news, because the Middle East is so prevalent in today's news—and yet, it seems that articles do not [do] justice to Muslims or the Islamic faith with regards to really informing people beyond the news.[21]

Finally, Carrie offered the following reflection in her final self-evaluation for the course.

> Talking with Farid over the copying machine . . . he said that my views of Islam have changed a lot over the course of this term. I agree wholeheartedly with this statement. Before taking this course, Islam was synonymous with Allah and Muhammad, distinguishable from Christianity and Judaism only by the regions in which it was practiced. Through our readings, discussions, and my two papers especially, I have come to appreciate the complexities of the Islamic faith, and have even found some of the ideas compelling. I have also come to a better understanding about religion in general, and the variety of concepts which it addresses beyond just "God". This course has left me with more questions than when I entered, but at the same time, it has been very gratifying and

rewarding. I have come away with the tools necessary to better appreciate and understand the role that Islam plays in our world today.[22]

Though all of the students in the course offered thoughtful and insightful reflections regarding their own learning, I was especially struck by those offered by Farid, Hope, and Carrie, who spoke explicitly about their learning in relationship to their own beliefs. Farid expressed appreciation for the opportunity to learn more about his own faith tradition from a religious studies lens. Hope spoke about how she found resonance with the questions engaged in the course with her own faith journey as a conservative Christian, and both commented about how their experience of faith was enhanced through participation in the course. Carrie, too, spoke about her deeper understanding of religion in general and Islam in particular in ways that enriched her understanding of the world.

Readers may recall that in Part One, I outlined the fears of conservatives and progressives alike who have voiced opposition to including the study of religion in the schools. Their fear is that teaching about religion will inevitably turn into a form of proselytizing that will have a negative impact on personal beliefs, including nonreligious ones. While I have not done a comprehensive study, I can say with confidence that in my 13 years of teaching about religion to secondary school students, I have discovered that responses such as those offered by Farid, Hope, and Carrie are common and widely representative. Adolescents hunger to ponder fundamental questions of meaning in an atmosphere where their views will be engaged and respected. The study of religion is not the only vehicle through which to invite such reflection but it is an excellent one that can serve the dual purpose of enhancing religious literacy while simultaneously engaging in issues of critical contemporary relevance and personal significance.

Conclusion

With the exception of the comparatively low ratings given to small group discussions, these evaluations and reflections confirm my belief that learner-centered methodologies in the form of discussion based pedagogies, reflection papers, and final projects that are student generated lead to deeper interest and investment in the learning experience by students, and better content understanding. Teaching about religion from a cultural studies lens that is learner-centered and inquiry-based is exciting for students and teachers alike. For students, they recognize that 1) they are taken seriously as individuals with thoughtful and meaningful ideas to share and 2) they can raise and address issues and questions that really matter to them. For me as a teacher, the material is ever fresh and dynamic as it comes alive in new ways through student interpretations, applications, and inferences. Together we wrestle with interpreting the profound role that religion played and continues to play in human agency throughout history and we often come to new understandings of our contemporary lives through such an inquiry. I come to class eager to hear what my students have to share and I am regularly moved by their insight, intelligence, and passion. This is one reason that I feel incredibly privileged to be a teacher.

There are many legitimate ways to teach about religion from a cultural studies perspective and I look forward to hearing from educators about their own ideas, strategies, successes, and failures. Sharing information in this way can help build collaborations across disciplines, regions, and grade levels in ways that have the potential to enhance all of our efforts. I have offered these reflections in this spirit and hope they will inspire other educators to share their practices as well.

CHAPTER SEVEN

Incorporating the Study of Religion Throughout the Curriculum: American History, Economics, Biology, and Literature

In Chapter Six I focused on how to teach about religion in courses where religion is the main topic of inquiry. In this chapter I offer reflections regarding how to incorporate the study of religion in disciplines that are commonly offered in secondary school curricula: American history, economics, biology, and literature. My most extensive commentary is focused on American history with shorter commentaries on the other disciplines given that I build upon frameworks already articulated.

Though my discussion here is more general in scope than it was in the previous two chapters, I continue to focus on specific content dimensions of the disciplines I examine in an effort to provide readers with particular examples of how religion is already embedded in most disciplines and to suggest ways for how to make the study of religion more explicit. In my own experience, incorporating the study of religion into courses that are not themselves explicitly focused on religion provides a fresh lens of insight into the material for students and teachers alike while simultaneously enhancing accuracy, critical thinking skills, and religious literacy itself. As I have articulated repeatedly throughout this book, the assumption that religion is a discrete and ahistorical human phenomenon is widespread, and the consequences of that misunderstanding are costly in social, moral, and intellectual realms. In this way, incorporating the study of religion throughout the disciplines should not be viewed as an "add-on" but rather a perspective that provides a more accurate and comprehensive representation of the topics themselves. I hope the examples I provide below will illustrate this claim in persuasive ways.

American History

In James W. Loewen's award winning bestseller *Lies My Teacher Told Me: Everything Your American History Textbook Got Wrong*, he documents his decade long research project studying 10 of the most widely used American history textbooks. His research stemmed, in part, out of his desire to learn why so many high school students "hate" history.[1] What he discovered will come as no surprise to many educators. First, most high school history courses are taught by teachers who use textbooks, and second, the textbooks are boring. "The stories that history textbooks tell are predictable; every problem has already been solved or is about to be solved. Textbooks exclude conflict or real suspense. They leave out anything that might reflect badly upon our national character. When they try for drama, they achieve only melodrama, because readers know that everything will turn out fine in the end."[2] In short, the 10 narrative textbooks that Loewen reviewed, present American history as a series of facts with little sense of causation or effect, save for an American triumphalism that is presented as an inevitable march of progress. When taught without critique or comparison, they represent the antithesis of critical thinking and engaged learning that I outlined in Chapter One as a central component of education for democratic citizenship. As Jonathan Zimmerman has insightfully shown, even those who challenged the Eurocentric and male dominated nature of the texts in the latter part of the twentieth century, rarely challenged the triumphal tone of the American narrative story as such. Immigrants, African Americans, and women of Western European ancestry simply wanted "their" heroes, heroines, and stories also included. "To be sure, the victory has never been complete. Jealousy guarding their own dominant position in the American narrative, old-stock white conservatives worked to block immigrant and black voices from school textbooks. Eventually most parties to the dispute reached a rough compromise: each racial and ethnic group could enter the story, provided that none of them questioned the story's larger themes of freedom, equality, and opportunity."[3]

As Loewen persuasively argues, this depiction of the American story as a "simple-minded morality play" made up of one dimensional heroes (and a few heroines) who are without significant blemish or complexity represents a lie that is both morally untenable and deadly dull. For example, he traces how Helen Keller is depicted in texts as the "blind girl" who overcame her disability by sheer willpower and not as the adult socialist who challenged the social conditions that led so many to live in poverty and destitution. In another portrait, Loewen decries how Woodrow Wilson is revered as a hero while his overt racism and his interventions in Russia and Latin America are downplayed or ignored. He asks why textbooks portray history in this way.

> Heroification itself supplies a first answer. Socialism is repugnant to most Americans. So are racism and colonialism. Michael Kammen suggests that authors selectively omit blemishes in order to make certain historical figures sympathetic to as many people as possible. The textbook critic Norma Gabler has testified that textbooks should "present our nation's patriots in a way that would honor and respect them"; in her eyes, admitting Keller's socialism and Wilson's racism would hardly do that.[4]

Similar to Gabler's view, in 1925, the American Legion claimed that the ideal textbook "must inspire the children with patriotism . . . must be careful to tell the truth optimistically . . . must dwell on failure only for its value as a moral lesson, must speak chiefly of success . . . "[5]

In spite of the current popularity of this particular portrayal of patriotism, I agree with Loewen when he asserts that

> the results of heroification are potentially crippling to students. Helen Keller is not the only person this approach treats like a child. Denying students the humanness of Keller, Wilson, and others keeps students in intellectual immaturity. It perpetuates what might be called a Disney version of history: The Hall of Presidents at Disneyland similarly presents our leaders as heroic statesmen, not imperfect beings. Our children end up without realistic role models to inspire them.[6]

Another consequence of this valorized representation is that "students also develop no understanding of causality in history. Our nation's thirteen separate forays into Nicaragua, for instance, are surely worth knowing about as we attempt to understand why that country embraced a communist government in the 1980s."[7] Similarly, students should be exposed to a more honest portrayal of U.S. intervention in the Middle East and Southeast Asia to place the current anti-American sentiments in those regions in context. As Loewen asserts, "textbooks should show history as contingent, affected by the power of ideas and individuals."[8] Instead, history is often presented as an inevitable culmination of forces. A critical question to pose is this: Who benefits from a depiction of American history that diminishes and distorts conflict in the service of representing our past as a steady march toward ever more consistent expressions of equality, opportunity, and freedom?

Loewen is not alone in his challenge to such a valorized approach to American history. Howard Zinn is perhaps the most well-known American historian to offer a more complex history of our past. In his widely read text *The People's History of the U.S.*, Zinn documents stories of resistance to slavery and oppression, government corruption well before Watergate and beyond, and the consequences of triumphalism.[9] Other authors of this genre include Ronald Takaki[10] and James Fraser.[11] All three provide a rich, complex, and yet ultimately optimistic view of human agency and capacity. I share their recognition that we simply must expose students to the ways that we in the United States have failed to live up to our highest aspirations *as well as* the ways that we have succeeded. Histories that depict only one or the other extreme leave students bored, discouraged, ill-informed, and ill-equipped to engage as responsible, active citizens accountable to helping make our highest ideals truly manifest.

Loewen's critique of history textbooks provides a springboard for my commentary regarding how to implement a cultural studies approach in history that addresses the religious dimensions of human agency from a nonsectarian perspective. Similar to the cultural studies model that I outline, the understanding of history that Loewen supports and embraces is one where complexity and causation are central rather than peripheral or altogether absent. As I mention in Chapter Five, history is ultimately a study of human nature and capacity. Unless we assume that history is somehow predetermined and simply a "done deal" as many textbooks portray, it offers us incredible insight into human agency and possibility. History as a long march of facts and events will become dull even to the most ardent connoisseur of trivia. But historical events that are approached with "why" and "how" rather than simply "what" kinds of questions invite an entirely new dimension of both engagement and relevance. This is where the question of religion comes in.

As we have already explored in Part One, religion has always been deeply imbedded in history, politics, and culture and remains a strong force today. When studying historical phenomena from a cultural studies perspective similar to the one Loewen advocates, questions regarding ideology inevitably arise. What were the ideological forces that shape agency in any given social/historical context? What assumptions about race, class, gender, and/or religion converge to lend credibility to certain choices over others? For example, Loewen paints a more fully complex (and much more disturbing) portrait of Columbus than even the recently "revised" textbooks he studied portray. How did assumptions regarding race, class, gender, and religion intersect in ways that allowed Columbus and his men to give thanks to God for their "discovery" while simultaneously justifying rape, slavery, theft, dismemberment, and colonization of the native peoples he encountered? Similarly, what were the influences that led Bartolome de las Casas, a young priest who participated in the conquest of Cuba and the transcriber of Columbus's journal, to make the following assertion: "What we committed in the Indies stands out among the most unpardonable offenses ever committed against God and mankind and this trade [in Indian slaves] as one of the most unjust, evil and cruel among them."[12] Remember that King Ferdinand and Queen Isabella mandated that the Spaniards were to read *El Requerimiento* to all natives that they encountered. Here is a translated excerpt from one version:

> I implore you to recognize the Church as a lady and in the name of the Pope take the King as lord of this land and obey his mandates. If you do not do it, I tell you that with the help of God I will enter powerfully against you all. I will make war everywhere and every way that I can. I will subject you to the yoke and obedience to the Church and to his majesty. I will take your women and children and make them slaves . . . The deaths and injuries that you will receive from here on will be your own fault and not that of his majesty nor of the gentlemen that accompany me.[13]

Contrast this with depictions of al-Andalus (Muslim Spain) from the mid-eighth century to 1492 prior to the reconquest. Though there were certainly horrors committed in the name of religion and of territorial expansion and protection during this time, there was also a thriving culture that emerged in the dynamic interaction of Muslims, Jews, and Christians who created a "culture of tolerance" in medieval Spain under Muslim rule.[14] Understanding the religious dimensions of the ideologies that shaped these expressions is critical to a fuller assessment of this significant period in world history and will give us tools to better understand the challenging religious dimensions of our own contemporary world.

Like Loewen, I am not promoting a particular set of answers to the questions regarding social context and points of interpretation. I am more interested in helping students cultivate their ability to articulate and pursue certain kinds of questions about any assertions of fact that they encounter (including assertions from me). Loewen identifies several questions that he encourages students of history to ask in relationship to historical materials themselves as well as secondary accounts of history. They serve as a good place to begin:

- First, why was the document written (or the picture painted, etc.)? Locate the audience in social/historical context. Consider what the speaker was trying to accomplish.
- Second, whose viewpoint is represented and what interests are served? What viewpoints are omitted?
- Third, is the account believable? Are there internal contradictions?
- Fourth, is the account backed up by other sources?
- Fifth, how does the account make you feel about the topic?[15]

To this excellent list of critical reading and thinking tools I would add only the following two in relationship to our topic:

- Sixth, how does your own lens of analysis shape your response to the account as presented? What are the sources of your own ideological frames of reference and analysis? And finally:
- Seventh, what role (if any) does religion play in the account? Remember to consider both explicit and inexplicit sources regarding the ideological context of the event (or events) being depicted, the narrator of that event (or events), and yours as interpreter.

In my view, it is important to situate the issues regarding how to teach about religion in American history within the context of this larger discussion. Like other dimensions of our history, religion cannot be depicted as separate from the social/cultural/political realities that have shaped our legacy nor can religion be represented in uniformly positive or negative terms. Religious influences are found in all corners of U.S. history and have served as ideological justifications and supports for the full range of human agency that Loewen, Zinn, and others highlight. By expanding the frameworks for analysis to include religion, teachers will find fresh resources to interrogate and ponder the rich complexity of America's many narratives.

Economics

In one regard, it could be argued that learning about economics suffers from some of the same challenges that Loewen leveled against learning about history through textbooks: much if not all of the mystery and complexity of the human condition is reduced to a basic formula that denies the legitimacy (or sometimes even the existence) of alternative views. For example, in *For the Common Good*, former World Bank economist Herman Daly teams up with process theologian John Cobb to challenge the hegemony of neoclassical economic theory that equates pursuit of private gain with rationality. They claim that assumptions regarding *Homo economicus* are rooted in unproblematized assertions about human nature. Most specifically, they assert that economists "typically identify intelligent pursuit of private gain with rationality, thus implying that other modes of behavior are not rational. These modes include other-regarding behavior and actions directed to the public good."[16]

They go on to state how this view of human nature was heavily influenced by Calvinism.

> Modern economic theory originated and developed in the context of Calvinism. Both were bids for personal freedom against the interference of earthly authority. They based their bids on the conviction that beyond a very narrow sphere, motives of self-interest are overwhelmingly dominant. Economic theory differed from Calvinism only in celebrating as rational what Calvinists confessed as sinful.[17]

In their text, Daly and Cobb challenge the unproblematized equation of private self-interest with rationality and propose an alternative theoretical framework that recognizes the relationship between individual and communal well-being. "[I]nstead of *Homo economicus* as pure individual we propose *Homo economicus* as person-in-community."[18] Contrary to popular belief, this framework does not automatically place them into a socialist versus neoclassical continuum as traditionally defined. They are, instead, challenging the legitimacy of that continuum as offering the only possible options for how to frame economic relationships.[19]

A second important contribution that Daly and Cobb make is to articulate how economic theories are fashioned more on scientific as opposed to social scientific methodologies. Even though many economists recognized the historically contingent nature of how economics functioned,

> economists on the whole wanted economics to become increasingly scientific, and their idea of science was based on physics rather than on evolutionary biology. That meant that economics had to focus on formulating models and finding laws "governing" present economic behavior rather than seeking laws "governing" the changes of economic systems or asking about contingent historical matters. As a result, when useful models have been found and when hypotheses have proved successful, they are treated as analogous to the models and hypotheses of the physicist. Their limitation to particular historical conditions is neglected.[20]

Daly and Cobb provide the foundation for me to address two problems regarding how economics is typically taught in schools. First of all, the social-historical conditions that have shaped current neoclassical economic theory and their attendant assumptions about human nature are rarely discussed in class. This is deeply problematic given that those conditions clearly had a significant formative impact on how economic theory developed and how it currently functions today. Second, alternatives to neoclassical theory are rarely seriously considered or engaged, save the occasional nod to the socialist end of the socialist-neoclassical continuum mentioned above and that Daly and Cobb challenge. As a result, generations of students are taught a certain representation of economic theory as a form of "science" equated with inevitability, objectivity, and neutrality. Even a cursory view of the history of classical and neoclassical thought reveals the ideological forces that helped shape the foundations that are now treated as inevitable rather than contingent. Students need to be exposed to this history and given the tools to think critically about how economic relationships are defined and how they function.

As Daly and Cobb have noted, religious worldviews played an important role in shaping these foundations and religion continues to play a significant role in both supporting neoclassical frameworks as well as offering sophisticated alternatives to them. The study of Islamic banking[21] and Roman Catholic positions on economic justice,[22] for example, provide rich bodies of resources that are worthy of attention and analysis. Considering these and other alternatives to neoclassical formulations will enhance critical thinking and enliven intellectual imagination regarding human agency.

Biology

Unfortunately, one significant manifestation of religious illiteracy in the contemporary age is the widespread assumption that religion and science are, by definition, fundamentally at odds. As I noted in Part One, there are many reasons for this belief. Most notably for us here in the United States, an important source of this assumption is the longstanding debate between some Protestant Christians and evolutionary scientists regarding human origins. The creation versus evolution debates were first dramatized in the famous Scopes trial in 1925 and have recently resurfaced in several attacks on the legitimacy of evolutionary theory via numerous manifestations of "Creationism" and "Intelligent Design." These widely publicized disputes have fostered the belief that they are categorically representative of the relationship between religion and science which they are not. Many Protestant, Roman Catholic, and Orthodox Christians have long ago reconciled science and faith.[23] Furthermore, many Muslims (for example) have never experienced a clash in the first place.[24]

Given this climate, it is no wonder that science teachers are especially leery of any talk about integrating the study of religion into science curricula. The mere mention of religion in this context raises suspicions that are often so overwhelming as to negate any possibility of their legitimate interface. Though highly unfortunate, it is naïve to ignore this widespread reality. Therefore my own suggestions regarding how to think about integrating religion into science curricula are relatively modest with the exception of specific contexts where there is wider latitude to engage in interdisciplinary and multidisciplinary explorations.

In standard Biology classes, my recommendation is that more explicit attention be given to the scientific method itself as a particular form of inquiry that addresses and engages phenomena in particular ways. By being clear about the domain of science and what it does and does not measure/address/engage, students will have a stronger foundation to understand how science and other forms of inquiry (including religious ones) can be complementary rather than antithetical frameworks of analysis. It will also provide the tools for students to critically reflect about both the possibilities and limitations of the scientific enterprise itself. Historian of science Donna Haraway's articulation of "situated knowledges" is an excellent framework to employ for such an inquiry. (See my discussion of her work in Chapter Three of this volume.) She clearly delineates the scope of scientific inquiry and exposes how failure to critically reflect about the scientific method has led to abuse and misrepresentation. For example, in other publications she documents how the failure of biologists to recognize that their own lenses of analysis are not neutral but shaped by their own social/historical circumstances led to ideologically laden "discoveries" under the guise of objective neutrality.[25] The eugenics movement is but one celebrated example of this abuse of the scientific enterprise historically and similar abuses are still practiced today under the guise of "objective inquiry."

For those with more inter and cross-disciplinary latitude, there are numerous possibilities. One example is to study ecology from an interdisciplinary perspective that includes the study of religion in shaping both worldview and human agency. An excellent set of resources for such an approach is the Forum on Religion and Ecology that is a multiyear, multidisciplinary initiative first launched at Harvard University through the Center for the Study of World Religions. Co-coordinators of the initiative are religious studies scholars Mary Evelyn Tucker and John Grimm who have established collaborations with several institutions, including the Harvard Center for the Environment under the directorship of Daniel Schrag, Harvard Professor of Earth and Planetary Sciences. The Forum on Religion and Ecology takes seriously contemporary challenges posed by global warming and other pressing environmental issues and seeks to both analyze and address these challenges from a multidisciplinary perspective. "The Forum recognizes that religions need to be in dialogue with other disciplines (e.g., science, ethics, economics, education, public policy, gender) in seeking comprehensive solutions to both global and local environmental problems."[26] There are numerous publications, papers, and conferences that are sponsored by or associated with the Forum that serve as excellent resources for educators in a variety of disciplines. See their website at http://environment.harvard.edu/religion/ for more information.

Literature

I have already outlined the importance of religious literacy in understanding both the literary and social/historical contexts of authors and subjects. Incorporating the study of religion into literature courses would result in giving students the tools to understand the religious dimensions of secular texts as well as giving them the opportunity to apply the methods of secular literary theory to the analysis of religious texts. Literature teachers know that whole dimensions of understanding are lost or misrepresented when religious allusions are incomprehensible and/or when religious contexts are unfamiliar. Whether reading authors that are included in Western European/American literary canon such as William Shakespeare, Jane Austin, F. Scott Fitzgerald, or Toni Morrison or from so-called World Literature authors such as Rumi, Chinua Achebe, Tayeb Salih, Rokeya Sakhawat Hossain, and Khaled Hosseini, the religious themes, metaphors, allusions, and/or contexts are significant. For example, how might one understand and interpret the significance of Lorca's decision to write ghazals without an understanding of the social/religious roots of this Persian poetic form or of the Muslim civilization that once flourished in his hometown of Granada that so inspired him?[27]

Incorporating the study of religion into literature courses also affords the opportunity to introduce students to the texts of the world's religious traditions through a nonsectarian lens. Such literacy is badly needed given the widespread and controversial uses of, for example, the Bible and the Qur'an as justifications for a wide diversity of often competing actions and claims. Students are rarely exposed to a nonsectarian study of the Qur'an in secondary education and thus have little to no understanding of its beauty as a literary text nor of its social/political influences. Although the Bible is more frequently taught in public school contexts, the nature of that instruction is often highly problematic as documented by two important studies: One was conducted by People for the American Way on Bible courses in Florida[28] and a second, more recent study focused upon Bible-related courses in Texas.[29] In this latter publication, Mark Chancey (a Professor of Biblical Studies at Southern Methodist University at Dallas) articulated the following findings:

1. Most bible courses taught in Texas public schools fail to meet even minimal standards for teacher qualifications and academic rigor.
2. Most bible courses are taught as religious and devotional classes that promote one faith perspective over all others.
3. Most bible courses advocate an ideological agenda that is hostile to religious freedom, science and public education itself.

4. A handful of Texas school districts show that it is possible to teach bible courses in an objective and nonsectarian manner appropriate to public school classrooms.[30]

Chancey found that though some districts utilized the problematic materials published by the National Council on Bible Curriculum in Public Schools that I discussed in Chapter Two, most drew from other similarly problematic but diverse sources that led to the findings cited above. My point in outlining this study under the literature section is to highlight the importance for literature teachers to be trained in being able to teach about the Bible and other religious texts from a nonsectarian perspective. As I have argued throughout this book and is clearly demonstrated here, religion is already being taught in the schools in often problematic ways. Therefore the question is not whether religion should be taught, but how it will be taught and what kinds of training teachers require to do so responsibly.

In this chapter I have articulated some of the ways that religion is a relevant topic of inquiry and/or lens of analysis in disciplines that are commonly taught in secondary schools. This discussion is clearly neither exhaustive nor comprehensive. It is, however, suggestive of the range of possibilities that exist when thinking about religion from a cultural studies lens. My hope is that educators will feel energized by these possibilities and inspired to rethink their own courses to incorporate religion in ways that are relevant, sound, and engaging for students and teachers alike.

Conclusion

My purpose in writing this book has been to articulate the ways in which religious literacy can serve to enhance efforts aimed at promoting the ideals of democracy in multicultural, multireligious America. Many may believe that the suggestions put forth here and the frameworks upon which they rest are too sophisticated for students and teachers to ever adopt, let alone successfully implement. One colleague was very enthusiastic about the manuscript but then offered the following lament: "We both know this will never take hold in public schools." I strongly disagree. My belief is rooted in my own experience over the past decade working with public and independent school teachers from across the country as well as across the world. It is true that these are challenging times for public school educators, but as I have argued throughout this book, they are too often underestimated, overregulated, and held accountable for enacting policies that they had no voice in constructing and that they recognize as educationally unsound. When expectations shift away from treating teachers as functionaries who need to be managed to capable scholars and professionals who need only the training, support, and resources to do their jobs, then classrooms can (and in my experience do) begin to transform.

I am speaking here of a shift in the culture of how we think about education itself and I am not naïve about the challenges associated with such an aim. Michael Apple is one among many educational theorists who has ably articulated how market economies are currently driving the move toward ever increasing standardization and regulation and the attendant shift from thinking of education as a public good to a private enterprise.[1] What is most disturbing to me about these and similar educational "reforms" is that they are often enacted in the absence of robust, transparent, and democratic public discourse and debate.

Teaching about religion provides a lens to ponder these larger challenges and opportunities. Because it is one of the most vexing and divisive issues in public discourses about education, the potential for it to serve as a catalyst for change is widespread and immediate. No matter what readers may think of the specific proposals and frameworks that I articulate in this book, I hope it will serve to promote a more informed, civil, imaginative, and probing public debate about the purpose of education itself in our multicultural, multireligious democracy.

If we fail to educate today's children with the skills to participate in and advance democratic citizenship that is defined as a political as opposed to an economic category, then the democracy that we Americans so cherish will inevitably erode into an empty shell of slogans without substance. No matter what one's political ideology, I hope that this specter is frightening enough to revive a true spirit of democratic patriotism in us all. There is much at stake, and our nation's teachers are our best resources for helping us to revitalize this central tenet of our identity.

Epilogue

I close this book with a brief review of a report published by the First Amendment Center entitled "Learning about World Religions in Public Schools."[1] Colleagues at the First Amendment Center have worked tirelessly over the past decade or more to help advance religious literacy and democratic citizenship in American education. All of us who care about these issues owe them a tremendous debt of gratitude. Though my approach to how to teach about religion in the schools differs in some significant ways to the one advanced by the First Amendment Center, our ultimate goals are quite similar and I offer these reflections in the spirit of promoting public discourse about how best to advance our mutually shared aims.

"Learning about World Religions in Public Schools" documents the effects on students who were enrolled in a required nine-week, ninth-grade world religions survey course in Modesto, California that the First Amendment Center was instrumental in helping to shape, organize, and launch. The course has been offered since 2000 and researchers Emile Lester[2] and Patrick Roberts[3] interviewed and collected written materials from students who participated in the course over the 2005–2006 academic year. They also interviewed teachers, administrators, school board members, and leaders of Modesto's religious communities to "examine how the course was taught and prepared, and the level of acceptance of the course within Modesto's community."[4] Here is a list of their major findings:

1. Modesto's course had a positive impact on students' respect for religious liberty.
2. Students emerged from the course more supportive of basic First Amendment and political rights in general.

3. The survey asked students six questions testing their basic knowledge of Eastern and Western religions and their understanding of the Bill of Rights. Average scores on this test increased from 37 percent correct before taking the course to 66 percent correct after.
4. Students left the course with an increased appreciation for the similarities between major religions.
5. Most students believed that their teachers presented the religions examined in a fair and balanced manner.
6. Modesto's world religion course has not stirred up any notable controversy in the community.
7. Implementing world religions courses could play a significant role in many communities in converting public schools from a battlefield in the culture wars into common ground.[5]

Though there is much to be celebrated about these findings, Lester and Roberts also issue a note of caution to temper the optimism represented above. They are especially concerned about the quality and consistency of teacher training. "The success of Modesto's course should not be exaggerated, nor does it mean that required world religions courses should or could be implemented in all school districts."[6] They go on to state the following:

> The school district could have been more careful in constructing its teacher-training process, and helping teachers to avoid any bias. Several of the course's positive effects were relatively modest, including several of the course's effects on students' support for religious liberty, and might not be long-lasting.[7]

Later in the report, the authors offer a more detailed discussion of the teacher-training program. Apparently there was some discrepancy between the first round of training in preparation for the initial year of implementation and subsequent years, most notably in the area of the promotion of religious freedom.[8] Also, one new teacher "complained of the lack of adequate in-service training" and said that the training consisted of "pretty much only videos." Another important critique came from one of the local Rabbis who expressed concern that the course presented a "warm and fuzzy" approach to religion. This was the result of the dual emphases to 1) avoid controversial topics and 2) to emphasize the similarities between traditions more than their differences.[9] Finally, teachers reported that they called upon students who were practitioners of religious minorities to share their experiences in order to give other members of the class "a more concrete understanding of these faiths"[10] and the researchers themselves recommended that speakers "from various religions visit classes" in order to further a more "concrete understanding of religion."[11]

At this point it will be obvious to readers of this book that the approach I am advocating differs in some significant ways from the one promoted by the First Amendment Center and adopted by Modesto, though as I stated earlier many of our ultimate aims are quite similar. Lester and Roberts articulate the following goals of world religions courses:

1. Safer and more inclusive schools and communities.
2. Enhance professional success.
3. More informed political decisions.
4. More civil discussions about religion.
5. Increased knowledge of world cultures and improved test scores.
6. Ensure neutrality and balance materialism.[12]

Many of these goals align well with my articulation of the purpose of the educational enterprise outlined in Chapter One. The differences in our approaches toward realizing those goals can perhaps be best summarized by the following four points: 1) how we understand and interpret the role of religious leaders and practitioners in relationship to promoting the study of religion in the schools; 2) whether religion should be represented both within and between traditions as diverse, complex and multivalent, or more uniform and universal with an emphasis on their positive manifestations; 3) whether or not methodological questions regarding classroom pedagogy are significant dimensions to consider when thinking about how to teach about religion in the schools; and, finally 4) how neutrality is defined and understood.

Readers will be familiar with my positions on these issues and my intention in articulating these differences is to help identify a range of approaches and their attendant frameworks. I also articulate these differences in order to invite public dialogue and discourse about them in the spirit of furthering the common goals of promoting religious literacy and strengthening democratic citizenship. Finally, I hope that educational researchers will focus their efforts on helping to analyze these and other approaches in ways that will help us all better understand and attend to the complex issues that arise when teaching about religion in the context of deeply rooted and widespread religious illiteracy.

APPENDIX

Compilation of Anonymous Student Evaluations of Islamic Cultural Studies

Please rate the following on a scale from 1–5:
1 = poor; 2 = fair; 3 = average; 4 = good; 5 = excellent.

Texts

Azim Nanji, "Islam," in Bush, et.al, *The Religious World*: 4.1
Carl Ernst, *Following Muhammad*: 4.3
Michael Sells, *Approaching the Qur'an*: 3.5
Fazlur Rahman, *Major Themes of the Qur'an*: 4.2
Readings on Gender: 4.6
Readings on Contemporary Issues: 4.6
John Esposito, "The Many Faces of Islam," in *Religion in the Modern World*: 4.4

Instructor

Knowledge of the material: 4.8
Skill as a discussion leader: 4.7
Enthusiasm for teaching the course: 5.0
Ability to stimulate interest in the subject: 4.8
Availability and helpfulness to students: 4.5
Respect for students' ideas: 4.8
Concern for students' learning: 4.8
Helpfulness of written feedback on papers and assignments: 4.6

Student Comments on Instructor

Note: These evaluations are anonymous so I numbered each one for reference. The numbers in the parentheses following each short answer response refer to the corresponding evaluation form.

Great energy! I enjoyed the explanations offered during our discussions when it seemed the class had gotten stuck on a particular idea. They helped move our discussions forward and in the right direction. (1)

Because of discussion nature of course, it would be nice to occasionally have lectures. This was done for explaining Sunni/Shi'ite split. (2)

Generally very good. No specific concerns/criticisms. (5)

Dr. Moore was always excited about the class and always led our discussions without having to speak much or bring things up of her own accord. She could always lead students into getting to the points that she wanted to discuss but never had to tell the class anything. She really seemed to enjoy teaching the class and made a great effort to be available and always help students learn. (6)

Dr. Moore is a stellar instructor. One of the best I've had at PA. (7)

Invited everyone's thoughts into discussions quite well. (8)

Fantastic instructor who took us seriously and asked us to really think. (10)

Organization of the Course

Please rate each of the following on a scale from 1–5 regarding its effectiveness as a learning tool.

Films: 4.5
Small Group Discussions: 3.8
Full Class Discussions: 4.4
Reflection Papers: 4.7
Qur'an Essay: 4.1
Gender Presentation: 4.1
Final Project: 4.7

Which section did you find most interesting and why?

The section on women because it is an issue that is so often falsely portrayed in the news. It was interesting to learn how culture integrates itself into religion. (1)

Those on fundamental, existential questions. Most rigorous intellectually. (2)

I found the gender articles, especially the ones for our presentation especially interesting. (3)

Final project allows students to indulge themselves. (4)

I found the final project most interesting. Short of that, I found the introductions about Islam and religion most interesting. (5)

I enjoyed the gender presentations, probably because they were very focused and I knew exactly what I was supposed to do—the rest of the course required giving myself direction, so this [the gender presentation] was a nice respite from the harder thinking of coming up with a topic and then writing on it. (6)

Anything concerning gender was great! (7)

I found the Qur'an paper to be most interesting to write. (8)

Rahman and the other sections on the Qur'an. I just learned a lot. (9)

I loved the section on gender. (10)

Which section did you find least interesting and why?

The early long readings about Islam in general. It felt like we were groping around in the dark trying to find something concrete when we might have been better off studying a few diverse specific cultures. (1)

The historical overview of the Sunni/Shi'ite split. Least rigorous intellectually. (2)

I found the constant repetition of history helpful but a little boring. (3)

Blank. (4)

I didn't think that the gender parts by themselves were all that interesting. I learned a lot about gender issues in the final project and in the intro readings, but I found the specific gender readings dull. (5)

I didn't really like the section on Sunni-Shi'a differences. I felt like just being told in class would have been much simpler and would have let me learn other thinks, rather than have problems figuring out the fundamentals. (6)

Sufism. The reading was dense and we never really talked about it. (7)

Beginning of the course was very reading intensive, sometimes the material was uninteresting. (8)

I wasn't as interested in the Sunni/Shi' distinctions, but it was ok. (9)

There weren't any that I didn't like. (10)

What did you like most about this course?

The incorporation of relevant modern day issues such as the discussions about the cartoon depictions of Muhammad and the election of Hamas. (1)

The classes. Discussion is effective. (2)

I enjoyed the discussions the most. (3)

The Ernst readings and films. (4)

I liked learning about the basic beliefs of Islam and how to approach the study of religion. (5)

I enjoyed class discussion. I felt like our class was very intelligent and most of the people contributed interesting things throughout the term. (6)

Dr. Moore (7)

Exclusively based on class discussion. (8)

The emphasis on our own views and ideas. (9)

The focus on discussion. (10)

What did you find most problematic?

Some of the class discussions seemed slow and circular and it didn't seem like we always had relevant, moving, or compelling comments. (1)

Blank. (2)

So much work . . . (3)

The full class discussion. (4)

It was difficult with the various levels of knowledge that people had coming in. This was much more the case in this class than any other I've taken at Andover. (5)

As you may have noticed from the section above, I had issues with the Sunni-Shi'a differences. I felt like it would have been much easier if I had just been told them and didn't think that finding them myself gave me any greater understanding than I would have had otherwise. (6)

Some people had a tendency to talk a lot, so much so that it was hard to get in any word at times. (7)

Blank. (8)

Trying to decide on a final paper topic. (9)

We always ran out of time! (10)

What suggestions do you have to strengthen the course?

Start with an in-depth study of specific Muslim cultures to show the diversity of the faith rather than just hear that it is diverse without understanding how and why for so long. (1)

More support on final projects. (2)

Watch more movies! Listen to more recitations! (3)

More time on the final project to allow for a real presentation. (4)

More "existential" questions/broad religious questions and how to approach those. (5)

I would suggest having a project right after midterms. Maybe it was just because [this] term is very short, but I felt like we could have one presentation on theological issues and one on applied Islam. (6)

Fewer presentations because those tended to be dull and repetitive. (7)

More videos during double period to compliment reading material. (8)

Give more time for group presentations. (9)

Offer it in the fall for a longer term. (10)

What were the two most significant things you learned in this class?

1) That many of the societal 'problems' with regard to women's rights that we attribute to Islam are actually helped by Islam and should be attributed to culture and tradition. 2) That Islam is an extremely diverse faith and the diversity doesn't make it less legitimate because the idea is that Islam and God are such huge concepts that by definition are impossible to understand. Each culture's attempt to understand a piece of it can be just as compelling as another's. (1)

The influence and implications of culture on Islam; fundamentals of Sunni/Shi'ite split. (2)

I learned that thinking and questioning religion is something shared by many, and I've learned about Islam and Muslims enough to understand we are all people and there are more than one or two sides to every story on the news. (3)

Five pillars of Islam and Sufism. (4)

1) Modernism does not mean liberalization/Westernization; 2) The impact of imperialism on Islam. (5)

I think that the idea of Muslim unity dominated my term, but also, in contrast to that idea, I found the differences within Islam provocative and found the contrast between these two, but the acceptance of both, particularly interesting. (6)

That's a really broad question. What is meant by significant? I loved learning about the treatment of veiling . . . (7)

The significance of the problems encountered in trying to fit Islam into the modern world—stereotypes; wide interpretations of Qur'an in different Islamic countries, but at the same time, their unity as Muslims. (8)

Muslim women aren't just victims; Muslims are very diverse in their views. (9)

The diversity within Islam and how to think about religion. (10)

Did your writing skills improve? 5-Yes; 4-No; 1-unsure.

Did your critical thinking skills improve? 10-Yes; 0-No.

Would you recommend this course to a friend? 10-Yes; 0-No.

Would you recommend this instructor to a friend? 10-Yes; 0-No.

Did you enjoy this class? 4.6

Overall rating for the course? 4.6

Other comments?

It was a lot of work but I have definitely gained much from this course. (3)

Great course overall. One of the better ones I've had at Andover. (5)

Thanks, it was fun. (6)

Great, great term! (7)

I learned a lot. Thank you. (9)

Thanks for a great class . . . my best at PA. (10)

NOTES

Introduction

1. Diana Eck, *A New Religious America* (New York: HarperCollins, 2001). Christian Smith takes issue with Eck's characterization of this diversity in his volume *Soul Searching: The Religious and Spiritual Lives of American Teenagers* (New York: Oxford, 2005). He claims that the United States is still overwhelmingly Christian in orientation. Though Smith may be right about numerical prominence (the numbers are notoriously difficult to accurately assess) there is no denying the fact that there is significant diversity of religious belief in practice in cities all across the United States. (See the Pluralism Project website at http://www.fas.harvard.edu/~pluralsm/ accessed December 3, 2006) I contend that no one is served when that diversity is ignored or downplayed.
2. See Edward Said, *Orientalism* (New York: Vintage, 1978/1994) and *Covering Islam* (New York: Vintage, 1981/1997). For contemporary expressions see the cross reference for hate crimes and violence in "Religious Diversity News" at the Pluralism Project website, http://www.pluralism.org/news/index.php?xref=Hate+Crimes+and+Violence accessed December 3, 2006.
3. George W. Bush, "Address to a Joint Session of Congress and the American People," September 20, 2001. "They hate our freedoms—our freedom of religion, our freedom of speech, our freedom to vote and assemble and disagree with each other." http:// www.whitehouse.gov/news/releases/2001/09/20010920-8.html, accessed March 20, 2005.
4. In November 2001, an organization founded by Lynn Cheney and Joseph Lieberman called *The American Council of Trustees and Alumni* (ACTA) issued a report entitled "Defending Civilization: How Our Universities Are Failing America And What Can Be Done About It." The report reproduced undocumented statements from 117 people from college and university campuses (many of them from faculty) who challenged or raised questions about the president's war on terrorism. The report called these and similarly minded academics who "blame America first" the "weak link" in the war against terror. For full text of the report see, http://www.totse.com/ en/politics/political_spew/162419.html, accessed April 3, 2005,. The ACTA website is http://www.goacta.org, accessed April 3, 2005.
5. *Abington Township v. Schempp* 374 U.S. 203 (1963).
6. For example, see http://www.hds.harvard.edu/prse/hstars (accessed December 3, 2006) for links to the history/social studies and English standards in Massachusetts, California, and Texas.
7. Most notably, James W. Fraser in *Between Church and State: Religion and Public Education in a Multicultural America* (New York: St. Martin's Griffin, 1999) offers an impressive historical context for the current debates and Warren Nord provides a good general overview of the issues

in *Religion and American Education* (Chapel Hill: University of North Carolina, 1995). More recently, Stephen Prothero's Religious Literacy (San Francisco: Harper, 2007), Kent Greenwalt's *Does God Belong in Public Schools?* (Princeton: Princeton University Press, 2005) and Joan DelFattore's *The Fourth R: Conflicts Over Religion in America's Public Schools* (New Haven: Yale University Press, 2004) all provide helpful overviews of current debates and their historical contexts. Nel Noddings advances the idea that engaging in ultimate questions of meaning should be an integral part of education in her now classic text *Educating for Intelligent Belief or Unbelief* (New York: Teachers College Press, 2000). In other volumes, Warren Nord and Charles Haynes address curricular questions in *Taking Religion Seriously across the Curriculum* (New York: Association for Supervision and Curriculum Development, 1998) and Diana L. Eck explores how religious pluralism is a defining factor in American contemporary life in *A New Religious America*.

One The Purpose of Education

1. *Webster's Third New International Dictionary*, s.v. "democracy."
2. Amy Gutmann, *Democratic Education* (Princeton: Princeton University Press, 1987/ 1999).
3. Ibid., 47.
4. Ibid., 42.
5. Ibid., xii.
6. Ibid., xiii.
7. Ibid., 52.
8. For her full discussion of these frameworks, see Gutmann, *Democratic Education*, "States and Education," 19–47.
9. Ibid., 42.
10. Ibid., 44.
11. Ibid., 45.
12. See chapter three in this text for a definition of these terms.
13. Gutmann, *Democratic Education*, 45.
14. See, for example, Gutmann's comments regarding the inclusion of the contribution of women in the curriculum in, "Sex Education and Sexist Education," *Democratic Education*, 107–115.
15. Gutmann, *Democratic Education*, 46.
16. Ibid., 54.
17. Paulo Freire, *Pedagogy of the Oppressed* (New York: Continuum, 1994).
18. Ibid., 54.
19. Ibid., 56–67.
20. Freire optimistically asserts that the vocation of humanity is humanization (25). This assertion is consonant with the optimistic view of human nature and capacity that is represented in our founding documents such as the Declaration of Independence and the Constitution.
21. Such transparency is applicable to all educational settings, including those that restrict teacher autonomy regarding content and method. If, for example, the state or local district mandates certain educational practices, then teachers should be open with students about these policies and how they are justified.
22. Freire, *Pedagogy*, 71.
23. Ibid., 68.
24. Sharon Welch, *A Feminist Ethic of Risk* (Minneapolis: Fortress, 1990). Welch has more recently challenged humility as a virtue but she still promotes the same values of confidence and self critique that the quote I cite here represents. See Sharon Welch, *Sweet Dreams in America: Making Ethics and Spirituality Work* (New York: Routledge, 1999).

25. Jonathan Kozol, *Savage Inequalities* (New York: Harper Reprint, 1992) and *The Shame of the Nation* (New York: Crown Publishers, 2005).
26. *Webster's Third New International Dictionary*, s.v. "democracy."

Two Why Religion Should Be Included in Public School Education

1. Marie Wachlin and Byron Johnson, *Bible Literacy Report* (Fairfax, VA: The Bible Literacy Project, 2005), 10.
2. Ibid.
3. Ibid., 15. Literacy is defined as "consisting of five components: (a) knowing the books of the Bible, (b) being familiar with common Bible stories, (c) being familiar with popular Bible characters, (d) being able to recognize common biblical phrases, and (e) being able to connect that knowledge to references in literature," 19.
4. See Mark Chancey, *Reading, Writing and Religion: Teaching the Bible in Texas Public Schools* (Austin: Texas Freedom Network Education Fund, 2006), http://www.tfn.org/religiousfreedom/biblecurriculum/texascourses/. Also, see the discussion regarding the National Council on Bible Curriculum in Public Schools later in this same chapter.
5. Nel Noddings promotes this same idea in *Educating for Intelligent Belief.*
6. See Jean Amery, *Suicide: A Discourse on Voluntary Death*, trans. John Barlow (Bloomington: Indiana University Press, 1999).
7. See Viktor Frankl, *Man's Search for Meaning* (New York: Pocket 1959/1984).
8. See Robert Gellately, *Backing Hitler* (New York: Oxford University Press, 2001).
9. Irving Greenberg, "Cloud of Smoke, Pillar of Fire," in John Roth and Michael Berenbaum, eds., *Holocaust: Religious and Philosophical Implications* (New York: Paragon, 1989), 318.
10. Many who agree with Greenberg's general critique of classical theism and secular humanism take issue with his somewhat uncritical support of the State of Israel.
11. "Sikh Student Allowed Ceremonial Dagger in Westchester School after Being Suspended," *Indian Express*, April 1, 2005, http://www.indypressny.org/article.php3?ArticleID=2010 accessed August 5, 2005.
12. U.S. Department of Education, "Guidance on Constitutionally Protected Prayer in Elementary and Secondary Schools," February 7, 2003, http://ed.gov/policy/gen/guid/religionandschools/prayer_guidance.html accessed March 13, 2003. I am not in full agreement with the interpretations of the First Amendment that the guidelines assume, but I appreciate the attempt to articulate guidance for educators that is specific and clear.
13. Personal email correspondence, October 3, 2002.
14. Samieh Shalash, "What It's Like to Wear a Head Covering in the Bluegrass," *Lexington Herald Leader*, July 17, 2005.
15. Gutmann, *Democratic Education*, 44.
16. James Davison Hunter characterizes the culture wars as divided into two camps that are both comprised of coalitions. He defines them as "orthodox" and "progressive." Though I generally agree with the soundness of his categorizations, I think the terms "conservative" and "progressive" are more aptly descriptive for our current context. James Davison Hunter, *Culture Wars: The Struggle to Define America* (New York: Basic, 1991). See especially 115, 122, and 124.
17. See, for example, M. Gabler, *Humanism/Moral Relativism in Textbooks* (Longview, TX: Educational Research Analysts, 1988); Stephen Carter, *The Culture of Disbelief: How American Law and Politics Trivialize Religious Devotion* (New York: Basic Books, 1993).

18. The course description reads as follows: "Islamic Cultural Studies, an introduction to modern Islamic influences in a variety of cultural contexts. Areas of focus could include the United States, Indonesia, Kenya, Pakistan, Iran, Central Asia, Turkey and Egypt. In this comparative study, we will give attention to both the unity and diversity of Islam as manifested in contemporary religious, political and cultural expressions in selected countries named above. Consideration will be given to origins, formative developments and religious thought and practice as well as the influence of Islam on gender and family life, economic structures and modern political conflicts and expressions. The first part of the course will focus on a general introduction to Islam. The second part of the term will be devoted to group projects where students will focus on Islamic cultural studies in one of the chosen countries." Phillips Academy *Courses of Study*, 1998–1999.
19. The Indonesian term for *madrasa*: a school for Islamic instruction.
20. Anonymous student evaluation, Philosophy and Religious Studies 530: *Islamic Cultural Studies*, Spring 2000.
21. See Hunter, *Culture Wars*, 176–196.
22. Alliance Defense Fund "Strategy and Coordination Make a Difference," http://www.alliancedefensefund.org/whatwedo/strategy/Default.aspx accessed August 6, 2005.
23. Ibid.
24. *Boy Scouts of America et al. v Dale*, 530 US 696 (2000).
25. Alliance Defense Fund, "Milestones," http://www.alliancedefensefund.org/about/History/Milestones.aspx accessed August 6, 2005.
26. Alan Sears and Craig Osten, *The Homosexual Agenda: The Principal Threat to Religious Freedom* (Nashville: Broadman and Holman, 2003).
27. See, for example, Bob Allen, "Leaders Declare War on Gay 'Agenda,'" *EthicsDaily.com*, November 6, 2003, http:www.ethicsdaily.com/article_detail.cfm?AID=3335, accessed August 6, 2005, and Michael Foust, "An Agenda? Book Shows How Homosexuals Advanced Cause," *BPNews*, October 23, 2003, http://www.bpnews.net/bpnews.asp?ID=16920 accessed August 6, 2005.
28. Sears and Osten, *Homosexual Agenda*, 46.
29. Ibid., 67. The authors cite the following as the source for the survey results: Christopher Michaud, "Survey: Students Hold Mostly Pro-Gay Views," *Reuters*, August 27, 2001.
30. Sears and Osten, *Homosexual Agenda*, 71.
31. American Civil Liberties Union Case Profile: *Boyd High GSA v. Boyd Co. Board of Education*, http://www.aclu.org/LesbianGayRights/LesbianGayRights.cfm?ID=17603&c=106 accessed August 6, 2005.
32. Ibid., and ACLU Case Profile: *Morrison v. Boyd Co. Board of Education* http://www.aclu.org/LesbianGayRights/LesbianGayRights.cfm?ID=18142&c=106 accessed August 6, 2005.
33. Day of Silence, "Frequently Asked Questions: What is the Day of Silence?" "The Day of Silence, a project of the Gay, Lesbian and Straight Education Network (GLSEN) in collaboration with the United States Student Association (USSA), is a student-led day of action where those who support making anti-LGBT bias unacceptable in schools take a day-long vow of silence to recognize and protest the discrimination and harassment—in effect, the silencing—experienced by LGBT students and their allies." http://www.dayofsilence.org/ accessed August 5, 2005.
34. Michael Janofsky, "Gay Rights Battlefields Spread to Public Schools," *The New York Times*, June 9, 2005, http://select.nytimes.com/search/restricted/article?res=F70E13FB3B5C0C7A8CDDAF0894DD404482 accessed June 9, 2005.
35. Bethan L. Mones, "Day Draws Fire," *Lexington Minuteman*, April 21, 2005.
36. See Edwin Gaustad and Mark Noll, eds., *A Documentary History of Religion in America to 1877* (Grand Rapids, MI: Eerdmans, 2003), 494–497.

37. Southern Baptist Convention, "About Us: Meet the Southern Baptists," http://www.sbc.net/aboutus/default.asp accessed August 6, 2005.
38. See Human Rights Campaign, "Southern Baptist Convention," http://hrc.org/Template.cfm?Section=Home&CONTENTID=21765&TEMPLATE=/ContentManagement/ContentDisplay.cfm accessed August 5, 2005.
39. Voddie Baucham, Jr. and Bruce N. Shortt, "Resolution on Homosexuality in the Public Schools," April 29, 2005, http://www.exodusmandate.org/20050503-resolution/20050503-resolution-homosexuals-in-public-schools.doc accessed August 6, 2005.
40. Bob Allen, "Family Groups Endorse SBC Resolution," *EthicsDaily.com*, June 15, 2005, http://www.ethicsdaily.com/article_detail.cfm?AID=5894 accessed August 5, 2005.
41. Bob Allen, "Southern Baptists Call for Investigation of Public Schools," *EthicsDaily.com*, June 22, 2005, http://www.ethicsdaily.com/article_detail.cfm?AID=5927 accessed August 5, 2005.
42. For examples, see the declaration published and endorsed by the ecumenical coalition entitled Religious Institute on Sexual Morality, "Religious Declaration on Sexual Morality, Justice and Healing," http://www.religiousinstitute.org/ accessed October 14, 2005; Unitarian Universalist Association, "Unitarian Universalist Association General Assembly Resolutions," http://www.uua., org/owl/uuares.html accessed October 14, 2005; General Synod XXV of the United Church of Christ, "Resolution in Support of Equal Marriage Rights for All (2005)," http://www.ucc.org/synod/pdfs/gs25minutes.pdf, 27–31 accessed October 14, 2005); Central Conference of American Rabbis, Resolution on Same-Gender Officiation (March, 2000), http://data.ccarnet.org/cgi-bin/resodisp.pl?file=gender&year=2000 accessed October 14, 2005.
43. Michael J. Perry, *Religion in Politics: Constitutional and Moral Perspectives* (New York: Oxford, 1999).
44. See Perry, *Religion in Politics* for an especially persuasive commentary on this insight as it relates specifically to homosexuality, 82–95. For a similar, more general articulation of this perspective see Ron Thiemann's important text, *Religion in Public Life: A Dilemma for Democracy* (Washington, DC: Georgetown University Press, 1996).
45. Perry, *Religion in Politics*, 96.
46. See Rob Reich, *Bridging Liberalism and Multiculturalism in American Education* (Chicago: University of Chicago Press, 2002).
47. Gutmann, *Democratic Education*, 45.
48. See, for example, Stephen R. Haynes, *Noah's Curse: The Biblical Justification of American Slavery* (New York: Oxford, 2002); Janet Duitsman Cornelius, *When I Can Read My Title Clear: Literacy, Slavery, and Religion in the Antebellum South* (Columbia: University of South Carolina Press, 1992); Lucille Salitan, Elizabeth Buffum Chace, Lydia Buffum Read, Lucy Buffum Lovell, Rebecca Buffum Spring, eds., *Virtuous Lives: Four Quaker Sisters Remember Family Life, Abolitionism, and Women's Suffrage* (New York: Continuum, 1994); Susan Hill Lindley, *"You Have Stept Out of Your Place": A History of Women and Religion in America* (Louisville, KY: Westminster John Knox Press, 1996). For suggested primary source material see Horace Bushnell, *Women's Suffrage: Reform Against Nature* (New York: Scribner, 1869); Elizabeth Cady Stanton, *The Woman's Bible* (Amherst, NY: Prometheus Books, 1999); Frederick Douglas, *Frederick Douglas: Selected Speeches and Writings* (Chicago: Lawrence Hill Books, 2000); Leonard E. Lathrop, *A Discourse on the Obligations of a Christian People: In View of the Divine Beneficence, Considered With Reference to the Subject of the Temperance Reform, War, of Capital Punishment, and of Slavery* (New York: R.G. and P.S. Wynkoop, Press of J.C. Merrell and Co, 1847); Charles Manson Taggart, *Slavery and the Law in the Light of Christianity: A Discourse Delivered Before the Congregation of Unitarian Christians of Nashville, Tennessee on Sunday Evening, June 22, 1851* (Nashville: J.T.S. Fall, 1851); Damon Y. Kilgore, *The Questions of Today, Caste, Suffrage, Labor, Temperance, Religion: An Oration Delivered Before the Wesleyan Academy Alumni Association at Wilbraham, Mass, June 29, 1870* (New York: Hurd and Houghton, 1870).
49. Greenwalt, *Does God Belong in Public Schools*, 147.

50. For example, Bob Jones University supported their policy of racial discrimination on religious grounds. The university believed that the "Bible forbids interracial dating and marriage." "To effectuate these views, Negroes were completely excluded until 1971. From 1971 to May 1975, the University accepted no applications from unmarried Negroes, but did accept applications from Negroes married within their race . . . Since May 29, 1975, the University has permitted unmarried Negroes to enroll; but a disciplinary rule prohibits interracial dating and marriage." *Bob Jones University v. United States* and *Goldsboro Christian Schools, Inc. v. United States*, 461 US 574 (1982) at 580 and 2022–23.
51. Gutmann, *Democratic Education*, 123.
52. Editorial, "The Evolution of Creationism," *New York Times*, May 17, 2005.
53. American Civil Liberties Union, "Pennsylvania Parents File First-Ever Challenge to 'Intelligent Design' Instruction in Public Schools," news release, December 14, 2004, http://www.aclu.org/ReligiousLiberty/ReligiousLiberty.cfm?ID=17207&c=139 accessed August 5, 2005.
54. Elisabeth Bumiller, "Bush Remarks Roil Debate on Teaching Evolution," *New York Times*, August 3, 2005.
55. *Tammy Kitzmiller, et al. v. Dover Area School District, et al.*, USDC, 342 (2005), 136.
56. Ralph Blumenthal and Barbara Novovitch, "Bible Course Becomes a Test for Public Schools in Texas," *New York Times*, August 1, 2005. Six thousand citizens signed a petition endorsing this curriculum.
57. Ms. Ridenour is the founder and president of NCBCPS and is licensed as a commercial real estate agent and certified paralegal. See "Biographical Sketch" at http://www.bibleinschools.net/sdm.asp accessed August 5, 2005.
58. National Council on Bible Curriculum in Public Schools, "President's Message," www.bibleinschools.net/sdm.asp accessed August 5, 2005.
59. National Council on Bible Curriculum in Public Schools, "Founding Fathers," www.bibleinschools.net/sdm.asp?pg=found_father accessed August 5, 2005.
60. Blumenthal and Novovitch, "Bible Course," *New York Times*.
61. Mark A. Chancey, The Bible and Public Schools: The National Council on Bible Curriculum in Public Schools (Austin: Texas Freedom Network) 2005, 2, http://faculty.smu.edu/mchancey/public_schools.htm accessed November 22, 2006. In another review published in *The Journal of Law and Education* the author summarizes her findings in the following way: "A widely used Bible course curriculum suffers from a number of constitutional infirmities and is likely to be found unconstitutional if used as written in public schools. The curriculum, which is produced and distributed by the National Council on Bible Curriculum in Public Schools (NCBCPS), fails to present the Bible in the objective manner required for public school courses that teach about religion. The curriculum favors Protestantism over Catholicism and a literal interpretation over nonliteralist approaches to the Bible. As written, the curriculum would require teachers and students to make a number of faith statements." Frances Paterson, "Anatomy of a Bible Course Curriculum," *Journal of Law and Education*, January, 2003, http://www.findarticles.com/p/articles/mi_qa3994/is_200301/ai_n9186918 accessed August 6, 2005.
62. National Council on Bible Curriculum in Public Schools, "Where it is implemented," http://www.bibleinschools.net/sdm.asp?pg=implemented accessed August 5, 2005. A rural school district in Frankenmuth, Michigan engaged in a year-long debate about adopting the NCBCPS curriculum and decided against doing so in January of 2005. The superintendent of schools, Michael Murphy, said that the school board did not believe that the curriculum was rigorous enough and that "It goes beyond talking about religion and becomes faith-based." See "Bible Class Idea Ditched in Mich. District," *Beliefnet.com*, January 11, 2005, http:www.beliefnet.com/story/159/story_15926_1.html accessed August 6, 2005.

63. "Texas School Board Adds Bible Class," *The Boston Globe*, April 27, 2005.
64. Gutmann, *Democratic Education*, 103.
65. Greenwalt, *Does God Belong*, 88–100.
66. Gutmann, *Democratic Education*, 103.
67. Ibid., 104.
68. A good resource to teach about the foundations of issues related to the separation of church and state for secondary students is Edwin S. Gaustad, *Church and State in America* (New York: Oxford, 1999). This is one of the volumes in the Oxford *Religion in American Life* series edited by Jon Butler and Harry S. Stout.

Three How to Teach About Religion in the Schools

1. The religious liberty clauses of the First Amendment to the United States Constitution.
2. For an excellent study on the controversy regarding these decisions and their role in the current culture wars, see DelFattore, *The Fourth R*. For a historical perspective, see Fraser, *Between Church and State*.
3. *School District of Abington Township, Pennsylvania, et al. v. Schempp et al.* 374 US 203 (1963).
4. See Nord, *Religion and American Education* and Nord and Haynes, *Taking Religion Seriously*.
5. See the First Amendment Center website at http://www.firstamendmentcenter.org accessed October 27, 2005.
6. First Amendment Center, *A Teacher's Guide to Religion in the Public Schools* (Nashville: First Amendment Center, 1999). Another useful general guidebook is Charles Haynes and Oliver Thomas, *Finding Common Ground: A Guide to Religious Liberty in Public Schools* (Nashville, TN: The First Amendment Center, 2001).
7. First Amendment Center, *A Teacher's Guide*, 3.
8. Donna Haraway, "Situated Knowledges: The Science Question in Feminism and the Privilege of Partial Perspective," in *Simians, Cyborgs, and Women: The Reinvention of Nature* (NY: Routledge, 1991), 183–202.
9. Diane L. Moore, "Overcoming Religious Illiteracy: A Cultural Studies Approach," World History Connected November 2006, http://worldhistoryconnected.press.uiuc.edu/4.1/moore.html accessed December 2, 2006.
10. James C. Carper, "History, Religion, and Schooling: A Context for Conversation," in James T. Sears and James C. Carper, eds., *Curriculum, Religion and Public Education: Conversations for an Enlarging Public Square* (New York: Teachers College Press, 1998), 11. Carper cites political scientist James Skillen as the author of this particular framework.
11. See Fraser, *Between Church and State*, 9–48.
12. Ibid., 43.
13. Carper, "History, Religion and Schooling," 16.
14. Fraser provides an excellent overview of Horace Mann and the controversies he encountered when he attempted to promote his own Unitarian theological assumptions under the guise of nonsectarianism. See Fraser, "Creating an American Common School and a Common Faith: Horace Mann and the Protestant Public Schools, 1789–1860," in *Between Church and State*, 23–48.
15. For an overview of the important role that the *McGuffey's Readers* played in promoting a common Protestant morality, see Fraser, *Between Church and State*, 40–43. For commentary on the role of the King James translation of the Bible and the practice of reading it without comment, see Fraser, "Creating an American Common School," in *Between Church and State* and DelFattore, *The Fourth R*.

16. David Tyack, "The Kingdom of God and the Common School," *Harvard Educational Review*, 36 (Fall, 1966), 454, quoted in Fraser, *Between Church and State*, 34.
17. Calvin Stowe, "The Religious Element in Education," (Boston, 1844), 26, quoted in Fraser, *Between Church and State*, 34–35. It is interesting to note how Stowe's sentiments mirror those in current debates.
18. Fraser, *Between Church and State*, 46.
19. J.D. Hunter, *American Evangelicalism: Conservative Religion and the Quandary of Modernity* (New Brunswick, NJ: Rutgers University Press, 1983), 37, cited in Carper, "History, Religion and Schooling," 19.
20. Carper, "History, Religion and Schooling," 19.
21. Ibid.
22. See Fraser, "Who Defines What Is Common? Roman Catholics and the Common School Movement, 1801–1892," 49–66; "Literacy in the African American Community: Church and School in Slave and Free Communities, 1802–1902," 67–82; and "Native American Religion, Christian Missionaries, and Government Schools, 1819–1926," 83–104 in *Between Church and State*.
23. The National Center for Education Statistics (NCES) has only recently begun to gather data on private schools and homeschooling in the United States. In a survey report published in October 2004, private schools were organized into three categories: Catholic, Other Religious, and Nonsectarian. The largest of the three was the category "Other Religious" which comprised 49.2 percent of all private schools. Of that group, Conservative Christian schools were the largest sub-category. They comprise 18.9 percent of all private schools in the United States. See S.P. Broughman and K.W. Pugh, *Characteristics of Private Schools in the United States: Results From the 2001–2002 Private School Universe Survey*, (NCES 2005–305), U.S. Department of Education (Washington, DC: National Center for Education Statistics), 9. These figures represent an increase from a report published in 1999 on the same topic. In that report the "other religious" category comprised 48.2 percent of all private schools and conservative Christian schools still comprised the largest sub-category, representing 18.2 percent. See S.P. Broughman and L.A. Colaciello, *Private School Universe Survey, 1997–98* (NCES 1999–319), U.S. Department of Education, (Washington, DC: National Center for Education Statistics), 2. In relationship to home schooling, the NCES published an Issue Brief in July 2004 entitled *1.1 Million Homeschooled Students in the United States in 2003*. The conclusion states the following: "From 1999 to 2003, the number of homeschooled students in the United States increased, as did the homeschooling rate. The increase in the homeschooling rate (from 1.7 percent to 2.2 percent) represents about 0.5 percent of the 2002–2003 school-age population and a 29 percent relative increase over the 4-year period . . . Nearly two-thirds of homeschooled students had parents who said that their primary reason for homeschooling was either concern about the environment of other schools or a desire to provide religious or moral instruction." See Institute of Educational Statistics, Issue Brief, *1.1 Million Homeschooled Students in the United States in 2003* (NCES 2004–115), U.S. Department of Education, (Washington, DC, National Center for Education Statistics) 2004.
24. Homeschools are regulated by the state and standards of accountability vary from no regulations at all to adhering to specific guidelines. See the Home School Legal Defense Association (HSLDA) for a listing of state laws: http://www.hslda.org/laws/default.asp accessed October 17, 2005.
25. Secular education thwarts democracy when religion is trivialized, banned or simply omitted from consideration as an important historical, cultural, and social phenomenon.
26. See Reich, *Bridging Liberalism*. As noted in chapter two, his definition of minimalist autonomy (91–92) and the importance for schools to develop autonomy as one of their primary functions (196) are especially pertinent to this debate.
27. See, for example, E.D. Hirsch, Jr., Chester Finn, Jr., and John T.E. Cribb. *The Educated Child: A Parent's Guide From Preschool Through Eighth Grade* (New York: Free Press, 1999), and other texts by these prominent authors.

28. David Stannard, *American Holocaust: The Conquest of the New World* (New York, Oxford, 1992).
29. See Sven Linqvist, *Exterminate all the Brutes* (London: New Press, 1997) and Adam Hochschild, *King Leopold's Ghost* (New York: Mariner Books, 1997).
30. See Gellately, *Backing Hitler*.
31. See, for example, Donald J. Dietrich, ed., *Christian Responses to the Holocaust* (Syracuse: Syracuse University Press, 2003); John Gager, *The Origins of Christian Anti-Semitism* (New York: Oxford University Press, 1983); William Brustein, *Roots of Hate: Anti-Semitism in Europe Before the Holocaust* (NY: Cambridge University Press, 2003); and John Shelby Spong, "The Bible and Anti-Semitism," in *The Sins of Scripture* (San Francisco: Harper, 2005), 183–212.
32. Bernard Lewis and Samuel Huntington are two prominent and popular contemporary scholars often associated with promoting "orientalist" views of Islam. See Samuel Huntington, *The Clash of Civilizations and the Remaking of the World* Order (New York: Simon and Schuster, 1998) and Bernard Lewis, *What Went Wrong? The Clash between Islam and Modernity in the Middle East* (New York: Harper Perennial, 2003) and *The Crisis of Islam: Holy War and Unholy Terror* (New York: Modern Library, 2003).
33. Said, *Orientalism*.
34. Ibid., 57.
35. There are some isolated incidents whereby Christian children were inappropriately forbidden to exercise their religious liberty rights in the schools, but these are rare in comparison to challenges that non-Christian students face.
36. For example, a school board member in Chattanooga, TN protested the administration's decision to allow a Muslim student at East Ridge High School to wear her hijab in school. "I think this opens up a Pandora's box for us. You may have Jewish students asking to wear yarmulkes and students from other religions making requests. I think we should stick to the dress code," stated school board member Rhonda Thurman. The student had previously been told she could not wear her hijab but the administration reversed its decision following an intervention by a Muslim civil rights group based in Washington, DC. "Rhonda Thurman Says Allowing Islamic Head Scarf Was Wrong Decision," January 18, 2005, *The Chattanoogan.Com* at http://www.chattanoogan.com/ articles/article_61195.asp accessed on October 27, 2005. In a similar story, in October 2003, Nashala Hearn was suspended from Benjamin Franklin Science Academy in Muskogee, Texas for refusing to remove her hijab at school. Nashala's parents, with the support of the Rutherford Institute, brought a lawsuit against the Muskogee Public Schools in protest. A little over a year later in November 2004, the Muskogee Public Schools settled the suit by agreeing to revise their dress code. "Muslim Girl Back to Wearing Head Scarf to School With Pride," *Dallas Morning News*, November 12, 2004.
37. Personal conversation during a teacher training session on Islam for world history teachers, July 12, 2005, University of Austin, Austin, Texas.
38. Personal conversation during a teacher training session on Islam for world history teachers, July 14, 2005, University of Austin, Austin, Texas.
39. Edmund Husserl is credited as the founder of this school of philosophical thought. Important phenomenologists of religion include Nathan Soderblom (1866–1931), Garardus van der Leeuw (1890–1950), Rudolf Otto (1869–1937), Friedrich Heiler (1892–1967), and Mircea Eliade (1907–1986).
40. Huston Smith, *The World's Religions* (San Francisco: Harper, 1958, 1991).
41. Several independent school teachers who participate in conferences held before the Annual Meeting of the American Academy of Religion report using the Smith text. Joseph Laycock, "Religious Studies in Secondary Schools" unpublished final paper for an independent reading and research course, Harvard Divinity School, Fall, 2004. The Smith text is also used by history and other religion teachers in California, Texas, and Massachusetts as reported in responses to a qualitative research project entitled the Harvard Study on Teaching About Religion in the Schools (H-STARS). For a description of the project and access to the online survey see http://www.hds.harvard.edu/prse/hstars/ accessed November 13, 2006.

42. Karen Russell is a mentor teacher who has worked with Program in Religion and Secondary Education at Harvard. This quote is taken from a profile of her found on the PRSE website at http://www.hds.harvard.edu/prse/people.html accessed November 13, 2006.
43. Reported in online survey of the Harvard Study on Teaching about Religion in the Schools (H-STARS) cited in n. 41 above.
44. Nord, *Religion and American Education*, 139–143.
45. See James A. Banks, *Educating Citizens in a Multicultural Society* (New York: Teachers College Press, 1997); James A. Banks, ed., *Multicultural Education: Transformative Knowledge and Action: Historical and Contemporary Essays* (New York: Teachers College Press, 1996); and James A. Banks and Cherry A. McGee Banks, eds., *Handbook of Research on Multicultural Education*, 2nd edition (San Francisco: Jossey-Bass, 2004).
46. In the authoritative *Handbook of Research on Multicultural Education* cited above, there are only a handful of references to religion in the index and most of these cite articles where religion is referenced in passing. A notable exception to this general trend of omission is an article by James K. Uphoff entitled "Religious Diversity and Education," in James A. Banks and Cherry A. McGee Banks, eds., *Multicultural Education: Issues and Perspectives* 4th edition (New York: John Wiley and Sons, 2001), 103–122.
47. Christine E. Sleeter and Carl A. Grant, *Making Choices for Multicultural Education: Five Approaches to Race, Class, and Gender*, 3rd edition (Upper Saddle River, NJ: Merrill, 1999).
48. Ibid., 37–75.
49. Ibid., 31.
50. Ibid., 76–109.
51. Ibid., 102.
52. Ibid., 110–149.
53. Ibid., 150–187.
54. Gollnick quoted in Sleeter and Grant, *Making Choices*, 150.
55. See Hirsch, *Cultural Literacy*; Diane Ravitch, "Multiculturalism: E Pluribus Plures," *The American Scholar*, 59 (3), 1990, 337–354; Arthur Schlesinger, Jr., *The Disuniting of America* (New York: Norton, 1991).
56. The inclusion of these categories and the language employed to describe them betrays an underlying assumption that the school is question is predominantly white and middle to upper middle class. This is a departure from the descriptions used in the other categories which speak more to the overall inclusion of diverse groups.
57. Sleeter and Grant, *Making Choices*, 189.
58. See Martin Luther King, Jr., "Letter From a Birmingham Jail" and "I Have a Dream," in James Washington, ed. *Testament of Hope: The Essential Writings and Speeches of Martin Luther King, Jr.* (San Francisco: Harper, 1990).
59. See Mohandas Gandhi, *The Essential Gandhi: An Anthology of His Writings on His Life, Work and Ideas*, Louis Fischer, ed., (New York: Vintage, 2002); Joan Bondurant, *Conquest of Violence: The Gandhian Philosophy of Conflict* (Princeton: Princeton University Press, 1988).
60. For Christian feminists, see works by Elisabeth Schussler-Fiorenza, Beverly Harrison, and Rosemary Reuther; for womanist perspectives see Katie G. Canon and Dolores Williams; for Jewish feminists see works by Judith Plaskow and Rebecca Alport; for Muslim perspectives see works by Amina Waddud.
61. Sleeter and Grant, *Making Choices*, 210–214.
62. Haraway, "Situated Knowledges", 191.
63. Cary Nelson, Paula A. Treichler, and Lawrence Grossberg, "Cultural Studies: An Introduction," in Lawrence Grossberg, Cary Nelson, and Paula Treichler, eds., *Cultural Studies* (New York: Routledge, 1992), 5.
64. Raymond Williams, "Adult Education and Social Change." *What I Came to Say*. London: Hutchinson-Radus, 157–166, quoted in Henry Giroux, "The Discourse of Critical Pedagogy," in Grossberg, et al., eds., *Cultural Studies*, 201.

65. Haraway, "Situated Knowledges," 191.
66. Ibid., 193.
67. This quote is attributed to German Christian mystic Gerhard Tersteegan (1697–1769).
68. Alliance Defense Fund, "Ten Commandments: Our History's Future on Trial," http://www.alliancedefensefund.org/actions/currentactions/default.aspx?cid=3319 accessed October 27, 2005.
69. Ibid.
70. Henry Giroux also recognizes how pedagogy is a critical dimension of cultural studies and one that is often overlooked by theorists outside of education. See Henry Giroux, "Doing Cultural Studies: Youth and the Challenge of Pedagogy," in Ruben A. Gaztambide-Fernandez, Heather A. Harding, and Tere Sorde-Marti, eds., *Cultural Studies and Education: Perspectives on Theory, Methodology, and Practice* (Cambridge, MA: Harvard Educational Review, 2004), 233–260.

Four Teacher Education: What Teachers Need to Know

1. For statistics on teaching salaries and other relevant data see the U.S. Census Bureau Newsroom article published on April 22, 2004 in honor of teacher appreciation week. http://www.census.gov/Press-Release/www/releases/archives/facts_for_features_special_editions/001737.html accessed October 17, 2005.
2. Jonathan Kozol cites the ideologically moderate advocacy institute Education Trust that reviewed recent trends in education finance. According to their findings, "the top 25 percent of school districts in terms of child poverty . . . receive less funding than the bottom 25 percent." Cited in Kozol, *Shame of the Nation*, 245.
3. See "The Prospect/FP Top 100 Public Intellectuals," in *Foreign Policy*, September, 2005, web exclusive, http://www.foreignpolicy.com/story/cms.php?story_id=3249 accessed December 3, 2006.
4. See website for Program in Religion and Secondary Education at Harvard Divinity School, http://www.hds.harvard.edu/prse/index.html accessed December 3, 2006.

Introduction to Part Two

1. For example, Phillips Academy and Phillips Exeter Academy both have extensive offerings in religious studies. Many other nonsectarian independent schools have course offerings in religion, such as Northfield Mount Herman, Deerfield Academy, etc.
2. My aim here is to provide readers with a focused opportunity to see how the elements of a cultural studies approach interact through a concrete example. This, therefore, is a narrative case study representing a paradigm and intended to be illustrative rather than exploratory.

Five Constructing a Learning Community

1. The original course description is included in footnote number 18 in chapter two.
2. Phillips Academy *Courses of Study*, 2004–2005.
3. I draw primarily from John Paul Sartre "Existentialism is a Humanism," 1946. There is a new volume published by Yale University Press: Jean Paul Sartre, *Existentialism is a Humanism*, Carol Macomber, trans., (New Haven: Yale University Press, 2007).

4. Immanuel Kant, *Anthropology from a Pragmatic Point of View*, 1798. I use an edition published in 2006 by Cambridge University Press.
5. Quote recorded in my personal class journal. All student quotes throughout Chapters Five and Six are drawn from this source.
6. Shiraz Hajiani (a then graduate Teaching Fellow for the course) prepared this video for Professor Ali Asani's freshman seminar entitled "Contemporary Muslim Voices in World Literature."
7. Carl Ernst, *Following Muhammad: Rethinking Islam in the Contemporary World*, (Chapel Hill: University of North Carolina Press, 2003), xvi.
8. Ibid., xvi–xvii.
9. Ibid., xvii.
10. Ibid.
11. Ibid., xix.
12. Phillips Academy *Courses of Study*, 2005–2006.
13. Greenberg, "Cloud of Smoke," 305–345, especially 335.

Six A Case Study: Teaching About Islam

1. Azim Nanji, "Islam," in Richard C. Bush, ed., *The Religious World: Communities of Faith*, 3rd edition (Upper Saddle Falls, NJ: Prentice-Hall, 1993), 361–412.
2. Ernst, "The Seal of the Prophets: The Prophet Muhammad," in *Following Muhammad*, 73–92.
3. Sayings attributed to the Prophet.
4. Michael Sells, *Approaching the Qur'an* (Ashland, OR: White Cloud Press, 1999).
5. John Esposito, "Islam: The Many Faces of the Muslim Experience," in Esposito, Fasching, and Lewis, eds., *World Religions Today* (New York: Oxford, 2002), 181–272.
6. Sometimes a student will try to claim the mantle of "expert" for her/himself, especially if s/he represents a minority tradition or view. It is very important for educators to swiftly address this dynamic as soon as it becomes apparent utilizing the same rationale I articulated in my own classroom when the focus was on Farid. I argue that it is never appropriate for a religious practitioner to be put in a situation where s/he is expected or allowed to represent the tradition simply by virtue of being a practitioner. This can be a delicate situation for an educator if a student claims that status for him or herself. It requires sensitivity, respect for the student's own beliefs and understandings and clarity on the part of the educator him or herself regarding why that role is an inappropriate one for a student to claim.
7. It is worth repeating here that some religious practitioners and leaders may *also* be trained as religious studies scholars who are well acquainted with an academic approach to religion and capable of speaking about their traditions from that perspective.
8. If students are introduced to Islam in the schools, they will usually learn about the tradition through this "five pillar" approach via textbooks.
9. Following are the relevant passages in Nanji that I asked them to focus on. The first addresses the place of humankind in relationship to the rest of creation: "Humankind has a special place within creation (95:4), because in creating human beings, God endowed them with a capacity to know and respond to Him greater than that given to other creatures. They are also special because built into the human condition was the notion of choice, by which they could either fulfill their potential as the most honored among God's creation or sink to a level farthest away from God by disobeying or denying Him." (372–373). Second, according to Nanji, the Qur'anic account of the Adam and Eve story portrays Adam and Eve exercising their freedom by "sinning" in response to temptations by Satan (*Iblis*) but they then "come to realize their error, are forgiven by God, and returned by Him to their original status." (373). It is important

to note here that Muslims do not believe in the Christian doctrine of "original sin." Third, regarding the Day of Resurrection, Nanji articulates that "on this occasion . . . all individuals will realize the fruits of their actions." He then offers the following quote from the Qur'an: "And the fate of every one We have made the individual's own responsibility . . . and We shall bring forth on the Day of Resurrection, a record that will reveal all. (Qur'an 17:13)" (373). Fourth, Nanji states that "when the Quran comes to define ideal human behavior, moral and spiritual perspectives ultimately determine whether one reflects Islamic goals or not." He then quotes from Yusuf Ali's translation of *The Holy Quran*, "By (the Token of) Time (through the Ages)/ Verily Man is in loss/ Except such as have Faith/ And do righteous deeds/ And join together/ In the mutual teaching/ Of Truth, and of/ Patience and Constancy." (373).

10. It is interesting to note that when studying Judaism these issues are not as prominent because interpretive discourses are themselves central to the tradition as exemplified in the Talmud. Similarly, when studying traditions that originated in Asian contexts the issue of multiple perspectives as problematic does not arise in the same way because multiplicity is itself a central dimension of these religions. I do find, however, that when studying Judaism or traditions that originated in Asia, students who self-identify across the full spectrum between "religious" and "nonreligious" are especially intrigued by the idea of multiple perspectives of interpretation regarding the divine and often note how "foreign" such a notion is to their understanding of religion more generally. This speaks to the ways that certain forms of Christian monotheism are profoundly imbedded in U.S. culture and the ways that they shape notions of religion itself.
11. See note 10 above.
12. Carrie, "RelPhil 530: Reflection Paper: Nanji 392–412" for session four.
13. See my discussion of Donna Haraway's assertions regarding objectivity and science in chapter three of this volume.
14. Sharon, "Reflection Paper #1" for session four.
15. There is some dispute regarding the authenticity of this hadith, but al-Khattabi has been quoted as recognizing that it has merit in the tradition. See Vardit Tokatly, "The A 'lam al-hadith of al-Khattabi: A Commentary on al Bukhari's Sahih or a Polemical Treatise?" *Studia Islamica*, 92 (2001), 84.
16. Erich Fromm, *You Shall Be As Gods* (NY: Henry Holt and Company, 1966).
17. Ernst, *Following Muhammad*, 72–105.
18. Depictions of Muhammad's "ascent" to God and return to the world are based on passages in the Qur'an whereby God "carried his servant [Muhammad] by night," (Qur'an, 17:1). See also surahs 53:1–21 and 81:19–25.
19. Ernst, *Following Muhammad*, 84.
20. Farid, untitled reflection for session 18.
21. Hope, "Three Things I Take Away From This Course" reflection for session eighteen.
22. Carrie, RelPhil 530 self-evaluation.

Seven Incorporating the Study of Religion Throughout the Curriculum: American History, Economics, Biology, and Literature

1. See James Loewen, *Lies My Teacher Told Me: Everything Your American History Textbook Got Wrong* (New York: Touchstone, 1995), note 4, 319.
2. Ibid., 13.
3. Jonathan Zimmerman, *Whose America? Culture Wars in the Public Schools* (Cambridge: Harvard University Press, 2002), 4.

4. Loewen, *Lies*, 33.
5. Zimmerman, *Whose America?* 272.
6. Loewen, *Lies*, 35.
7. Ibid.
8. Ibid.
9. Howard Zinn, *A People's History of the United States* (New York: HarperCollins, 1980), 2003.
10. Ronalk Takaki, *A Different Mirror: A History of Multicultural America* (Boston: Little, Brown and Company, 1993).
11. James Fraser, *A History of Hope* (New York: Palgrave MacMillan, 2002).
12. Bartolome de las Casas, *History of the Indies*, trans. Andree M. Collard (New York: Harper and Row, 1971), 289. Quoted in Loewen, *Lies*, 38.
13. Quoted in Loewen, *Lies*, 43.
14. See Maria Rosa Menocal, *The Ornament of the World: How Muslims, Jews, and Christians Created a Culture of Tolerance in Medieval Spain* (Boston: Little Brown and Company, 2002) and Salma Khadra Jayyusi, *The Legacy of Muslim Spain*, volumes 1 and 2 (Leiden: Brill, 2000). For primary source material see Olivia Remie Constable, ed., *Medieval Iberia: Readings from Christian, Muslim and Jewish Sources* (Philadelphia: University of Pennsylvania Press, 1997), and Maria Rosa Menocal, Raymond Scheindlin, and Michael Sells, eds., *The Literature of Al-Andalus* (Cambridge: Cambridge University Press, 2000).
15. Loewen, *Lies*, 316–317.
16. Herman Daly and John Cobb, Jr., *For the Common Good* (Boston: Beacon, 1994), 5.
17. Ibid., 6.
18. Ibid., 7.
19. Ibid., 8–21.
20. Ibid., 30.
21. See, for example, Munwar Iqbal and Philip Molyneux, *Thirty Years of Islamic Banking: History, Performance and Prospects* (New York: Palgrave MacMillan, 2005); Mahmoud A. El-Gamal, *Islamic Finance: Law, Economics, and Practice* (Cambridge: Cambridge University Press, 2006); and Mohsin Khan and Abbas Mirakhor, eds., *Theoretical Studies in Islamic Banking and Finance* (Oneonto, NY: Islamic Publications International, 2005).
22. See National Conference of Catholic Bishops, *Tenth Anniversary of Economic Justice for All* (NJ: Hunter Publishing, 1997) and Albino Barrera, *Modern Catholic Social Documents and Political Economy* (Washington, DC: Georgetown University Press, 2001).
23. For an excellent overview of the issues related to science and religion (primarily Christianity) see Ian G. Barbour, *Religion and Science*, revised edition (San Francisco: Harper, 1997).
24. For example, see Fazlur Rahman, "God," in *Major Themes of the Qur'an* (Minneapolis: Bibliotheca Islamica, 1980), 1–17. Also, see Ayatullah Murtaza Mutahhari, *Fundamentals of Islamic Thought: God, Man and the Universe* (New York: Mizan Press, 1985).
25. See, for example, Donna Haraway, *Primate Visions: Gender, Race and Nature in the World of Modern Science* (New York: Routledge, 1989).
26. Forum on Religion and Ecology website at http://environment.harvard.edu/religion/ accessed December 3, 2006.
27. Frederico Garcia Lorca, *The Tamarit Poems: A Verson of Divan Del Tamarit*, (New York: Dedalus, 2000).
28. People for the American Way, *The Good Book Taught Wrong: Bible History Classes in Florida Public Schools* (2nd printing, 2000), available at http://www.pfaw.org/pfaw/general/default.aspx?oid=1345 accessed December 3, 2006.
29. Mark Chancey, *Reading, Writing and Religion: Teaching the Bible in Texas Public Schools* (Texas Freedom Network Education Fund) 2006, available at www.tfn.org/religiousfreedom/biblecurriculum/texascourses/ accessed December 3, 2006.
30. Ibid.

Conclusion

1. See, for example, Michael Apple, *Educating the "Right" Way: Markets, Standards, God, and Inequality*, 2nd edition (New York: RoutledgeFalmer, 2006), and *The State and Politics of Knowledge* (New York: RoutledgeFalmer, 2003).

Epilogue

1. Emile Lester and Patrick S. Roberts, "Learning About World Religions in Public Schools: The Impact on Student Attitudes and Community Acceptance in Modesto, California," (Nashville: First Amendment Center, 2006). Available at www.firstamendmentcenter.org/about.aspx?id=16863 accessed December 3, 2006.
2. Emile Lester is an Assistant Professor in the Department of Government at the College of William and Mary.
3. Patrick S. Roberts is an Assistant Professor in the School of Public and International Affairs at Virginia Tech.
4. Lester and Roberts, "Learning," 6.
5. Ibid., 6–8.
6. Ibid., 8.
7. Ibid., 8.
8. Ibid., 49.
9. Ibid., 52.
10. Ibid., 51.
11. Ibid., 63.
12. Ibid., 14–17.

BIBLIOGRAPHY OF WORKS CITED

Abington School District v. Schempp 374 US 203 (1963).

Améry, Jean. *Suicide: A Discourse on Voluntary Death.* Translated by John Barlow. Bloomington: Indiana University Press, 1999.

Apple, Michael. *Educating the "Right" Way: Markets, Standards, God, and Inequality.* 2nd edition. New York: RoutledgeFalmer, 2006.

——. *The State and Politics of Knowledge.* New York: RoutledgeFalmer, 2003.

Barbour, Ian G. *Religion and Science.* Revised edition. San Francisco: Harper, 1997.

Barrera, Albino. *Modern Catholic Social Documents and Political Economy.* Washington, DC: Georgetown University Press, 2001.

Bennett, William, Jr. *The Educated Child: A Parent's Guide from Preschool through Eighth Grade.* New York: Free Press, 1999.

Blumenthal, Ralph and Barbara Novovitch. "Bible Course Becomes a Test for Public Schools in Texas." *New York Times,* August 1, 2005.

Bob Jones University v. United States and *Goldsboro Christian Schools, Inc. v. United States,* 461 US 574 (1982) at 580 and 2022–23.

Bondurant, Joan. *Conquest of Violence: The Gandhian Philosophy of Conflict.* Princeton: Princeton University Press, 1988.

Boyer, Peter J. "Jesus in the Classroom." *The New Yorker,* March 21, 2005.

Boy Scouts of America et al. v. Dale 530 US 696 (2000).

Browning, Christopher. *Ordinary Men: Reserve Battalion 101 and the Final Solution in Poland.* New York: Harper Perennial, 1998.

Brustein, William. *Roots of Hate: Anti-Semitism in Europe before the Holocaust.* New York: Cambridge University Press, 2003.

Bumiller, Elisabeth. "Bush Remarks Roil Debate on Teaching Evolution." *New York Times,* August 3, 2005.

Bushnell, Horace. *Women's Suffrage: Reform against Nature.* New York: Scribner, 1869.

Carper, James C. "History, Religion, and Schooling: A Context for Conversation." In *Curriculum, Religion and Public Education: Conversations for an Enlarging Public Square.* Edited by James T. Sears and James C. Carper. New York: Teachers College Press, 1998. 11–24.

Carter, Stephen. *The Culture of Disbelief: How American Law and Politics Trivialize Religious Devotion.* New York: Basic Books, 1993.

Chancey, Mark. *The Bible and Public Schools: Report on the National Council on Bible Curriculum in Public Schools.* Austin: Texas Freedom Network Education Fund, 2005.

Chancey, Mark. *Reading, Writing and Religion: Teaching the Bible in Texas Public Schools.* Austin: Texas Freedom Network Education Fund, 2006.

Constable, Olivia Remie, ed. *Medieval Iberia: Readings from Christian, Muslim and Jewish Sources.* Philadelphia: University of Pennsylvania Press, 1997.

Cornelius, Janet Duitsman. *When I Can Read My Title Clear: Literacy, Slavery, and Religion in the Antebellum South.* Columbia: University of South Carolina Press, 1992.

Daly, Harman and John Cobb, Jr. *For the Common Good: Redirecting the Economy toward Community, the Environment, and a Sustainable Future.* 2nd edition. Boston: Beacon Press, 1994.

DelFattore, Joan. *The Fourth R: Conflicts over Religion in America's Public Schools.* New Haven: Yale, 2004.

Dietrich, Donald J., ed. *Christian Responses to the Holocaust: Moral and Ethical Issues.* Syracuse: Syracuse University Press, 2003.

Douglas, Frederick. *Frederick Douglas: Selected Speeches and Writings.* Edited by Philip Foner. Abridged and adapted by Yuval Taylor. Chicago: Lawrence Hill Books, 2000.

Eck, Diana. *A New Religious America: How a "Christian Country" Has Now Become the World's Most Religiously Diverse Nation.* New York: HarperCollins, 2001.

Ernst, Carl. *Following Muhammad: Rethinking Islam in the Contemporary World* Chapel Hill: North Carolina Press, 2003.

Esposito, John, L. "Islam: The Many Faces of the Muslim Experience." In *World Religions Today.* Edited by John L. Esposito, Darrell J. Fasching, and Todd Lewis. New York: Oxford University Press, 2002. 181–272.

First Amendment Center. *A Teacher's Guide to Religion in the Public Schools.* Nashville: First Amendment Center, 1999.

Flender, Harold. *Rescue in Denmark.* New York: Holocaust Library, 1963.

Frankl, Viktor. *Man's Search for Meaning.* New York: Pocket, 1959/1984.

Fraser, James. *Between Church and State: Religion and Public Education in a Multicultural America.* New York: St. Martin's Griffin, 1999.

——. *A History of Hope: When Americans Have Dared to Dream of a Better Future.* New York: Palgrave MacMillan, 2002.

Freire, Paulo. *Pedagogy of the Oppressed.* New York: Continuum, 1970/1994.

Fromm, Erich. *You Shall Be As Gods.* New York: Henry Holt and Company, 1966.

Gabler, M. *Humanism/Moral Relativism in Textbooks.* Longview, TX: Educational Research Analysts, 1988.

Gager, John. *The Origins of Christian Anti-Semitism.* New York: Oxford, 1983.

Gandhi, Mohandas. *The Essential Gandhi: An Anthology of His Writings on His Life, Work and Ideas.* Edited by Louis Fischer. New York: Vintage, 2002.

Gaustad, Edwin. *Church and State in America.* New York: Oxford, 1999.

Gaustad, Edwin and Mark Noll, eds. *A Documentary History of Religion in America to 1877.* Grand Rapids, MI: Eerdmans, 2003.

Gellately, Robert. *Backing Hitler: Consent and Coercion in Nazi Germany.* New York: Oxford, 2001.

Giroux, Henry. "Doing Cultural Studies: Youth and the Challenge of Pedagogy." In *Cultural Studies and Education: Perspectives on Theory, Methodology, and Practice.* Edited by Ruben A. Gaztambide-Fernandex, Heather A. Harding, and Tere Sorde-Marti. Cambridge: Harvard Educational Review, 2004. 233–260.

Greenberg, Irving. "Cloud of Smoke, Pillar of Fire." In *Holocaust: Religious and Philosophical Implications.* Edited by John Roth and Michael Berenbaum. New York: Paragon, 1989, 305–348.

Greenwalt, Kent. *Does God Belong in Public Schools?* Princeton: Princeton University Press, 2005.

Gutmann, Amy. *Democratic Education.* Princeton: Princeton University Press, 1987/1999.

Haraway, Donna. "Situated Knowledges: The Science Question in Feminism and the Privilege of Partial Perspective." In *Simians, Cyborgs, and Women: The Reinvention of Nature*. New York: Routledge, 1991. 183–202.

Haynes, Charles and Oliver Thomas. *Finding Common Ground: A Guide to Religious Liberty in Public Schools*. Nashville: The First Amendment Center, 2001.

Haynes, Stephen R. *Noah's Curse: The Biblical Justification of American Slavery*. New York: Oxford, 2002.

Hershman, Marcie. *Tales of the Master Race*. New York: Harper Perennial, Reprint, 1992.

Hirsch, E.D., Jr. *Cultural Literacy: What Every American Needs to Know*. New York: Vintage, 1998.

Hochschild, Adam. *King Leopold's Ghost: A Story of Greed, Terror, and Heroism in Colonial Africa*. New York: Mariner Books, 1997.

Hunter, James Davison. *Culture Wars: The Struggle to Define America*. New York: Basic, 1991.

Huntington, Samuel. *The Clash of Civilizations and the Remaking of the World Order*. New York: Simon and Schuster, 1998.

Iqbal, Munwar and Philip Molyneux. *Thirty Years of Islamic Banking: History, Performance and Prospects*. New York: Palgrave MacMillan, 2005.

Jackson, Robert. *Rethinking Religious Education and Plurality: Issues in Diversity and Pedagogy*. New York: RoutledgeFalmer, 2004.

Janofsky, Michael. "Gay Rights Battlefields Spread to Public Schools." *New York Times*, June 9, 2005.

Jayyusi, Salma Khadra. *The Legacy of Muslim Spain*, volumes 1 and 2. Leiden: Brill, 2000.

Kant, Immanuel. *Anthropology from a Pragmatic Point of View*. New York: Cambridge University Press, 2006.

Khan, Mohsin and Abbas Mirakhor, eds. *Theoretical Studies in Islamic Banking and Finance*. Oneonta, NY: Islamic Publications International, 2005.

Kilgore, Damon Y. *The Questions of Today, Caste, Suffrage, Labor, Temperance, Religion: An Oration Delivered Before the Wesleyan Academy Alumni Association at Wilbraham, Mass, June 29, 1870*. New York: Hurd and Houghton, 1870.

King, Martin Luther, Jr. "I Have a Dream" and "Letter From a Birmingham Jail." In *Testament of Hope: The Essential Writings and Speeches of Martin Luther King, Jr.* Edited by James Washington. San Francisco: Harper, 1990, 217–220 and 289–302.

Kitzmiller, et al. v. Dover Area School District, et al, USDC, 342 (2005).

Kozol, Jonathan. *Savage Inequalities: Children in America's Schools*. New York: Harper Reprint, 1992.

——. *The Shame of the Nation*. New York: Crown, 2005.

Lathrop, Leonard. *A Discourse on the Obligations of a Christian People: In View of the Divine Beneficence, Considered With Reference to the Subject of the Temperance Reform, War, of Capital Punishment, and of Slavery*. New York: R.G. and P.S. Wynkoop Press of J.C. Merrell and Co, 1847.

Lester, Emile and Patrick S. Roberts. "Learning About World Religions in Public Schools: The Impact on Student Attitudes and Community Acceptance in Modesto, California." Nashville: First Amendment Center, 2006.

Lindley, Susan Hill. *"You Have Stept Out of Your Place": A History of Women and Religion in America*. Louisville, KY: Westminster John Knox Press, 1996.

Lindqvist, Sven. *"Exterminate All the Brutes": One Man's Odyssey into the Heart of Darkness and the Origins of European Genocide*. Translated by Joan Tate. London: New Press, 1997.

Loewen, James W. *Lies My Teacher Told Me: Everything Your American History Textbook Got Wrong*. New York: Touchstone, 1996.

Lorca, Frederico Garcia. *The Tamarit Poems: A Version of Divan Del Tamarit*. New York: Dedalus, 2000.

Menocal, Maria Rosa. *The Ornament of the World: How Muslims, Jews, and Christians Created a Culture of Tolerance in Medieval Spain*. Boston: Little, Brown and Company, 2002.

Menocal, Maria Rosa. Raymond Scheindlin and Michael Sells, eds. *The Literature of Al-Andalus*. Cambridge: Cambridge University Press, 2000.

Moore, Diane L. "Overcoming Religious Illiteracy: A Cultural Studies Approach." *World History Connected*, 4 (1), November, 2006. http://worldhistoryconnected.press.uiuc.edu/4.1/moore.html

Mutahhari, Ayatullah Murtaza. *Fundamentals of Islamic Thought: God, Man and the Universe*. New York: Mizan Press, 1985.

Nanji, Azim. "Islam." In *The Religious World: Communities of Faith*, 3rd edition. Edited by Richard C. Bush. Upper Saddle River, NJ: Prentice-Hall, 1993. 361–412.

National Conference of Catholic Bishops. *Tenth Anniversary of Economic Justice for All*. NJ: Hunter Publishing, 1997.

Nelson, Cary, Paula A. Treichler, and Lawrence Grossberg. "Cultural Studies: An Introduction." In *Cultural Studies*. Edited by Lawrence Grossberg, Cary Nelson, and Paula A. Treichler. New York: Routledge, 1992, 1–16.

Noddings, Nel. *Educating for Intelligent Belief or Unbelief*. New York: Teachers College Press, 2000.

Nord, Warren. *Religion and American Education: Rethinking a National Dilemma*. Chapel Hill: University of North Carolina, 1995.

Nord, Warren and Charles Haynes. *Taking Religion Seriously across the Curriculum*. New York: Association for Supervision and Curriculum Development, 1998.

Paterson, Frances. "Anatomy of a Bible Course Curriculum." *Journal of Law and Education*, January, 2003. http://www.findarticles.com/p/articles/mi_qa3994/is_200301/ai_n9186918 accessed August 6, 2005.

Perry, Michael. *Religion in Politics: Constitutional and Moral Perspectives*. New York: Oxford, 1999.

Rahman, Fazlur. "God." In *Major Themes of the Qur'an*. Minneapolis: Bibliotheca Islamica, 1980, 1–17.

Ravitch, Diane. "Multiculturalism: E Pluribus Plures." *The American Scholar*, 59 (3), 1990: 337–334.

Reich, Robert. *Bridging Liberalism and Multiculturalism in American Education*. Chicago: University of Chicago Press, 2002.

Said, Edward. *Covering Islam*. New York: Vintage, 1981/1997.

——. *Orientalism*. New York: Vintage, 1978/1994.

Salitan, Lucille, Elizabeth Buffum Chace, Lydia Buffum Read, Lucy Buffum Lovell, and Rebecca Buffum Spring, eds. *Virtuous Lives: Four Quaker Sisters Remember Family Life, Abolitionism, and Women's Suffrage*. New York: Continuum, 1994.

Sartre, Jean Paul. *Existentialism Is a Humanism*. Translated by Carol Macomber. New Haven, Yale University Press, 2007.

Schlesinger, Arthur, Jr. *The Disuniting of America: Reflections on a Multicultural Society*. New York: Norton, 1991.

Sears, Alan and Craig Osten. *The Homosexual Agenda: The Principal Threat to Religious Freedom*. Nashville: Broadman and Holman, 2003.

Sells, Michael. *Approaching the Qur'an: The Early Revelations*. Ashland, OR: White Cloud Press, 1999.

Sleeter, Christine E. and Carl A. Grant. *Making Choices for Multicultural Education: Five Approaches to Race, Class and Gender*, 3rd edition. Upper Saddle River, NJ: Merrill, 1999.

Smith, Christian. *Soul Searching: The Religious and Spiritual Lives of American Teenagers*. New York: Oxford, 2005.

Spong, John Shelby. "The Bible and Anti-Semitism." In *The Sins of Scripture*. San Francisco: Harper, 2005. 183–212.

Stannard, David. *American Holocaust: The Conquest of the New World*. New York: Oxford, 1992.

Stanton, Elizabeth Cady. *The Woman's Bible*. Amherst, NY: Prometheus Books, 1999.

Taggart, Charles Manson. *Slavery and the Law in the Light of Christianity: A Discourse Delivered Before the Congregation of Unitarian Christians of Nashville, Tennessee on Sunday Evening, June 22, 1851.* Nashville: J.T.S. Fall, 1851.

Takaki, Ronald. *A Different Mirror: A History of Multicultural America.* Boston: Little, Brown and Company, 1993.

Thiemann, Ronald. *Religion in Public Life: A Dilemma for Democracy.* Washington, DC: Georgetown University Press, 1996.

Uhlman, Fred. *Reunion.* New York: Farrar, Straus, and Giroux, 1997.

Uphoff, James K. "Religious Diversity and Education." In *Multicultural Education: Issues and Perspectives*, 4th edition. Edited by James A. Banks and Cherry A. McGee Banks. New York: John Wiley and Sons, 2001. 103–122.

Wachlin, Marie and Byron Johnson. *The Bible Literacy Report.* Fairfax, VA: The Bible Literacy Project, 2005.

Welch, Sharon. *A Feminist Ethic of Risk.* Minneapolis: Fortress, 1990.

——. *Sweet Dreams in America: Making Ethics and Spirituality Work.* New York: Routledge, 1999.

Wiesenthal, Simon. *The Sunflower: On the Possibilities and Limits of Forgiveness.* Revised edition. New York: Schocken, 1998.

Williams v. Vidmar, USDC, Northern District, San Jose, Case No. C044946.

Zimmerman, Jonathan. *Whose America? Culture Wars in the Public Schools.* Cambridge: Harvard University Press, 2002.

Zinn, Howard. *A People's History of the United States.* New York: HarperCollins, 1980/2003.

ABOUT THE AUTHOR

Diane L. Moore is Professor of the Practice in Religious Studies and Education and Director of the Program in Religion and Secondary Education at the Harvard Divinity School. In addition to her appointment at Harvard, she is also on the faculty of Phillips Andover Academy where she teaches in the Philosophy and Religious Studies department. Professor Moore serves as chair of the Religion in the Schools Task Force for the American Academy of Religion and is on the editorial board of the journal *Religion and Education.* She has written several articles and lectures widely on how to enhance the public understanding of religion through education in middle and secondary school contexts. She has also conducted numerous teacher education seminars on how to teach about religion here in the United States as well as in Kenya and Pakistan. Dr. Moore has been the recipient of numerous teaching awards, including "Outstanding Teaching in Secondary School" from the University of Chicago in 2000 and is corecipient of the Harvard Divinity School award for "Outstanding Teaching 2006–2007".

INDEX

Printed in the United States
131106LV00001B/36/P

9 781403 963499